The Cultural Work
of Corporations

THE CULTURAL WORK
OF CORPORATIONS

Megan Brown

THE CULTURAL WORK OF CORPORATIONS
Copyright © Megan Brown, 2009.

A version of Chapter 3 originally appeared as "Survival at Work: Flexibility and Adaptability in American Corporate Culture" in *Cultural Studies* 17, no. 5 (2003): 713–733. The chapter appears here with kind permission of Taylor & Francis Group, and *Cultural Studies* is available at http://www.informaworld.com.

A version of Chapter 4 originally appeared as "Taking Care of Business: Self-Help and Sleep Medicine in American Corporate Culture" in the *Journal of Medical Humanities* 25, no. 3 (2004): 173–187. The chapter appears here with kind permission of Springer Science and Business Media.

First published in 2009 by
PALGRAVE MACMILLAN® in the
United States - a division of St. Martin's Press LLC,
175 Fifth Avenue, New York, NY 10010.

Where this book is distributed in the UK, Europe and the rest of the world, this is by Palgrave Macmillan, a division of Macmillan Publishers Limited, registered in England, company number 785998, of Houndmills, Basingstoke, Hampshire RG21 6XS.

Palgrave Macmillan is the global academic imprint of the above companies and has companies and representatives throughout the world.

Palgrave® and Macmillan® are registered trademarks in the United States, the United Kingdom, Europe and other countries.

ISBN: 978-0-230-61872-5

Library of Congress Cataloging-in-Publication Data is available from the Library of Congress.

A catalogue record of the book is available from the British Library.

Design by Macmillan Publishing Solutions

First edition: October 2009

10 9 8 7 6 5 4 3 2 1

Printed in the United States of America.

Transferred to Digital Printing in 2009

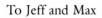

To Jeff and Max

CONTENTS

ACKNOWLEDGMENTS

This book was written with the generous support of the Drake University Center for the Humanities tenure-track support program; the Drake University Office of the Provost research grant; the Pennsylvania State University Science, Medicine, and Technology fellowship program; and the Amherst College Memorial and John Woodruff Simpson fellowship programs. I thank all of these programs for helping me through the research and writing process.

My graduate advisor, Susan Squier, guided my research in innumerable ways, far beyond the typical "suggestions for further reading" and assistance with writing and editing. She modeled a certain sensibility—unabashed enthusiasm and curiosity—that shaped this book from start to finish.

Conversations with Jane Juffer sparked many of my best ideas, and I thank her for sharing her wisdom and insights with me.

Jeff Nealon really, really knows how to teach critical theory, and showed me that the only way out is through.

Dan Conway is a thoughtful, careful, and endlessly patient reader.

Ron Lembo taught me that popular culture should be taken seriously.

Cynthia Spina taught me to love learning. I will always miss her.

I am deeply grateful to friends, colleagues, editors, professors, teachers, and reviewers who offered their suggestions, advice, and support. My thanks to Marco Abel, Susan Baumgartner, Michael Berubé, Betsy Blanchard, Tony Ceraso, Richard Doyle, Robert Dunn, Jeremiah Dyehouse, Valerie Hanson, Bernice Hausman, Debra Hawhee, Doug Henwood, Catherine and Tim Knepper, Lon Larson, Joseph Lenz, Melissa Littlefield, Melissa Longhi, Janet Lyon, Yasmina Madden, Bruce Martin, Elizabeth Mazzolini, John Muckelbauer, Ryan Netzley, Jodie Nicotra, Craig Owens, Aaron Panofsky, Nancy Reincke, Elizabeth Robertson, Marika Seigel, Dina Smith, Jillian Smith, Carol Spaulding-Kruse, Jody Swilky, Chandra Tobey, Evan Watkins, and Beth Younger.

My love and thanks to my family: my parents, Catherine and Russell Brown; my sister and brother-in-law, Heather and Jonathan Gibson; my grandmothers, Marjorie Buddenhagen and Gertrude Brown; my aunts and uncles, Anne Buddenhagen, Frosty Glass, Janet and Vinny Ambrosio, and Deanie Ross; my cousins, Laura, Amy, and Crista Ambrosio, Dana Rowe, and Jamie Ross. I am especially grateful to my parents and sister for their support, love, and great senses of humor.

Finally, I thank Jeff and Max, who make everything worthwhile.

CHAPTER 1

CORPORATE CULTURE AND BUSINESS STUDIES

A TRIP TO PLANET ANDERSEN

In 1997, when I first clicked my cheap high heels across the tasteful marble floor of Andersen Consulting's lobby, I did so exclusively for financial reasons. As the elevator whisked me up to the building's top floor, I reminded myself of my slightly overdue rent check, which was why I was about to spend my week answering consultants' ever-ringing phones and formatting endless Excel spreadsheets. My temp agency had excitedly explained that Andersen paid its executive assistants quite well and that the firm would probably extend my work assignment if I proved to be reasonably efficient, obedient, and friendly. In fact, the agency representatives said many a bright-eyed temp eventually applied and was accepted to "go perm" at Andersen as a full-time, full-fledged employee. I had no such goals. I meant to stay there for five days, as scheduled. Instead, I stayed for almost a year, shuttling between various departments, filling in wherever I was needed, and leaving only when I moved out of state. During that time, I found myself living on Planet Andersen, fully immersed in what I can only describe as a foreign culture. I truly felt like an exchange student or even an intergalactic explorer. I was presented with a colorful new vocabulary, was given a sense of the politics between local fiefdoms, and was introduced to a set of values and customs fairly different from those I knew. I even got a sweet going-away party when I left the company, as if I was returning to my home world.

My experience at Andersen was relatively brief but intense. I spent the first two months assisting the codirector of the campus recruiting division of human resources. This assignment turned out to be my crash course in all things Andersen. As college seniors visited the office for tours and interviews, I learned along with them about the firm's departments and divisions, commonly used phrases, policies, expectations, and philosophies. Curious about the information I was (perhaps unwittingly) absorbing, I began to read the brochures and pamphlets I'd been asked to stuff into envelopes for mailing. These documents revealed more mysteries: the everyday activities of something called a "Change Management Team," the purpose of the "Products Group," and the innumerable "work-life" benefits available to full-time consultants. I had worked for several companies before my stint at Andersen, but had never previously encountered so much jargon or such wide-ranging policies and practices.

After a week or two, the lengthy training process to which new permanent hires were subjected no longer surprised me, given the immense amount of Andersen lore they were expected to know by heart. Later, when I switched departments and filled in for the vacationing assistants of various upper-level executives, I was able to use the appropriate lingo and follow the necessary guidelines. As a temp, however, I was not expected to embrace fully the philosophy set forth in the training and publicity manuals. I was at Andersen but not of it. There clearly was a way to be "of it," and most of my colleagues and supervisors—other than the small cadre of temps brought in to fill empty desks—had achieved "of it" status. For example, I noticed the unusually intense devotion to their jobs that the Andersen staff—from partners to receptionists—seemed to have. Other than the temps, many of my coworkers often skipped lunch, remaining at their desks almost all day, and regularly stayed in the office at least two hours after official closing time. Some of the partners I assisted almost never visited their home office and would call to check in from all sorts of far-flung locations: Paris, Singapore, Rio de Janeiro, or Battle Creek, Michigan. There were many people who had seemingly devoted every aspect of their lives to Andersen, and they gave the impression of being more than just employees, more than just executives. They were part of something—a community, an environment, or, perhaps, a culture.

Andersen Consulting (now known as Accenture) was where I became intrigued by the concept of "corporate culture"—often defined as the prevalent values and customs of an organization—and also where I first heard the phrase used in conversation. Although my work at Andersen was often secretarial rather than directly related to the firm's overall business goals, as an outsider I had a unique position from which to observe what corporate culture might mean at the workplace level. Since those months in 1997, I have learned how the phrase is used in business-related academic fields—administration, management, and industrial/organizational psychology, to name a few—but these scholarly approaches have never given me as strong a sense of "culture" as being in that Andersen office once did. Also, at Andersen, even while I admired my coworkers' abilities and attitudes, I felt deeply conflicted about the atmosphere I was breathing in. The long hours seemed somehow inhumane, the frequent travel caused family and personal relationship conflicts, and the unflagging enthusiasm about work (and more work and more work) as well as the overarching presence of Andersen in employees' everyday lives within and outside the office made me suspicious. I wondered, did a strong corporate culture eventually become a corporate cult? Did the many worker-friendly policies make up for the colonization of workers' time? Were my colleagues being duped into sacrificing their feelings and personal interests to the almighty gods of consulting? Or, was I just being paranoid, after all?

With the memory of all of those questions in mind, this book examines corporate cultures from many angles, focusing on what companies have to say about their own cultures as well as how organization theorists, management gurus, business self-help writers, and others have analyzed versions and aspects of the concept. My main goal is to investigate the effects of various manifestations of corporate culture on workers and managers. Ultimately, variations on two key themes emerge in the book; corporate culture becomes a form of worker governance (even when corporations explicitly state the opposite) and allows for the extension and strengthening of work's presence in all aspects of life, even aspects generally characterized as "personal" or "private." For example, as upcoming chapters will argue, there are corporate cultural phenomena that affirm and reward certain personality traits while punishing others, that inspire managers to value "progress" above all else, and that bring workers' physical health into the realm of business management. Corporate culture may sometimes seem to be little more than a convenient catch-all category invented for the sole purpose of selling business advice books, but the idea has had a truly profound effect on the American business world. Corporate culture has changed how managers think about employee relations and has altered how workers conduct themselves both in and out of the workplace—even if such changes and alterations are difficult to predict, never occurring exactly the same way twice. The chapters to come will look at some specific corporate cultural trends, such as a celebration of employee individuality and nonconformity, an encouragement of flexibility and adaptability for workers and organizations, an emphasis on the importance of worker wellness, and a particular view of business progress as the be-all and end-all of human activity. But, before delving into these trends, an outline of some fundamental issues and a historical background of the concept seem appropriate—the following sections of this chapter will provide these. Also, at the end of this chapter, I will examine the current status of corporations as a *research topic* in the humanities; specifically, I will situate this study within the context of contemporary cultural studies and suggest what a book such as this one can contribute to the field.

Writing about the influence of the stock market on American corporate practices in his book *After the New Economy* (2003), Doug Henwood distinguishes between micro- and macro-effects. For Henwood, the market does indeed dictate some of the strategic decisions of specific corporations: hiring and firing, the creation or dissolution of departments, mergers and acquisitions, et cetera. To call these decisions "micro" is not to diminish their importance to workers, managers, and stockholders, but rather to underscore the direct impact of a large, diffuse body (the market) on a relatively smaller and more centralized one (the corporation). Henwood is also interested, however, in the macro-level of effects, which "induce a climate of fear and deference. Workers who read stories of massive layoffs at brand-name firms may be more inclined to do whatever the boss asks—toil harder, longer, cheaper—than they would otherwise be . . . Restructuring CEOs may not be expanding their own bottom lines, but they're doing a favor to their class when they announce 5,000 layoffs" (216). In short, even when corporate restructuring strategies inspired by market demands do not immediately improve a particular company's profit margins, they do create an overall environment that encourages employees—*not just those at the company in question*—to play it safe, to keep their jobs by following the rules (whether explicit or implicit) and making extra efforts to impress. This study, while it will look at the inner workings of specific companies, is more invested (excuse the pun) in things *macro*—in the wide-ranging effects of various corporate cultural trends. When best-selling business book authors exhort managers to seek creativity and flexibility in job applicants, what might be the impact of this recommendation on the U.S. labor force? More broadly, when research scientists employed by a multinational pharmaceuticals manufacturer are pressured to speed up their work so that the company can introduce a new product, how does the current thinking on risk, accountability, and progress change? These are just a few examples of the kind of inquiry to be found in these pages.

And now for an important disclaimer: I want to emphasize here the impossibility of offering wholly definitive answers to the questions posed in this book. For one thing, arguments about influence are notoriously slippery; for instance, years of research have been unable to forge a definite link between the slapstick violence of Saturday morning cartoons and the aggressive behavior of many school-aged television viewers. Similarly, I cannot predict the exact actions, reactions, and responses of U.S. workers as they navigate the alternately smooth and shark-infested waters of American corporate culture. Because of the for-profit nature of most corporate work (no matter how low and even exploitative the wages may sometimes be), it's probable that many people will have to fall in line with what the business world wants—the alternative is far too risky, especially in uncertain economic times. Also, previous scholarly work and current evidence do strongly suggest certain outcomes. Those outcomes will be explored in this book, which focuses on specific values and attitudes that have recently emerged or become common in the corporate world. Some of these values have heritage dating back to the late nineteenth century or even earlier, while others are of newer vintage. But first, a macro-look—with some micro-examples—at "corporate culture" as a concept, at the history and implications of defining of business as "cultural," and at the future of corporate cultural studies.

"THE WAY WE DO THINGS AROUND HERE": DEFINING CORPORATE CULTURE

"Corporate culture," in this book, names a series of phenomena that range from official corporate policies to the less tangible values, attitudes, and philosophies of companies and industries—values that often comprise the driving force behind company policies and decisions. Taken together, my chapters on some of the more prevalent "themes" in (or aspects of) contemporary American corporate cultures provide an overview of what the phrase means today and also trace the significance of business's status as a "cultural" field, distinct from such relatively neutral terms as commerce or trade. I am particularly interested in how governance works through corporate culture, for example, how workers might shape their conduct in certain ways or how people are rewarded or punished for their adherence or lack thereof to certain values propounded by their workplace. The study as a whole focuses on the for-profit sector in the United States, which is where many of the management approaches described below were initially developed.[1]

Are some companies more "cultural" than others? In *No-Collar: The Humane Workplace and Its Hidden Costs* (2003), Andrew Ross describes the philosophy and day-to-day operations of Razorfish, a digital consultancy firm based in Silicon Alley (New York City's version of Silicon Valley). At the height of its success in the late 1990s, Razorfish epitomized "corporate culture" as it was gleefully depicted in news and business media of that era: casually dressed Generation X and Y employees mixing work with creative play in a nonhierarchical office with the latest high-tech gadgets. While this is precisely the kind of culture that dominated *Business Week* during the bubble years (a culture archly parodied by Razorfish, which kept a foosball table—a then popular symbol of the cool dot-com workplace—in the office as a joke), the office environment, values, and structure of Razorfish were by no means representative of corporate culture as usually envisioned by organization theorists and management gurus. Companies of all stripes, from web design companies in San Francisco to aluminum plants in Pittsburgh, have identified, labeled, and even advertised their cultures in mission statements, official policies, and corporate websites. A corporation does not have to be "hip," like Razorfish, to claim a culture, though the best-known elements of hipster corporate culture did spread from the bleeding-edge dotcoms into other, seemingly stodgier industries and organizations. At the Flint, Michigan tool and die plant of the venerable General Motors Corporation, line workers are encouraged to take breaks for yoga.[2] Universities and colleges—seen by some as a last bastion of uncorporatized space—have embraced the corporate value of "excellence" as they assess instructor performance and characterize students as customers to be served and satisfied.[3] The general definition of corporate culture below demonstrates the concept's applicability to a variety of contexts:

> By the early 1980s, companies were being encouraged to develop "strong cultures," with the aim of forging emotional bonds among employees and with the company that would feel just as meaningful as those encountered outside the workplace, among families or friends. Theoretically, the result, from the side of management, would be a boost in productivity and company loyalty. As for employees, they were supposed to acquire newfound respect, garner support for personal initiatives, and enjoy the kind of on-site dignity that had been auspiciously lacking in the age of the organization cog. (Ross 2003, 26)

Management theorists have pointed out that there are many different corporate cultures—as many as there are corporations. Each company has a culture, even if some companies might never define themselves using that term. It is also possible to speak of corporate culture more generally—as in "American corporate culture"—because the cultures of American companies tend to have a lot of traits in common. Consider, for instance, these three eerily similar descriptions of culture from three different corporations, from the early 2000s:

> As part of a global organization, with one underlying mission, the people of Deloitte share a common vision and set of beliefs. These fundamental elements define who we are and distinguish us in the eyes of our clients and our people. Our culture is our competitive advantage. (Monster.com 2008)
>
> Our firm's long-standing values of teamwork, client focus, excellence and entrepreneurship remain codified in our business principles... We believe that our culture, built on teamwork and excellence, affords opportunities for everyone to have an important impact on the building of our businesses. (Goldman Sachs Annual Report 2000)
>
> AT&T has culture. In fact, it has a mosaic of cultures, held together by a common identity. Our Common Bond is a major component of the glue that holds it all together. With the tenets of Our Common Bond as a solid foundation, the principles of culture provide the guide to the kinds of behaviors and attitudes that lead to great customer service, quality and reliability, open communication, teamwork, continuous improvement, innovation, and growth. (AT&T 2002)

Because of strong resemblances—and nearly content-free phrases—like those referenced above, getting a sense of what "corporate culture" may entail, rather than struggling to define it per se, seems to be the most relevant task.[4] For Deloitte, Goldman Sachs, and AT&T, culture is clearly equated with a set of values—values purportedly shared by all employees. (It is impossible to predict whether the employees in question really do share those values.) Culture is simultaneously a foundation that inspires teamwork and an outward-looking, customer-oriented attitude. Other corporations, like Microsoft and Yahoo, describe their culture as a two-fold focus on community service: what the company can contribute to charitable organizations and how the company's products and/or services enhance customers' lives. General Electric and General Motors define their cultures as commitments to learning. Both boast of their training facilities—corporate universities where new employees discover how to implement these practices and thus improve customer service. Already, in just these few examples, it is clear that a variety of ideas can fall within the broad category of corporate culture. The wording used by these businesses often sounds the same, but the areas of emphasis differ at least slightly from company to company.

To further complicate matters, the term (and the phenomena it invokes) also varies according to context. For example, by examining the online applicant recruitment materials of the top 20 *Fortune* 500 corporations (primarily multinationals with U.S. headquarters), one can trace how businesses' usage of the term "corporate culture" is affected and altered by context, most notably by the different audiences targeted by those businesses. The "careers" (or human resources) sections of many *Fortune* 500 corporations' websites include distinct—yet often hauntingly similar—versions of corporate culture, used strategically to appeal to particular groups of readers, be they college graduates, African Americans, or working parents. Of course, the effectiveness of the appeal is unpredictable; Ross describes downsized dot-commers scoffing at cultural "code words": "[They] were especially adept at picking apart recruitment ads... designed to draw gullible young inductees into the bondage of seventy-hour work-weeks" (Ross 2003, 202). Some firms emphasize the creative energies flowing within their offices, while others boast of their devoted attention to work-life balance issues, particularly for employees with families. Some businesses appeal to long-standing traditions of service and reliability (as noted earlier, corporate culture doesn't have to be hip or glamorous). Others choose to focus on the ethnic diversity of their employees and the welcoming and nurturing atmosphere they foster within their office walls. The human resources departments of countless corporations use *all* of the aforementioned aspects of office life and management to appeal to potential job applicants. Companies also group these aspects under the general rubric of corporate culture, usually labeled on their websites as "Our Culture."

The word "culture" itself constitutes an audience appeal, since the term is generally associated with community (as in societal culture), fun (as in pop culture), and even rebellion (as in subculture). "Corporate culture" conjures a picture quite different from popular images of business as bureaucracy and boredom. The appealing, empowering language of contemporary corporate culture contributes to its wide circulation; for example, business literature is a perennially best-selling genre, and motivational speakers and seminars (both live and televised) continue to be extremely popular with American audiences. In "Corporate Pleasures for a Corporate Planet" (1995), Christopher Newfield wonders why he so infrequently hears criticisms of business self-help writers and gurus. His answer is simple: people like business self-help, and the corporate culture it advocates, because it's fun and exciting. His description of best-selling author Tom Peters nicely encapsulates the issue: "Liberation management offers specific steps for more freedom, creativity, and prosperity in the place where you get paid. It constantly describes your life after the revolution, where oppressive authority is gone and there's even more money coming in" (Newfield 1995, 37).

Given the appeal of the concept, most major corporate websites include at least a brief mention of corporate culture and more often a lengthy and detailed account of what the company's culture is all about. AT&T is careful to insist that it has "an innovative, forward thinking spirit and culture" (AT&T 2008). On the same webpage, that culture is said to include such traits as dedication to customer service, the highest standards of integrity, respect for individuals, and community service. Principal Financial Group, meanwhile, announces its "commitment to integrity, team work, inclusion and the pursuit of excellence" (Principal Financial Group 2008). Running counter to many long-standing stereotypical portrayals of corporate America as the realm of the gray flannel-suited, conformist bureaucrat, Goldman Sachs's homepage trumpets, "Innovative thinking finds innovative companies" (Goldman Sachs 2008). Before it was felled by scandal in 2002, WorldCom once described its ideal workers as members of "Generation d... an attitude that enables the under-standing and embracing of the power of digital communications" (WorldCom 2001). Interestingly, in an analysis of WorldCom's woes, *Business Week's* May 2002 special report on "The Crisis in Corporate Governance"—like the websites of many well-known corporations, such as Microsoft, Yahoo, and Boeing—characterizes corporate cul-ture as a space of ethics. In other words, the conventions and values of these companies guide the behavior of employers and employees. The *Business Week* reporters argue that CEOs should take moral exemplar roles and lead their company cultures away from the stop-at-nothing competitiveness that may have contributed, to cite just two particularly dramatic examples, to WorldCom and Enron's "creative accounting" scandals in the early 2000s.[5]

Ultimately, given all of the issues described above, I get a sense that the phrase "corporate culture" is highly mutable. The category can encompass both official policies and procedures (e.g., flextime programs meant to help ensure healthy work-life balance for single parents in the workplace or diversity management training modules designed to improve communication skills) and those less tangible qualities that make corporations unique, or at least somewhat distinct, from each other. In corporate rhetoric, those intangibles include values ranging from creativity and openness to healthy balance and symbiosis—traits not typically associated, at least until fairly recently, with corporations. As Terrence Deal and Allan Kennedy put it in their groundbreaking 1982 book, *Corporate Cultures: The Rites and Rituals of Corporate Life,* corporate culture is "the way we do things around here" (4). Clearly, this deceptively simple definition is wide open to interpretation and is not without controversy. Meanwhile, Stanley Davis, who claims to have coined the term "corporate culture" in the first place, argues, "Every organization will have its own word or phrase to describe what it means by culture; some of these are: being, core, culture, ethos, identity, ideology, manner, patterns, philosophy, purpose, roots, spirit, style, vision, and way. To most managers, these mean pretty much the same thing" (Davis 1984, 1). The past three decades have seen some heated debates over how to interpret (and utilize) corporate culture—debates that began much earlier with the emergence of organization theory as a discipline.

ON THE HUMAN SIDE OF ENTERPRISE: 1910S–1960S

Business writers such as Deal and Kennedy have been discussing corporate culture for a long time; in fact, given the term's frequent association with the booming 1990s "New Economy," it's important to note that corporate culture is an older idea than many observers might expect. Though it is tempting to pinpoint 1982 as the year of corporate culture's birth (I will explain the particular significance of that date later), similar ideas emerged as early as the 1910s. As I hope to demonstrate, a look at the history of corporate culture helps to explain the current definitions of—and debates over—the concept itself. Also, the cultural trends described in the chapters of this book have a long, rich, and frequently disquieting history; even fairly recent developments, like casual Fridays and workplace napping, have heritage in older business philosophies—heritage that helps to illuminate the potential effects of their emergence.

Today, discussion of corporate culture occurs in three main arenas: within corporations themselves (as noted in the previous section of this chapter), in popular business literature, and in organization theory. The last of these arenas is worth examining in some detail here, because some of the issues explored by even the earliest organization theorists point the way toward current versions of corporate culture. Jay M. Shafritz and J. Steven Ott, editors of the *Classics of*

Organization Theory anthology, contend that organization theory (also sometimes known as management theory) first became a distinct field in 1776, with the publication of Adam Smith's *The Wealth of Nations* and the start of the search for the "one best way" to manage large groups of people (Shafritz and Ott 1987, 24). As Shafritz and Ott note, Smith's book outlines approaches to the emerging factory system of production—a system that, Smith argued, would require new management strategies, such as a division of labor into small, uncomplicated tasks, to ensure optimum efficiency and output.

The Wealth of Nations laid the groundwork for later theorists who also focused on efficiency in factory environments, such as the notorious Frederick W. Taylor, the father of so-called scientific management. Taylor devised a series of methods carefully calculated to increase the productivity of individual workers through measuring and timing each motion within a set physical task.[6] The classical school of organization theory, which includes Taylor and his adherents, was at its prime in the late nineteenth and early twentieth centuries. Chapter 2 discusses popular and industry responses to Taylor in detail, but the strong criticisms leveled at scientific management are worth briefly noting here. While Taylor's supporters cited the productivity improvements in scientifically managed factories, other observers worried about the dehumanizing aspects of the approach, arguing that workers were being treated like cogs in a vast apparatus rather than as people who needed and deserved on-the-job fulfillment and respect. These criticisms mark a turning point in the philosophy underlying organization theory; nineteenth-century views of workers were not known for their humanism. As Shafritz and Ott put it, "It was well into the twentieth century before the industrial workers of the United States and Europe began to enjoy even limited 'rights' as organizational citizens. Workers were viewed not as individuals but as interchangeable parts in an industrial machine whose parts were made of flesh only when it was impractical to make them out of steel" (21). Later, humanistic approaches would exhibit some serious problems of their own and would even be lambasted by a few critics as outraged as Taylor's. But, as we will see, the critics of humanism were neither as numerous nor as vocal as those of scientific management.

One writer normally grouped within this classical school, the French civil engineer Henri Fayol, is unusual in that he includes a rudimentary version of what might now be called "corporate culture" within his principles for successful management. The last of Fayol's 14 principles—originally written in 1916—could, with updated jargon, appear in a 1990s business self-help book:

Esprit de Corps. "Union is strength." Business heads would do well to ponder on this proverb. Harmony, union among the personnel of a concern, is great strength in that concern. Effort, then, should be made to establish it. Among the countless methods in use I will single out one principle to be observed and two pitfalls to be avoided. The principle to be observed is unity of command; the dangers to be avoided are (a) a misguided interpretation of the motto "divide and rule," (b) the abuse of written communications. (Fayol 1916, 64)

Like his contemporaries, Fayol was primarily concerned with questions of worker energy and output, but his work also stresses the importance of face-to-face contact between managers and employees and the success that managers can find if they encourage employees to take initiative, invent projects, and work together to follow tasks through to completion. In an era when Taylor was *discouraging* certain types of worker unity (for fear of "systematic soldiering," otherwise known as deliberate work slowdowns undertaken by groups of employees), Fayol acknowledged the possibility that worker attitude—and a positive workplace environment that fostered certain types of attitudes—could have significant effects on productivity.[7] (Interestingly, another of Fayol's principles is the subordination of individual interests, so that workers would think only about work while at the factory. One has to wonder about the effects of this principle on attitude.)

In the 1930s, increasing numbers of organization theorists picked up on ideas like Fayol's and began to emphasize the "human" side of management.[8] The newly surfacing ideas soon came to be known as the basic principles of Human Relations theory. This theory, at the time of its emergence and after the fact, was depicted as a refreshing, healthy change for the business world, leaving behind the cold mechanism of scientific management and moving toward a gentler, more human approach to the workplace.[9] Some writers, like Elton Mayo, presented findings with a radically different slant than Taylor's. Mayo and his colleagues from Harvard University's Graduate School of Business Administration conducted a series of experiments at the Hawthorne Plant of the Western Electric Company from 1927 to 1932. Their findings, published by Mayo in 1933 as *The Human Problems of an Industrial Civilization*, suggest that opportunities for workers to provide management with input and to enjoy a sense of community in the workplace are integral factors in individual and organization productivity. Mayo and his cohorts also found that within all formal organizations dwell "informal organizations" made up of personal relationships between coworkers; these informal groups dictate workers' behavior and perceptions of management and organization goals. The humanistic impulse remains central to theorists' comments on organizational culture today; it might even be said that Mayo's "informal organizations" are precursors of today's corporate cultures.[10] But, as Ross points out and as I will discuss in the chapters to come, the legacy of Human Relations is not necessarily a happy story: "In an exclusively market civilization, the *humane* workplace (with its feel-good stimulation and tests of mettle) has taken precedence over the *just* workplace (with protection for all, democratic control over the enterprise, and assurances of security beyond the job)" (Ross 2003, 20, italics in original). In other words, the humane treatment of workers comes with considerable costs. I would argue that the steepest of these costs include the colonization of workers' time by work-related activities, the extension of corporate control, and the perpetuation of a system wherein employees are encouraged to put up and shut up (even when their opinions are expressly sought and acknowledged).

Some writers further developed ideas culled from Mayo's work and even more strongly emphasized aspects of work that would now be characterized as "cultural." Chester Barnard, a former president of New Jersey Bell Telephone Company and a supporter of Mayo's, published a book in 1938, *The Functions of the Executive*, that painstakingly (and rather tediously) applied Human Relations tenets to everyday organizations.. Despite the book's inelegant, snail's pace prose, as of 1968 *Functions* "appear[ed] in virtually every bibliography on organization and [was] cited in such popular works as J.K. Galbraith's *The New Industrial State*... which credits [Barnard] with 'the most famous definition of an organization'" (Andrews 1968, vii). Barnard's work combines Mayo's account of employee belongingness and motivation with Fayol's earlier ideas about worker initiative (and organizational environments that foster said initiative). He argues that Mayo's "informal organizations," groups that affect how their members think and behave, are the bases for all formal organizations—in other words, organizational climate or culture is the foundation on which official organizational structures and policies rest. Recalling lessons learned during his experiences in management, Barnard focuses on possible means to encourage worker motivation and concludes that executives must fulfill three main functions to create a coherent, healthy, and loyalty-inspiring organization. The first executive function is to provide and articulate a purpose or mission for the organization as a whole: "Willingness to cooperate, except as a vague feeling or desire for association with others, cannot develop without an objective" (Barnard 1938, 86). The second is the development and maintenance of a strong communication system, so that information about the organization's objectives flows smoothly between employees and managers.

Central to Barnard's argument and to his influence on later organization theorists up to and including today's corporate culture gurus is the third function: offering both "objective" and "subjective" incentives to motivate employees. Whereas Taylor's scientific management principles exclusively relied on objective incentives—specifically, bonus pay for working at or above the desired production level— Barnard surmised that a variety of subjective incentives should be used to keep employees motivated and devoted to the organization. In *Functions,* he describes these subjective incentives:

> Inducements of a personal, non-materialistic character are of great importance to secure cooperative effort above the minimum material rewards essential to subsistence. The opportunities for distinction, prestige, personal power, and the attainment of dominating position are much more important that material rewards in the development of all sorts of organizations. (Barnard 1938, 145)

He also stresses that managers must create the kind of organization where workers can satisfy their "personal ideals," including "pride of workmanship, sense of adequacy, altruistic service for family or others, loyalty to organization in patriotism, etc., aesthetic and religious feeling" (146). Here, Barnard anticipates late twentieth-century developments in business discourse; first and foremost, he names many of the intangible elements now commonly associated with the development of strong corporate cultures. Earlier writers provided the basis for Barnard's theories, but he makes an explicit link between employee desires and a particular type of worker-friendly environment—a link that remains at the core of corporate culture theories today. But Barnard's strong emphasis on intangible rewards conjures the troubling image of workers being asked to contribute their ideas and energy without appropriate monetary compensation. Furthermore, his celebration of informal organizations full of motivated, "cooperative" employees raises questions about the place of unions and workplace democracy in the humane factory or office. These troubling aspects of Human Relations largely go unremarked in later organization theory.

Barnard's work also introduces a crucially important idea that often remains unsaid in contemporary writings about corporate culture, even though it underlies many management theories and business self-help books: employee belonging and enthusiasm as control mechanisms. He describes what he calls a "zone of indifference" wherein employees will accept and obey orders without question. This zone "will be wider or narrower depending upon the degree to which the inducements exceed the burdens and sacrifices which determine the individual's adhesion to the organization. It follows that the range of orders that will be accepted will be very limited among those who are barely induced to contribute to the system" (169). In other words, in Barnard's view, people who feel like they're motivated, respected, and valued will be more likely to heed what organizational authorities say. Though feeling motivated may well be more pleasant than feeling bored, overworked, or coerced, the important question is not so much a matter of "better" or "worse" approaches and effects. Much as losing 20 pounds, while a noteworthy accomplishment, does not mean you can ignore the other 400 pounds that the doctor ordered you to lose, *some* improvements to workplace policies and practices do not exclude the need for more improvements, even serious ones. And the "humane" corporate culture may well inspire workplace apathy or oversight of important issues... those 10 hours per week of unpaid overtime may not seem to matter when management throws a party to celebrate your department's productivity, just as the other 400 pounds may not seem that significant when you're enjoying kudos for the lost 20. Dangers lurk in pleasant workplaces and in brutal ones.

Although Barnard and Mayo before him are certainly influential figures in the realm of organization theory, their ideas did meet with significant criticism. In the 1950s, several well-known business writers called into question various tenets of the Human Relations approach. In *Organizations* (1958), James G. March and Herbert A. Simon challenge the efficacy of managerial boosting of employee motivation: "High morale is not a sufficient condition for high productivity, and does not necessarily lead to higher productivity than low morale" (48). They describe a complex and dynamic work model in which employees' reactions to organizational stimuli are highly personal and thus unpredictable—or much less predictable than Mayo or Barnard might have thought. March and Simon claim that managers have to inspire workers to *identify* with the organization: "The stronger an individual's identification with a group, the more likely that his goals will conform to his perception of group norms" (65). Personal motivation and enjoyment at work clearly does not matter in this model—only peer-pressured obedience (or, as Antonio Gramsci might put it, "winning consent") does. March and Simon's statement on conforming is made without a trace of skepticism or irony—a surprising lack, given the strong anti-conformity argument outlined just two years earlier by William H. Whyte in his famous book, *The Organization Man* (1956).

Whyte, whose work is discussed again in Chapter 2, diagnoses a serious problem inherent in Human Relations theory; he argues that the techniques for employee motivation espoused by Mayo and his cohorts are harmful because they create a culture of conformity. Managers as well as employees lose the ability to express their opinions because their need for group belonging supersedes any desire to challenge the status quo. Companies become deeply conservative as managers endeavor to maintain peace and avoid conflict—and ignore the potentially productive aspect of conflict in the workplace. Whyte also spells out what was implicit in Barnard's and Mayo's work: the motivational aspect of Human Relations theory can also be used as a form of governance—"Implicit in this technique is the assumption that the worker's problems can indeed be talked out. He is to adjust to the group rather than vice versa; and the alternative of actually changing reality is hardly considered" (Whyte 1956, 37). Again, the question of worker rights arises—will these allegedly humanely treated employees challenge management when problematic edicts are issued, and will they blow the whistle on unethical behavior? Whyte thinks not. In short, he asks, has humanism always been part of the *problem* in corporate America, rather than the solution? Whyte worries that the Human Relations approach makes workers docile while simultaneously allowing organizational problems to deepen—without sufficient challenge from anyone in the workplace.

Douglas McGregor hints at these problems of Human Relations and its offshoots, but ultimately relies on a somewhat different version of the same basic philosophy in his 1960 book, *The Human Side of Enterprise*. This book represents an important link between older forms of organization theory, such as those discussed above, and the culture-based approaches that came to dominate management books in the 1980s. According to McGregor, older management theories, whether mechanistic or humanistic, rested upon a particular set of assumptions about employee behavior: people inherently dislike work, have to be coerced into working, would rather avoid responsibility, like to be directed, and have little ambition. McGregor calls these assumptions "Theory X." McGregor's assertion about organization theory up to 1960 as Theory X-laden rings true; even in Mayo's work, there is a reliance on coercive tactics—however gentle and "humanistic"—to persuade employees to stay motivated at all times.

In *Personality and Organization* (1957), well-known organizational psychologist Chris Argyris even goes so far as to claim that "there is an inherent conflict between the personality of a mature adult and the needs of modern organizations"—a claim that underscores the basic worker/manager antagonism that McGregor describes (Shafritz and Ott 1987, 14). And, in *The Functions of the Executive*, Barnard reluctantly concedes that employee enthusiasm is not a naturally occurring phenomenon:

> Willingness... means self-abnegation, the surrender of control of personal conduct, the depersonalization of personal action... Activities cannot be coordinated unless there is first the disposition to make a personal act a contribution to an impersonal system of acts, one in which the individual gives up personal control of what he does.   (84)

Barnard goes on to say that individuals are more likely to make contributions if managers foster the proper environment. McGregor also emphasizes the significance of workplace environment, but argues that managers need to acknowledge certain truths about human nature (and the nature of work) before they can effectively lead a healthy organization. He advocates management strategies based on what he calls "Theory Y," a more generous interpretation of employee behavior *and* of the basic appeal of work activities. For McGregor, workers are capable of engaging in creative problem solving and are naturally oriented toward work, an arena in which they can achieve goals and find a sense of personal satisfaction. He writes that the aim of management strategies based on Theory Y is "to encourage integration, to create a situation in which a subordinate can achieve his own goals best by directing his efforts toward the objectives of the enterprise" (McGregor 1960, 61). As shown in this quotation, for McGregor there need be no basic conflict between individual "subordinate" and organization; with the help of effective management that encourages peoples' natural predilection toward work and amply demonstrates the connections between organizational and personal goals, there will be no reluctance or doubt to overcome, no barriers impeding motivation, no need to coerce employees with outlandish incentives.

As implied earlier, a friendly and peaceful workplace may be a pleasant location to spend at least eight hours per day, five days per week, but such a workplace (and the theories offering tips for its development) can be problematic. Certainly, McGregor's "Theory Y" appears to be a healthy attitude toward work and workers. McGregor jettisons the paternalism of Human Relations and the condescension of scientific management, instead acknowledging the talents and intelligence of workers at all organizational levels. But his insistence that with proper management there should be *no conflict* between individuals and the institutions that shape their lives is deeply disturbing. First, the strategic alignment of work and personal goals smoothly inserts work into life outside office or factory walls. As Nikolas Rose notes in *Powers*, governance relies "upon establishing relays between the calculations of authorities and the aspirations of free citizens" (Rose 1999, 49). Similarly, both Rose and Arlie Hochschild, among others, have asserted that the work-life boundary, if it was ever substantial to begin with, is barely discernable at this point—"the individual was to conduct his or her life, and that of his or her family, as a kind of enterprise, seeking to enhance and capitalize on existence itself through calculated acts and investments" (Rose 1999, 164). Hochschild's analysis of working mothers enjoined by self-help books to "invest" emotions and quality time in a few well-chosen people more vividly tells the same story as Rose's remark. And the issue extends well beyond family life and into civic and community issues; as Hochschild notes, "One trend in the American economy today is toward cultural consolidation of life around work, to make the workplace into a little town and meet all needs there" (2003, 210). With personal goals and social needs addressed in the workplace, thanks to a strong corporate culture, the public sphere seems to shrink.

The second problem is that McGregor overlooks the importance of various kinds of conflict—from everyday skepticism to overt protest to the securing and maintenance of worker rights. Especially in a country like the United States with lax governmental regulation of business, without the safeguards of skepticism and complaint, it would be far easier for management gradually to erode rights to fair wages, adequate benefits, and a safe work environment, to cite just a few examples. To situate this argument in a more contemporary context, it was angry Wal-Mart workers who challenged the store chain's dangerous nighttime worker lock-in policy and exposed the retail giant's unethical activities to the American media through interviews and legal action (Greenhouse 2004). Whether or not their bravery will make a lasting difference in policy remains to be seen, but Wal-Mart clearly fears lasting damage to its reputation (and the profit loss and stock depreciation that usually accompany said damage). The company's PR people had to scramble to improve the chain's image (Kaiser 2004). Without conflict of the sort that McGregor wants to manage away, this much-needed challenge to corporate authority would never have happened. As a famous, oft-quoted phrase goes, "The price of liberty is eternal vigilance." Leaving aside the loaded question of the existence of "liberty," the docility that McGregor wants managers to foster excludes such vigilance.

Problems aside, McGregor had a profound influence on the development of corporate culture as a concept. As with all of the theorists previously discussed (with the exception of Taylor), McGregor's work frequently refers to the paramount significance of workplace environment or climate; he insists that managers must learn more "about the creation of an organizational climate conducive to human growth" (McGregor 1960, vi). As of 1960, the similarly used word "culture" had yet to make its mark on management theory. Whyte occasionally uses the phrase "organizational culture" in *The Organization Man*. Shafritz and Ott, in the introduction to the "Organizational Culture" chapter of their anthology, refer to Elliott Jaques' *The Changing Culture of a Factory* (1951) as another early example of the term's use and also describe various books from the 1960s and the 1970s that examined "professional socialization processes" in different professional fields. They note, "As useful as these books were, they *assumed* the presence of organizational or professional cultures, and proceeded to examine issues involving the match between individuals and cultures" (Shafritz and Ott 1987, 376, italics in original). In the early 1980s, business writers began to explore that assumption and to theorize about the "human side of enterprise" as something specifically cultural. As the next section will show, a number of debates arose, mostly pertaining to the same key issue raised by earlier organization theorists: the conflict (or lack thereof) between individual desires and organizational goals.

"HE WHO HAS A *WHY* TO LIVE FOR CAN BEAR ALMOST ANY *HOW*": HEADING FOR THE BUBBLE YEARS

The Nietzsche quotation in the above heading appears in an especially peculiar passage of the frequently bizarre *In Search of Excellence* (1982), the best-selling business self-help book by Tom Peters and Robert H. Waterman, Jr.[11] In a chapter detailing the usefulness and appeal of corporate culture as a concept, Peters and Waterman link Nietzsche's words with their strategy for achieving business nirvana. Here's their epiphany: if a corporation can provide its workers with that "why"—with fulfillment of personal and social needs—that corporation will be rewarded with intense worker devotion. For Peters and Waterman, employees are deeply needy and naïve—a harsh claim somewhat softened by their use of the first person plural: "We desperately need meaning in our lives and will sacrifice a great deal to institutions that will provide meaning for us. We simultaneously need independence, to feel as though we are in charge of our destinies, and to have the ability to stick out" (Peters and Waterman 1982, 56). Culture, they argue, is the ideal provider of group belonging *and* a sense of autonomy—even if workers don't realize it, culture is the thing that makes them satisfied with their lot and happy to go to work each day.

This idea is unsettling in its blithe disregard for worker intelligence, perhaps, but Peters and Waterman's book points toward a more complex version of the "why" of work than previous organization theory. Where early and mid-twentieth century management scholars concentrated on the importance of worker motivation, business writers of the 1980s began digging deeper, investigating the many intangible elements that *inspire* and *maintain* those feelings of motivation. These newer writers claimed to look at employees and managers as whole people and went further than earlier writers in suggesting how work could satisfy social and personal desires, spark creativity, and—as seen in the Peters and Waterman quotation above—fulfill the simultaneous need to fit in and to stand out. The question of individual worker personality (or attitude) became central to the logic of corporate culture as management scholars and business self-help writers delineated the kinds of people most appropriate for cultural membership and the ability of certain personality types to perpetuate culture in the future. All of the aforementioned elements contributing to motivation had, of course, been introduced in earlier organization theory, but the increase in discussion of culture itself brought with it more detailed and specific analyses of organizational effectiveness than ever before. Indeed, like corporations themselves, corporate culture discourse has expanded and intensified in the past three decades. This section of the chapter will examine the issues described above, as well as the rise of the corporate culture concept, its staying power, and its multiple roles in the business world just before the "New Economy." This brief history of 1980s management theory points toward corporate cultural trends of the 1990s and the 2000s, specific discussion of which will largely be left for upcoming chapters.

Earlier, I mentioned that 1982 might be an appropriate date to mark the emergence of corporate culture as a popular term in management literature. Management trends from the late 1960s and the early 1970s set the stage for it—particularly systems theory, which was central to the business world's shift away from certain long-standing organizational traditions, like vertical, hierarchical structures.[12] In their organization theory anthology, Shafritz and Ott note that corporate culture became "a very hot topic" in the management field that year "almost overnight" thanks primarily to two books: Terrence E. Deal and Allan A. Kennedy's *Corporate Cultures: The Rites and Rituals of Corporate Life* and Peters and Waterman's aforementioned *In Search of Excellence: Lessons from America's Best-Run Companies* (Shafritz and Ott 1987, 377). The former of these was one of the first books to focus exclusively on culture, while the latter is often credited with ushering in the era of cultural organization theory. *In Search of Excellence* remains one of the best-selling American management books of all time.

The field's immediate impact and popular appeal affected its reputation. For example, Massachusetts Institute of Technology professor Edgar Schein, now considered to be one of the founders of organizational culture theory, saw the fledgling movement's credibility as shaky and endeavored to bolster it by using the tools of social scientists to provide evidence for culture's influence on corporations. Shafritz and Ott's anthology criticizes many of the corporate culture theorists for lacking scientific vigor and characterizes this school of thought as the rebellious youngster in the organization theory family: "[This] perspective represents a 'counterculture'... Its assumptions, theories, and approaches are very different from those of the dominant 'modern' structural and systems schools" (373). In keeping with its allegedly countercultural aspect, the overall style of corporate culture studies differs significantly from that of earlier management theory. Whereas older work aspired to academic credibility by maintaining an "objective" tone and basing claims on quantifiable evidence, some 1980s writers (many of whom also came to be known as "management gurus") deliberately fashioned themselves as nonconformists by writing in a more colloquial style, referring to empirical data less and less frequently and making eccentric appearances on the public speaking circuit. Tom Peters epitomizes this phenomenon. Also, the 1980s writers worked within a context that the earlier writers could never have anticipated. Concerns about competition from Japanese companies (most of which were nonhierarchical in structure), coupled with interest in ideas culled from systems theory, led to the increased appeal of horizontal, flat, or matrix organizational strategies. In the absence of structural hierarchy, many authors posited corporate culture as the glue holding companies together. So, the corporate culture movement of 1982 was indeed a new development, even if many of its tenets were based on older theories.

Deal and Kennedy's *Corporate Cultures*, which heralded this new organizational approach and brought the phrase "corporate culture" into popular usage, begins with a description of a then successful Silicon Valley company called Tandem.[13] The authors interview Tandem employees who all express intense enthusiasm for their work. "I feel like putting a lot of time in… I'm not a workaholic—it's just the place. I love the place," says one, while another proclaims, "I don't want anything in the world that would hurt Tandem. I feel totally divorced from my old company, but not Tandem" (Deal and Kennedy 1982, 9). Deal and Kennedy, then a Harvard University Graduate School of Education professor and a principal at McKinley & Company consulting firm, respectively, confess the reason for their fascination with these workers: "What is it about Tandem's organization that exerts such a grip on its employees?" (13). Ultimately, they find that the "grip" in question is corporate culture.

Culture, in the context of the book, denotes organizational values, heroes (people who exemplify those values), rites and rituals (which "show employees the kind of behavior that is expected of them… examples of what the company stands for"), and communication networks (14–15). Strong mission statements are highlighted; like Barnard before them, Deal and Kennedy recommend that managers clearly announce and try to personify company objectives, so that workers have something to believe in. (Of course, it's difficult to determine whether employees can actually benefit from "believing in" such empty yet frequently cited values as "excellence" or "service.") The authors also recall earlier theorists by insisting upon the strong influence of environment on companies: "A corporate culture embodies what it takes to succeed in [the] environment. If hard selling is required for success, the culture will be one that encourages people to buy and sell hard" (107). Finally, Deal and Kennedy make a case for corporate culture as the new "one best way" for companies to flourish. Culture ensures that order is maintained in the absence of traditional hierarchy, and culture increases productivity by motivating employees and making sure that they feel a strong bond to the organization and to each other.

> Without strong cultural bonds, atomized work units would fly off in a centrifugal plane. The winners in the business world of tomorrow will be the heroes who can forge the values and beliefs, the rituals and ceremonies, and a cultural network of storytellers and priests that can keep working productively in semi-autonomous units that identify with a corporate whole. (193)

As suggested in the quotation above, corporate culture, for Deal and Kennedy, is a form of *governance*. It's what keeps the company organized when traditional centers of authority are dispersed. It's what instructs and advises workers on how to act, how to think and make decisions, and how to get things done. Note, for example, that all of the key elements of culture as defined by Deal and Kennedy— values, heroes, rites, and communication networks—are things that can be dictated, decided, or at the very least advocated by management.[14] What the authors describe is not the gradual growth of culture over time, but a series of strategic maneuvers calculated to enhance the corporation: "A strong culture is a series of informal rules that spells out how people are expected to behave... by knowing exactly what is expected of them, employees will waste little time in deciding how to act in a given situation... The impact of a strong culture on productivity is amazing" (15). This is not to say that the strategy will inevitably be successful or that employees will always be receptive to management's messages. As Edgar Schein observed after the publication of Deal and Kennedy's book, "All the recent writings about improving organizational effectiveness through creating 'strong' and 'appropriate' cultures continue to proliferate the possibly quite *incorrect* assumption that culture can be changed to suit our purposes" (Schein 1985, 383).[15] Still, as Deal and Kennedy are clearly aware, corporate culture as a concept has a certain seductiveness, in part because it supposedly fosters employee satisfaction and a pleasant sense of identification with the job and the workplace (as in the Tandem example). The authors describe how people feel better about their jobs knowing that their company has an identifiable "personality"—and how those people will therefore make sacrifices for the organization. "The next time they have the choice of working an extra half hour or sloughing off, they'll probably work," they gleefully report (Deal and Kennedy 16).

This final point brings me to the more disturbing aspects of Deal and Kennedy's work and of corporate culture theory in general. Distinct from earlier organization theory based on empirical data, *Corporate Cultures* takes on an overtly moralistic tone, expressing nostalgia for supposedly simpler times when people trusted the institutions that shaped their lives: work, school, family, religion, and the like. Work, of course, is Deal and Kennedy's special concern; they claim, "Unlike workers ten or twenty years ago, employees today are confused... they feel cheated by their job; they allow special interests to take up their time; their life values are uncertain; they are blameful and cynical; they confuse morality with ethics" (16). Here, Deal and Kennedy hearken back to the nastier elements of McGregor's Theory X, pitting manager against worker and evincing basic mistrust of corporate employees. They argue that corporations should be the entities to swoop in and save the day, providing the strong and reliable values now allegedly lacking in other aspects of everyday life in the United States. In their model, corporate culture triumphantly stands in for other modes of culture: "Strong culture companies remove a great deal of that uncertainty... In fact, corporations may be among the last institutions in America that can effectively take on the role of shaping values. We think that workers, managers, and chief executive officers should recognize this need and act on it" (16). Peters and Waterman, among others, similarly posit corporate culture as a savior in uncertain times.

I see several problems with this argument. First, Deal and Kennedy were writing at a time when corporations were not doing much to earn the workers' trust (or the public's trust, for that matter). The 1970s marked the beginning of a long period of layoffs in a variety of fields, from manufacturing to corporate management. Fears of Japanese and German competition spurred yet more job losses in the early 1980s—what Ross calls a "sacrifice to the gods of cash flow and profit maximization" (Ross 2003, 8). Thus, the worker "cynicism" and "blamefulness" that Deal and Kennedy describe with such irritation may have been quite justified during that period of unpredictability and anxiety. Second, benefits accrue to corporations that, through a strong culture or any other management strategy, alleviate worker "uncertainty." When corporations, following Deal and Kennedy's advice, insist that their workers must become "more flexible and less job-dependent" (180), why shouldn't those workers be angry? Docile workers made comfortable by their company's culture may provide much needed compliance, especially, again, in a rocky economy. For example, a culture like Tandem's may keep employees away from the union office or even the suggestions box. Worker satisfaction is not a cause for alarm in and of itself, but as Michel Foucault often argued, things that seem benevolent should be regarded with suspicion, for these things have multiple effects—some of which may not be so benevolent.[16]

The most important problem here, though, is Deal and Kennedy's intimation that corporate values are the only values that matter.[17] *Corporate Cultures* urges managers to be more aggressive in usurping the traditional roles of teachers and parents: "In today's self-conscious world, where things are supposed to be 'laid back' and 'easy-going,' few managers have the conviction to set any standard for behavior" (76).

While the influence of families or schools is not entirely unproblematic in itself, I shudder to think of work as the most influential and far-reaching presence in people's lives. I am not saying that corporations are always consciously plotting to trick people into working longer and harder and applying efficiency standards to all aspects of their everyday lives, but I would argue that much of the network of values and discourses produced by managers and management gurus is not necessarily useful as a guide for ethical decision making or as a guide for living—a point dramatically illustrated by the infamous Enron debacle.

Before its stunning collapse, Enron was a leading U.S.-based energy firm repeatedly named "America's Most Innovative Company" by *Fortune* magazine. The company went bankrupt in 2001 due to allegations of massive accounting fraud: top executives hid Enron's debts and inflated its profits. Once the full story of Enron was revealed by employees, journalists, and executive testimonials during government hearings, the fraud hardly seemed surprising, given the hypercompetitive culture fostered by former CEO Jeffrey Skilling and other managers. In Bethany McLean and Peter Elkind's *The Smartest Guys in the Room: The Amazing Rise and Scandalous Fall of Enron* (2003), many former Enron workers describe the company's workplace environment in the mid- to late 1990s as cutthroat—so much so that colleagues lost sight of their ethics: "Gradually, people who valued teamwork were weeded out... and those who stayed and thrived were the ones who were the most ruthless in cutting deals and looking out for themselves" (121).

While Enron is an extreme example of corporate malfeasance and of the impact of an unethical culture on workers' lives, the application of more typical business values to family relationships, friendships, community service, national government, and the natural environment can be destructive. Hochschild has demonstrated the insidious effects of corporate capitalism on family life and childcare. Paul Hawken has argued that the way business conceptualizes nature—as a resource—contributes to the ongoing pollution of our air and water, deforestation, species extinction, and global warming. Barbara Ehrenreich has shown how companies, eager to improve profit margins, keep wages low, thereby helping to create a vast population of "the working poor" in the United States. Clearly, an uninterrogated embracing of business values has far-reaching implications in a variety of crucially important areas.

Likewise troubling is corporate culture advocates' notion that companies can and should foster certain personality traits that may further company interests—a concern voiced by Whyte back in 1956 that remains vital today. The active encouragement of particular personality types in the business world may conjure alarming images of brainwashed corporate zombies, but is quite typical in 1980s and 1990s management thinking. Oddly, for all of their talk of moral standards, Deal and Kennedy celebrate those who cast aside standards (in the name of company innovation and progress, of course): "While business certainly needs managers to make the trains run on time, it more desperately needs heroes to get the engine going" (38).[18] This encouragement of nonconformity and innovation is also central to Peters and Waterman's corporate culture book of the same era, *In Search of Excellence*. (In fact, Deal and Kennedy once described themselves as "intellectual godsons" of Peters.)[19] But creativity is not the only personality trait encouraged by the cultures of American corporations. Dave Arnott, author of *Corporate Cults*, describes an army of friendly, enthusiastic Southwest Airlines employees who, despite the company's casual and nonrestrictive dress code, were all wearing the same clothes: khakis and a polo shirt with the corporate logo on it. Management theorists Caren Siehl and Joanne Martin explain the process by which corporate cultures reward certain types of people: "[They] teach, support, and demonstrate behavior and attitudes that are appropriate for a particular cultural context... culture helps to maintain boundaries. In- versus out-groups arise that help to define who is and who is not behaving appropriately" (1984, 434). The in- and out-groups mentioned here are powerfully reminiscent of teenagers' social cliques, raising the question of just how pleasant it is to work in such a "cultural" workplace. Speaking of high school social life, Henwood notes that the reinforcement and training of particular business-friendly personalities may begin earlier than the first job and even earlier than college. He finds that surveys of both employers and high school teachers show approval of employees (or students) who are "steadfast, dependable, consistent, punctual, tactful, and who identify with work and show sympathy for others" (2003, 76). Schools are expected, Henwood notes, to teach students those traits, to model enthusiastic and obedient behavior (while, one assumes, punishing the opposite sort of behavior). Although Henwood's findings don't precisely match the theories of Deal, Kennedy, Peters, and Waterman, the same point comes across: corporations are asking for certain kinds of people, and they're getting what they ask for.

The management gurus of the 1980s also found, though, that corporations can't *always* get what they want—not without concerted effort and the ability and willingness to change. For example, Peters and Waterman strengthened the environment-culture link alluded to by Deal and Kennedy, thus establishing a theme that later became central to corporate culture discourse: the need for flexibility. The standard argument—initially introduced in the 1980s—is as follows: organizations, managers, and employees must all become flexible in order to survive changes in the business world. *In Search of Excellence* uses Darwinian imagery to describe the need for corporate change: "To the extent that culture and shared values are important in unifying the social dimensions of an organization, managed evolution is important in keeping a company adaptive" (Peters and Waterman 1982, 106). This is an early example of the flexibility discourse that will be discussed in Chapter 3. Peters and Waterman also worry about a potential evolution problem in strong corporate cultures: these cultures may resist environmental changes and fall behind quicker, more agile cultures. This worry is an interesting moment in the book, because despite all of their praise of culture-based organizational management, the authors ultimately sound like aforementioned business doomsayer William Whyte. They acknowledge the inherent dangers of corporate culture: blind adherence to cultural dictates and the possibility that managers will enforce loyalty through coercive tactics ("now that you're like the rest of us, you won't be able to fit in anywhere else"). Peters and Waterman even refer to the notorious obedience experiments of Stanley Milgram as they fret about unthinking corporate conformity.

In keeping with their comments on company and employee evolution, Peters and Waterman argue that the conventional management wisdom must become less conventional, must demonstrate its own form of flexibility and adaptability to environmental (market) conditions: "[Management] Theory is not tight enough to consider the role of rigidly shared values and culture as the prime source of purpose and stability... At the same time, most current theory is not loose enough to consider the relative lack of structure and the need for wholly new management logic to ensure continuous adaptation in large enterprises" (106). Organization theory and business self-help discourses did become "loose" in the 1990s, both in terms of style (Peters, prone to strange digressions and outlandish imagery, was a trendsetter) and content. But before delving into contemporary trends in corporate culture discourse, one more detour: a look at academic approaches (or lack thereof) to corporate culture, from *outside* the discipline of management/organization theory.

CORPORATE CULTURAL STUDIES

In his critique of American business practices, *One Market under God: Extreme Capitalism, Market Populism, and the End of Economic Democracy* (2000), Thomas Frank complains that the field of academic cultural studies has all but ignored corporate culture as a subject of inquiry. "For all its generalized hostility to business and frequent discussions of 'late capital,'" he writes, "cultural studies failed almost completely to produce close analyses of the daily life of business. Convinced that the really important moment of production was not in the factory or in the TV studio but in the living rooms and on dance floors as audiences made their own meanings from the text of the world around them, the cult studs generally left matters of industry up to the business press" (Frank 2000, 290–291). Frank's provocative characterization of cultural studies seems somewhat unfair; especially since the late 1990s, an increasing number of researchers in the field have devoted time to analyzing and engaging with texts and phenomena from the business world. Some examples of these will be discussed below. Also, the field of "cultural policy studies," while still a subject of significant debate, has contributed to a movement away from theories of fandom and rebellion and toward sustained encounters with forces of production and distribution.[20] Policy researchers do precisely what their moniker implies—they examine and even contribute ideas to the institutions and regulations that shape our lives; of course, this interest leads many of these researchers to focus on corporations.

Still, despite noteworthy exceptions, Frank's feeling of dissatisfaction with cultural studies seems justifiable. As Eric Guthey asks, "Why have so many highly trained, intelligent and critical cultural scholars... chosen to overlook so completely the burgeoning corporatization of American culture? Isn't this a bit like oceanographers refusing to acknowledge the existence of water?" (qtd. in Frank 2000, 291). In short, U.S. culture is steeped in corporate values and strongly influenced by corporate practices. The average American adult spends more than one-third of his/her waking life at work.[21] And there simply aren't enough researchers attending to these facts of American life.

So, regardless of misgivings, I initially began this study with Frank in mind, because I also feel that the effects and manifestations of the business world merit a much closer look. As Avery Gordon notes in an article on diversity management,

Those of us in academic cultural studies have not been paying enough attention to the fact that there is a whole parallel intellectual sphere where writing and thinking about culture... occurs. Not paying attention means we may be missing the opportunity to learn from it and to influence it. In short, I think academic cultural studies would benefit from greater corporate literacy. (1995, 4)

Frank and Gordon lament a shortage of "close," specific analyses of business culture—a shortage that I have also noticed in my research. But, as noted earlier, there are exceptions—and these exceptions point toward a trend that has been gaining momentum for more than a decade. Though the business world remains an undertheorized, underanalyzed subject area within cultural studies, increasing numbers of researchers from a variety of disciplines have been scrutinizing aspects of corporate culture and practice since about 1990. The growing list includes practitioners from sociology (Arlie Hochschild, Avery Gordon, Nikolas Rose), American studies (Andrew Ross), anthropology (Emily Martin), psychology (Nancy Tippins), public policy (Randy Martin), English (Evan Watkins, Christopher Newfield), and outside the academy (Jill Andresky Fraser, Doug Henwood, Thomas Frank). There are business, economics, and management scholars who pay careful and critical attention to corporate culture and could be added to my list; the journal *Management Communication Quarterly* and the edited collection *Foucault, Management and Organization Theory* provide representative illustrations of their work. Also, to varying degrees, the listed writers are influenced by the ideas of earlier philosophers and critical theorists, many of whom analyzed not only capitalism as a system but also the apparatuses of the workplace. A very incomplete list of these thinkers could include Karl Marx, Max Weber, Thorstein Veblen, Michel Foucault, and Gilles Deleuze. I categorize all of the above writers as belonging to the nascent field of *cultural studies of business* or *business studies*.

My definition of business studies owes a great deal to Joseph Rouse's painstaking discussion of "cultural studies of scientific knowledge" (hereafter referred to as "cssk"). In a 1993 article, Rouse describes cssk as "various investigations of the practices through which scientific knowledge is articulated and maintained in specific cultural contexts, and translated and extended into new contexts" (58). Replacing the word "scientific" with the word "business" provides me with a workable illustration of what business studies researchers do. In short, these researchers examine the origins, mechanisms, and effects of business knowledge, discourse, and practice. This very general definition is appropriate because, as Rouse is careful to emphasize in the context of his analysis of cssk, the field encompasses a rich variety of methodologies, guiding philosophies, and political stances. Indeed, Rouse's comments on the diversity within cssk and my view of business studies resonate with definitions of "cultural studies" itself; as Tony Bennett wrote, cultural studies is "a term of convenience for a fairly dispersed array of theoretical and political positions... which, however wildly divergent they might be in other respects, share a commitment to examining cultural practices from the point of view of the intrication with, and within, relations of power" (qtd. in Nelson, Treichler, and Grossberg 1992, 3). As a branch of cultural studies, business studies, as I envision it, benefits from its diversity and interdisciplinarity—from the interaction between scholars from various fields (including business itself) and from the exchange of research sources.

Fittingly, this book—my own foray into business studies—uses a wide variety of sources, ranging from self-help best sellers to novels to human resources pamphlets to philosophy and cultural theory.[22] The corporate, theoretical, administrative, and literary sources that I refer to in upcoming chapters would not traditionally be thought of as a coherent group of research subjects. Yet, I hope to show over the course of the chapters how these areas might be grouped together and why it would be fruitful to do so. Because the world of work—time spent doing some sort of paid labor—encompasses such a significant portion of most Americans' daily lives, it makes sense that many of the sources I use to examine corporate culture stem from the realm of the everyday and the popular. By "everyday" I do not mean "unenlightened" or "simplistic" or "common," but, following Michel de Certeau, "specific" or "concrete" or, quite literally, "everyday"—emerging from what people tend to encounter and practice day in and day out. Literature may therefore be "everyday," as may official corporate documents or self-help books. Also, as might be expected, much of my work on corporate culture—and the work of business studies in general—situates its inquiry at the level of the corporation: mission statements, human resources materials, official policies, business-related self-help or advice books, and the like.

If business studies includes such an assortment of disciplines, approaches, and sources, what are the commonalities that allow me to posit it as a distinct field? What, if anything, might its practitioners have in common? First, business studies researchers take business seriously. This point may sound obvious, but the "generalized hostility" toward business that Frank observes in cultural studies is probably why corporate discourses remain underanalyzed in contemporary academia. Instead of dismissing all corporate rhetoric as yet more ideological trickery from some nebulous and thoroughly evil version of "The Man," business studies researchers (with some exceptions) specifically attend to the production, distribution, and effects of corporate thought. Instead of repeatedly insisting only on the repressive aspects of corporate power (of which, to be sure, there are many), the most interesting work in business studies conducts a more nuanced examination of the multiple and simultaneous effects of business practices and discourses. After all, to label any and all management theory or New Economy rhetoric as merely ideology is to simplify it and thereby run the risk of ignoring its far-reaching, manifold impact. As Evan Watkins notes,

> Taking [business] seriously means more than unmasking new disguises for familiar ideological agendas. There is a sense in which corporations, like Kurt Vonnegut characters, are what they pretend to be. The question is what exactly are they pretending to be. What do they promise? What do they appeal to? How do they work? (1995, 2)

In the spirit of contemporary cultural studies, Watkins goes on to say that even the most seemingly "degraded" business discourses—popular self-help books for managers, for instance—should be taken seriously as valuable sources of insight into the effects of business on society. Watkins's argument brings me to another important commonality shared by business studies writers: the idea that business and society are mutually determining forces. In short, the traffic between corporations and societies is two way, and both entities have permeable if not invisible boundaries; corporate culture shapes and is shaped by public life. While many people might wish that work life were completely separate from "private" life, business studies writers generally acknowledge the fact that such a distinction is impossible to uphold. Late twentieth century developments—such as the increase in U.S. work hours and the widespread availability of communication technologies and "cybercommuting" options—made the interrelationship between business and society more apparent. Corporate presence in schools, communities, and governments cannot be cast aside, shut down, or locked out. Similarly, business discourses and practices are cultural formations strongly impacted by societal values and contexts. American corporate culture can be affected by common attitudes about race or gender, by popular books and television programs, or by a Congress dominated by a particular political party. As

James Livingston notes, "Corporate culture is no more impervious to the larger society than the most self-conscious ethnic enclaves, and so cannot be studied (or exhorted) as if it represents the uncomplicated Other that once enabled our disciplines" (1995, 67).

Another commonality to be found in business studies is admittedly quite general but nonetheless significant: an interest in power and governance. Following Foucault, most business studies writers, such as Emily Martin and Nikolas Rose, paint a detailed picture of how governance works—often at a distance rather than in a clear and direct manner—through corporate discourses. As Nelson, Treichler, and Grossberg note, "Cultural studies cannot be used to denigrate a whole class of cultural objects, though it can certainly indict the uses to which those objects have been put" (1992, 13). Upcoming chapters will further illustrate and clarify some of the uses of corporate "cultural objects"—various modes of governance within American corporate culture.

Assuming that this account of the main features of business studies is persuasive, an important question may still remain: why is business studies necessary or useful? Why add another subfield to an already long and often bewildering list of academic disciplines? Why call for business studies to foster its own academic courses, conferences, journals, and edited collections? Watkins claims that the "study of corporate culture yields necessary knowledge for academics—for those in the humanities and the social sciences no less than for those in professional schools" (Watkins 1995, 2). But what might that "necessary knowledge" be? Certainly, the sociologists and anthropologists among business studies scholars have good reason to investigate corporate culture. As James March and Herbert Simon pointed out back in 1958, social scientists "are interested in explaining human behavior... in what influences impinge upon the individual human being from his environment and how he responds to these influences. For most people formal organizations represent a major part of the environment" (2). Thanks primarily to cultural studies, researchers in the humanities (e.g., in English and comparative literature departments) are also showing interest in human behavior—particularly in the everyday workings of power and governance in terms of race, gender, and (to a lesser extent, I'd argue) social class. Business studies could become an integral part of those inquiries about power, precisely because of the field's relatively mundane area of focus. As Rose puts it, "It is, most often, at this vulgar, pragmatic, quotidian and minor level that one can see the languages and techniques being invented that will reshape understandings of the subjects and objects of government" (Rose 1999, 31).

While, as claimed earlier, business and society are mutually determining rather than mutually exclusive, the thought that schools and universities might wholeheartedly, unskeptically embrace business values gives me pause. University-level business studies programs could provide students with valuable information about the corporate sector while simultaneously encouraging them to maintain a healthy skepticism about business. If, as Bill Readings argues, corporate presence in American universities is already pervasive and influential, then it makes sense for professors to take a closer look at manifestations of corporate culture—its rhetoric, its policies—in order to engage with it more carefully and strategically. But there is more than one way to engage, and some strategies are more balanced than others. Consider, for example, the contrast between business studies, as I have described it, and an argument espoused by Daniel Rabuzzi in the journal *Liberal Education*. Rabuzzi writes that liberal arts professors should cooperate with the future employers of our students as we design and teach courses. Teaming with campus placement offices, liberal arts departments could develop relationships with corporations and government agencies to persuade them to hire more humanities graduates. Humanities professors could talk with corporate and agency officers about how those skills either are or might be taught (Rabuzzi 2001).

On one hand, as said earlier, there is no point in pretending that corporations have no presence in today's universities. Similarly, it is pointless (and misguided) to assume that corporate presence is *always* problematic and harmful. Given the reality of economic instability, it's also highly likely that many students, including liberal arts majors, are concerned about their postgraduation employability; therefore, Rabuzzi's encouragement of "job training" in fields that aren't traditionally categorized as preprofessional makes some sense. But Rabuzzi's article overlooks a crucial problem: if corporations are allowed to have direct input into classroom activities and syllabi, what kinds of knowledge will they tend to privilege over others, and what kinds of knowledge might be cast aside? What will teachers be discouraged from teaching? And what about critical thinking skills? It is a mistake to believe that students don't have critical thinking skills before they enter the college classroom, but it's also the case the college can sharpen those skills. Do corporations want critical thinkers? As Henwood found in his research for *After the New Economy*, the answer to that question is a resounding "no." My hope is that by honing their skills of close observation and analysis, business studies students will not only act as much needed workplace watchdogs, but also work toward changing the most troubling aspects of contemporary business—the colonization of workers' time, the erosion of workers' rights, and the destruction of the natural environment, to give a few examples.[23] As I hope this book will demonstrate, we need to go well beyond current work-life and environmentally friendly strategies. Perhaps business studies students and scholars will be the people to accomplish this important goal. In fairness to Rabuzzi, his argument eventually seems to arrive at a similar conclusion—he writes that corporations want to develop "learning organizations" and creativity in the workplace, but are unsure how to do so. And he claims that liberal arts graduates with corporate literacy can lead the way.

Rose once described his own work as "a suspicious attention to the petty humiliations and degradations carried out in the name of our own best interests" (Rose 1999, 60). This statement has guided me in my research and underlies my sense of what business studies could be—suspicious attention, rather than a simplistic debunking or an unproductive attack. Certainly, there are many serious allegations that one could level against specific corporations and against corporate business in general—exploitation of workers, destruction of the natural environment, and unethical conduct, to give a few prominent examples. In my mind, all of these accusations would be accurate to one degree or another.[24] But to halt the inquiry at the act of accusation and exposure would be to fall short of conducting a rigorous and nuanced investigation of what corporations—particularly, corporate cultures—can do. I hope that I have already demonstrated such a "beyond critique" endeavor here. This book will suggest ways to approach corporate rhetoric and policy without stopping at the act of critique and without allowing squeamishness to obstruct analysis and discussion. While I admit that I am tempted in this book to seek and skewer easy targets—the proverbial fish shot in a barrel—I am committed to examining self-help books, corporate publicity statements, and human resources propaganda with an eye for nuance and complex implications. I also acknowledge that people have much to be suspicious or critical of in corporate culture; there are many elements of corporate rhetoric and policy that people might find infuriating or even repugnant. My conclusions will not always be rosy. However, even potentially destructive elements of corporate culture—the justification of downsizing espoused in Spencer Johnson's mega best seller, *Who Moved My Cheese?* or Citigroup's proud trumpeting of its "scale" and "strength," even after announcing plans to lay off over 50,000 employees worldwide, for example—might somehow be leveraged to other ends (Citigroup 2008). Therefore, in the chapters to follow,

I intend to conduct a thorough analysis of corporate culture's multiple and simultaneous effects.

Each chapter discusses a particular theme within contemporary corporate discourse. Chapter 2, "From Organization Man to Liberation Management: An Examination of Individuality and Conformity in the Workplace," explores a trend that has gained momentum in American business discourses: an increasing emphasis on the individuality, diversity, and uniqueness of corporate employees. The celebration of individuality manifests itself in three main ways: work-life policies and rhetoric, diversity management, and individual creativity and self-expression in the workplace. Using Foucault's ideas about disciplinary power and Wendy Brown's concept of the "liberal subject" as a theoretical backdrop, my aim in the chapter is to trace how these corporate appeals to individualism can become forms of governance, affecting how workers act, think, and live their lives. Corporate appeals to individualism have many possible effects, including the promotion of worker loyalty, the encouragement of consumer spending, and the improvement of corporate image.

Chapter 3, "Survival at Work: Flexibility and Adaptability in American Corporate Culture," elaborates on the individuality theme by analyzing the emphasis on individual workers' "adaptability" and "flexibility" in corporate culture and the use of terms culled from Social Darwinism—most notably, "survival of the fittest"—in business advice books and management theory. First, I discuss the history of natural selection as a business concept. The chapter then examines more recent forays into Darwinian corporate philosophy; many of the most successful self-help business books from the late 1990s argue that flexibility—willingness to embrace change—is central to "survival" in the corporate world. Finally, I suggest that the point to take away from this analysis of Darwinian imagery in business discourses is the same point that frightened so many of Darwin's contemporaries when *On the Origin of Species* was first published: when it comes to evolution, no one gets to *choose* to survive.

Chapter 4, "Taking Care of Business: Corporate Performance, Self-Care, and the Healthy Workplace," examines another "survival"-related issue: the intersection between corporate governance and self-help or self-care. Increased attention to worker health—eating, sleeping, and exercise habits—is one example of how the emerging relationship between corporate policy and self-help discourse (including advice purportedly based on the findings of medical science) is fraught with complexities and contradictions. The overarching theme of this chapter is how corporations encourage the micromanagement of workers' daily habits and what are the implications and effects of this strategy, including the cultivation of efficiency and the optimization of productivity. Both employees and their supervisors are encouraged to improve themselves in the name of greater personal success, but, as Deleuze helps us to see, that success benefits organizations as well as individuals.

Chapter 5, "Everything to Gain: The Intensification of Corporate Progress, Presence, and Risk," broadens the book's scope by scrutinizing the ways in which corporate notions of "progress" constitute a movement toward an ever increasing ubiquity of business values and interests outside of the workplace, outside of workers' homes, out in the world at large. This is the new progress: a network of linked processes (and consequences) that intensify corporate presence to the point where corporations themselves become invisible forces, paradoxically everywhere and nowhere. The "progress" ideal functions as a conduit for the spread of business influence and values in a world where corporate authority and responsibility are increasingly difficult to pin down. Through a discussion of two "case studies"—the American mega corporation Procter & Gamble (P&G) and Clare International, novelist Richard Powers's thinly disguised fictional version of P&G—I illustrate how the contemporary version of progress functions, examine some of its many effects, and analyze one of its end results: intensified business presence. Ultimately, I argue that today's corporate progress and presence are becoming boundless despite the risks involved and may, one day, even be unfettered by the human hands that once kept the process moving steadily, perhaps inexorably, forward.

The chapters described above all touch upon dominant practices and values in the contemporary business world, and Chapter 6, "Students and Stakeholders: Business Writing Courses and Corporate Cultural Literacy," considers the role of university-level business writing courses in the *dissemination* of these practices and values. I examine business writing's power to naturalize values, to affect what counts as "truth," to advise which ideas should be believed or disregarded, and to foster particular types of workplace environments. I suggest the ways in which business writing conventions, whether learned in the university classroom or onsite in the workplace, can help to construct corporate values and enculturate students and new employees into the business world. Finally, I discuss what should change in professors' and administrators' approaches to business writing instruction. The chapter also explores the current tensions surrounding business writing curricula—the serious conflicts between scholars from various fields (such as English, communication, and business) that teach writing skills.

Chapter 7, "Corporate Culture Out of Control?", concludes the book by revisiting earlier themes in light of the global financial crisis of 2008. Using the examples of Lehman Brothers and American International Group (AIG) as touchstones, this chapter examines the role of corporate culture in hastening the downfall of these firms and speculates about the future of "corporate culture," as a concept, when so many companies and industries are struggling to stay solvent.

As noted earlier, two key themes unite the chapters. First is the idea that corporate culture, even when it seems to be doing otherwise, operates in the service of governance. The second idea is that corporate culture extends and strengthens work's presence in people's everyday lives. This book considers the mechanisms that perform this work, looks at the everyday phenomena of corporate culture, and analyzes what their effects are, without rushing to make value judgments. It is my hope that business studies—through closer attention to the corporate realm—could, as Nietzsche once wrote, act "counter to our time and thereby on our time, and let us hope, for the benefit of a time to come" (Nietzsche [1874] 1997, 60).

CHAPTER 2

FROM ORGANIZATION MAN TO LIBERATION MANAGEMENT: AN EXAMINATION OF INDIVIDUALITY AND CONFORMITY IN THE WORKPLACE

Something is provided for all so that none may escape.
—*Theodor W. Adorno and Max Horkheimer*[1]

"THINK DIFFERENT"[2]

In the "careers" section of its corporate website, Accenture, a *Fortune* 500 consulting firm, proudly announces that its employees are diverse and forward thinking: "We value the uniqueness of each individual and rely on these differences to drive our innovation, growth and performance among our client base." Exxon Mobil exults that it "hire[s] exceptional people, and every one of them is empowered to think independently, take initiative and be innovative." Boeing's online publicity emphasizes the company's participatory atmosphere, where workers can and should feel free to contribute their ideas. Chevron-Texaco focuses on the corporation's wish to fulfill workers' individual needs through flexible policies. Fannie Mae promises to "put your unique talents to good use." The Altria Group, parent company of Philip Morris USA, somewhat cryptically tells its website visitors, "We encourage everyone to think about things differently and to think about different things, bringing vigorous challenge to everything we do… We are receptive to new ideas, and applaud those who dare to think differently."[3]

The above paragraph may seem painfully repetitive, but this collection of quotations underscores a trend that has gained momentum in business discourses: an increasing emphasis on the individuality, diversity, and uniqueness of corporate workers. A sunny outlook on employee individuality, creativity, autonomy, and even rebellion has become de rigueur for even the largest transnational corporations. Despite (or, perhaps, partially because of) the overwhelmingly enthusiastic tone that characterizes these discourses, I find that there is much to be suspicious of in comments like those quoted above. My aim in this chapter is to demonstrate how corporate appeals to individualism can become forms of governance, potentially affecting how workers act, think, and live their lives. As corporations faced with large applicant pools and slashed budgets decide who gets hired and fired, contemporary management theory encourages companies to seek and reward certain "individualist" personality types: people who are creative, assertive, and even outspoken. Hopeful applicants and current employees alike may therefore feel inspired or compelled to display these same traits. Similarly, emphasis on diversity in business—a field traditionally dominated by white men—can also operate in the service of governance; identity is now more or less explicitly made "useful" for business purposes, including attracting target markets (women, African Americans, 20-somethings, etc.) and allowing corporations to benefit from new perspectives. Contemporary management theory also suggests that diversity enhances overall corporate performance. After all, when the "same old thing" is no longer lucrative—thanks to new and emerging industries and markets—businesses become eager to pursue new, less-explored avenues for success. One of these avenues has been to acknowledge and take advantage of demographic changes in the American workforce, in hopes that the "new blood" will invigorate American business.

I hope to show that corporate appeals to individualism have many other possible effects as well, including the promotion of worker loyalty, the encouragement of consumer spending, and the improvement of corporate image. As made abundantly clear by news headlines and dwindling 401Ks, we live in a time of corporate collapses and shaky stock markets—and a time when few Americans retain the same job, or even the same career track, for life. The logic of the corporate emphasis on individualism helps to counteract the effects of these circumstances—the possible drop in employee loyalty and the rampant cynicism about corporate ethics. Meanwhile, individualism has long occupied a central position in advertising and marketing. Just as individualism discourses help to cultivate an environment where certain types of workers succeed, so too do they nurture particular tastes and sensibilities, which then become a focus in product design and promotion.

After tracing the twentieth-century history of individuality and conformity in American business discourses, I will describe several significant contemporary manifestations of this issue: discussions about the importance of maintaining "work-life balance," the stress placed on employee diversity, and the notion of individual self-expression at work. Through this examination, I wish to challenge the traditional, oversimplified dichotomy between individualism and conformity to organization norms, where individualism is usually considered the healthy and admirable term. Rather, I will argue that, like conformity or homogeneity, individualism carries a price, for it operates in the service of business interests, perpetuates an ideal of independence and autonomy that is difficult (if not impossible) for most people to attain, and may even help to foster docility in workers while seeming to do the opposite. In short, the rhetoric of individualism effectively binds people to their jobs, their workplaces. While encouraging rebellion and nonconformity, corporate individualism discourses can also keep people working long hours—and this mechanism meshes smoothly with the trend toward privatization of human services in the United States and the concomitant dismantling of any public sphere outside of work. To paraphrase the Adorno and Horkheimer quotation at the beginning of this chapter, something is provided at work for all, so that none may escape. Though one could argue that the positive results of corporate policies that give workers a voice or actively foster workplace diversity outweigh the negative aspects, to do so would mean missing a larger point: we cannot simply choose some effects over other, less appealing ones. The question of intensified workplace individualism, whether through the active encouragement of nonconformity, the celebration of the diversity of workers' voices, or the policies tailored to ease employees' family responsibilities, is not a question of "good" or "bad." It is not a question of what's preferable. It just is. Simply put, corporate policies have a variety of effects, and they cannot be separated from each other. After a discussion of the theoretical and historical contexts of these ideas, I will return to contemporary examples of individualism-as-governance in American corporate cultures. I will also examine the fate and future of workplace individualism in today's uncertain economy.

It's Not Easy Being Me

Many philosophers have articulated the problems bound up in the process of subject formation and of naturalizing the idea that each person is a unique individual. More importantly for my purposes here, many of these same philosophers have explored the dangers inherent in the encouragement of (or even the belief in) unique human selfhood—how these tactics contribute to the regulation and replication of certain types of subjects. Louis Althusser, for example, demonstrates how the concept of selfhood is always already beholden to the concept of otherness: a person's individuality and uniqueness do not matter—or even register as concepts—unless they are recognized by another person. His famous illustration of interpellation—a police officer hailing a passerby and the passerby halting and turning to look when the officer calls—also highlights the significant role of established authorities (the law in this example, but one's government or employer could be others) in the formation of subjects. Even employers who encourage workers to express their uniqueness remain *employers*, authority figures who seek and reproduce certain traits in their workers, including, possibly, individual decision making, innovation, and creativity. As mentioned earlier, advocating individualism can also foster the desirable trait of loyalty in workers; after all, people generally enjoy working in environments where they may dress as they choose and contribute new ideas at staff meetings. Corporate governance can thus make use of discourses of individualism and freedom. As employees, we may feel free to "be ourselves," in part because that's precisely the attitude many corporations want to cultivate.

But what *sort* of individual is typically cultivated, idealized, and naturalized by contemporary American corporate discourses? Through her analysis of western political theory in *States of Injury* (1995), Wendy Brown offers the following definition of the liberal subject—a definition very much in line with the individualism celebrated by today's businesses:

> A rational calculator, driven by passionate self-interest, and expressive of the possessive individualism perfectly tailored to bourgeois acquisitiveness and accumulation: he also bears an array of character attributes that confer his specifically masculine status. Fiercely autonomous and diffident, he is unencumbered by anyone or anything, independent in both senses of the term (free of dependents and dependency in civil society). (149)

Brown also adds that despite the influence of socializing forces, this notion of the liberal subject retains a precultural, transcendent nature—some kernel of authentic selfhood that survives. Other key aspects of liberalism, for example, the notion that all men are free and equal, simultaneously depend upon and perpetuate this particular version of subjectivity, but, Brown argues, this definition of subjectivity is *itself* dependent upon the unacknowledged subordination of some values—and some people—to others. Liberal subjectivity presupposes rigid (and gendered) binaries between public and private, individual and family/group, rights and responsibilities. In short, for the liberal subject to feel free and unencumbered, someone else must be unfree, encumbered, and excluded. Someone must take responsibilities and care for dependents if these ideal individuals of liberalism are to express fully their autonomy and independence. And, even though people may feel that they are autonomous individuals always able to make choices freely, the model of liberal subjectivity is a trap, for it constantly reinvokes and thereby strengthens assumptions about what it means to be man or woman, white or black, et cetera. This "trap" image is particularly germane to corporate strategies for approaching individual difference through work-life initiatives and diversity programs—points to which I will return later.

As Brown notes, it is very much this liberal definition of the autonomous subject that Michel Foucault challenges in much of his work. Foucault explores the consequences of strategies and developments—like liberalism's cultivation of a sense of individualism—that seem altruistic at first glance. He examines institutional projects, such as psychoanalysis and social reform, which aim to help people by allowing and inviting them to speak for themselves. In *Discipline and Punish: The Birth of the Prison* (1975), Foucault uses the historical shift from public torture rituals to the incarceration and surveillance of criminals as an example of how a relatively humane strategy can be as nefarious as an overtly brutal one. His description of the goal of European legal reform, "to make of the punishment and repression of illegalities a regular function... not to punish less, but to punish better... to insert the power to punish more deeply into the social body," implies how increased opportunities for governance can work through social improvements that supposedly give individuals greater access to human rights and privileges (Foucault 1975, 82). Giving individuals a voice (e.g., in their therapeutic treatment, in their democratic government, or in their workplace) is one possible example of such an improvement. Self-expression in the workplace makes workers more visible, thus increasing their chances of becoming targets of surveillance and control. Similarly, in Volume I of *The History of Sexuality* (1978), Foucault shows how subjects are produced through discourse: the injunction to talk about one's individuality—including one's sexuality—produces far-reaching governance tactics: labeling and categorizing people according to their predilections and thereby creating norms against which people can be assessed. In short, Foucault argues, though many people insist that society is repressive, certain "subversive" discourses and behaviors are encouraged, for they contribute to the process of managing citizens without resorting to the relatively inefficient tactic of overt force.

While he does not directly mention the business world in the books cited above, Foucault's ideas have clear applications and implications for this study of individualism in the workplace. A key question posed in *The History of Sexuality* suggests a compelling parallel with my line of inquiry: "Why do we say, with so much passion and so much resentment against our recent past, against our present, and against ourselves, that we are repressed?" (8–9). Indeed, much of today's business discourse about individualism is predicated on the idea of repressive corporate conformity—a state that is at least partially mythical, as I will demonstrate in the next part of this chapter.[4] For now, I will highlight just one important aspect of this corporate conformist issue: the idea that in the not-too-distant past, most workplaces were naturally repressive, but now the best, most successful companies are both liberated and liberating, for they foster self-expression, diversity, and creativity. What are the effects of depicting business as liberation? As Foucault's work suggests, fostering certain types of individualism can allow for the effective management and control of the individuals in question. To borrow and recontextualize a phrase from *The History of Sexuality,* the idea of corporate nonconformity causes workers to be "inserted into systems of utility, regulated for the greater good of all" (24). In this model, people characterized as "individuals"—free thinkers, creative minds, and nonconformists—might foster dissent or foment change, but they also work to increase their employer's profits, their workplace's productivity. Of course, they may also work to make money and spend it (perhaps on some of the many items strategically marketed toward nonconformists), thus keeping the wheels of consumerism well oiled.[5] In addition, the very act of encouraging individuality and nonconformity at work can have impressive market value—as evinced by the popularity of management self-help books like Tom Peters's *Liberation Management* (1992) and *The Circle of Innovation* (1997). Peters, who has been an obvious influence on many well-known business writers (including Spencer Johnson, best known for *Who Moved My Cheese?,* and Kevin Kelly, *Wired* editor and author of *New Rules for the New Economy*) makes a lot of money by telling people how to be workplace individuals and by showing managers how creativity and individuality can lead to business success. After all, many readers probably enjoy Peters's message and like to be told that work need not be boring, stifling, or repressive.

With a nod to Peters-like self-help discourses, Nikolas Rose, in *Governing the Soul: The Shaping of the Private Self* (1989), applies Foucauldian concepts to the work world and explicitly links the governance of workers with the concept of human individuality. Rose's work, to which my ideas in this chapter owe a great deal, is a genealogy of the belief that we are unique individuals imbued with free will. He notes that a focus on individuality has always been integral to the workings of governance: "Thoughts, feelings, and actions may appear as the very fabric and constitution of the intimate self, but they are socially organized and managed in minute particulars" (1). But Rose does not consign the technologies on which this management depends—psychology, management science, and others—to the realm of false ideas or ideology. Instead, these technologies are part of a vast apparatus for constituting and disseminating truths—Western truths about what it means to be human, to be a citizen, to be a worker or family member. As he writes,

> Citizens shape their lives through the choices they make about family life, work, leisure, lifestyle, and personality and its expression. Government works by "acting at a distance" upon these choices, forging a symmetry between the attempts of individuals to make life worthwhile for themselves, and the political values of consumption, profitability, efficiency, and social order. (10)

In his chapters about subjectivity in the workplace, Rose traces the history of how work became one "essential element" in this "path to self-fulfillment" (118). His history begins with significant changes in management theory at the start of the twentieth century that eventually led to a reconfiguration of the idea of "the worker." Instead of seeing workers as interchangeable parts in the churning, grinding whole of an industrial organization, management started thinking of employees as subjects who must be respected. In the wake of this reconfiguration came "increased efforts to make work pleasurable" (56). Then, developments in the field of psychology, alongside these advances in management science, contributed to "new ways of relating the feelings and wishes of individual employees to the fate of the enterprise" (60). These methods included increased "democracy" in the workplace (through participatory management, employee ownership, and such) and intensified attention to employees' individual welfare (physical and psychological health, job satisfaction, and opportunities for career advancement). In time, the bond between personal and organizational goals was further strengthened by the growth of consumerism. Just as individuals were presented with product choices in the marketplace, so too were they presented with a wider selection of career tracks: "The individual is not to be emancipated *from* work, perceived merely as a task or a means to an end, but to be fulfilled *in* work, now construed as an activity through which we produce, discover, and experience ourselves" (103, italics in original). Contemporary American management theory has picked up on this link between individuality and work, expanding its scope so that, as Rose argues, work becomes an attractive prospect not only because it offers monetary compensation or the pleasures of belonging to a social group, but because it promises a better self. A crucial question remains, what might be the costs and implications of the drive toward self-betterment through work?

One way to approach this question is to consider how individualism connects with individual *risks* as well as individual "choices." Ulrich Beck's *Risk Society* (1992) and *The Brave New World of Work* (2000), taken together, help to illuminate potential costs of individuality and self-actualization in the workplace. In *Risk Society*, Beck criticizes the distribution of risks to individuals, but he also seems invested in the ideal of individual agency: "Risk positions create dependencies... the affected parties are becoming incompetent in matters of their own affliction. They lose an essential part of their cognitive sovereignty" (53). However, the characterization of individual sovereignty as "essential" is part of the problem he convincingly describes elsewhere. In other words, a dependence on the concept of individuality itself contributes to the sloughing off of governmental and corporate responsibilities onto citizens and workers, who are often denied the resources to respond effectively to those responsibilities. In *The Brave New World of Work*, Beck implies as much. Here, he describes 1990s business as freewheeling and unpredictable, fond of trumpeting the virtues of its increasing informality and flexibility.[6] Meanwhile, he argues, workers facing the growing instability of their workplaces suffer from the constant threat of downsizing, their lack of job security "discursively sweetened... by the rhetoric of independent entrepreneurial individualism" (4). The risk of allowing work to become integral to one's self-definition is likewise grave: people who lose their jobs often feel they have also lost their sense of identity—and this loss can have devastating effects.[7] When work is configured as the place where one is supposed to find fulfillment and a sense of community, unemployment becomes an especially bleak prospect. As James Paul Gee, Glynda Hull, and Colin Lankshear point out in their book on "the language of new capitalism,"

> The newly empowered and newly "critical thinking" workers cannot really question the goals, visions, and values that define the very parameters of the new capitalist business in the new global work order. Such questioning might well mean exiting the new capitalist world and seeking employment in the Third World-like, low-wage, marginal jobs in the remaining backwaters of the old capitalism, or having no employment at all... The worker's "freedom" is fixed within the margins of the goals, ends, and vision set by the new capitalism and its theoreticians. (Gee, Hull, and Lankshear 1996, xvi)

All of these theoretical perspectives point toward strategic reasons why American corporations are currently so invested in the idea of worker individuality. By encouraging workers to express themselves, organizations obtain valuable input while redirecting potentially damaging dissent and downplaying the possibility of outside loyalties (e.g., to unions). Also, workers who express their ideas become more "visible" to authorities—easier to watch, control, and utilize for corporate benefit. By strategically aligning corporate and personal interests, companies foster worker enthusiasm and devotion—perhaps even at the expense of workers' non-work interests. And, by insisting that workers are unique, autonomous subjects, the corporate world works toward shifting responsibilities and burdens from organizations to individuals. These sinister possibilities are by no means hidden from view—workers are not being tricked or coerced by corporate individualist sentiments. As Evan Watkins has pointed out, corporations are what they pretend to be; the question is *what* they pretend to be.[8] The attendant risks and problems of individualism are belied by the benevolent tone of discourses such as those referenced in this chapter's first paragraph.

"Imprisoned in Brotherhood"

Before we can fully understand why the contemporary business world is so invested in the concept of worker individuality and uniqueness, it is also necessary to examine the background story: the fear that the very nature of corporate work might produce an army of zombie-like conformists. This may sound like a melodramatic idea, but many early and mid-twentieth-century sources, running the gamut from sociological texts to popular magazines, suggest that workplace individuality was not always so encouraged as it appears to be today. Mid-century sources in particular also indicate a sense of alarm: what, ultimately, would be the effects of corporate norms and conformity? Certainly, parts of this story have been told before, but my aim here is to synthesize the disparate elements leading up to today's corporate obsession with individualism. In terms of its twentieth-century history, the problem of worker individuality and conformity may first have emerged with the dissemination of Frederick Winslow Taylor's management strategies. Taylor's principles of "scientific management" (slowly developed over the course of several decades and published in book form in 1911) met with strong responses, both laudatory and harshly critical.[9] Supporters praised Taylor's elaborate tactics for optimizing worker efficiency through time-motion techniques and minutely regimented work schedules, noting that when workers knew exactly what was expected of them at each possible moment, they would be more likely to succeed—and more satisfied with their jobs as a result.[10] Indeed, Taylor saw himself as a savior of industry; as biographer Robert Kanigel writes, "In [Taylor's] mind, an impersonal arbiter—cool, neutral science—would step in, take the hands of workman and boss, whisper truth to each, and return them gently to the garden to live in peace" (1997, 220).

Many observers, however, saw Taylor's "science" as anything but cool and neutral and claimed instead that the application of Taylorism to factories would result in a work environment of spirit-crushing monotony and conformity. After Taylor's book appeared in 1911, many labor activists, politicians, and scholars—including Upton Sinclair and Samuel Gompers—argued that scientific management aimed to reduce skilled workers to interchangeable, mindless automata, less-than-human beings trained and designed solely to further the interests of American industry.[11] One anonymous critic writing for *American Machinist* magazine summed up much of what Taylor's critics had to say in one simple phrase; time study, he noted, "practically eliminates the operator's or mechanic's personality" (Kanigel 1997, 445). The controversy surrounding scientific management grew so rancorous that, in 1912, the House Labor Committee of the U.S. government held hearings to assess Taylorism's effects on workers. Though ultimately the committee did not agree to launch factory investigations, the damage to Taylor's reputation was done—and was certainly not ameliorated when, during World War II, critics drew parallels between scientific management and the horrible efficiency of Nazi concentration camps (532). Critiques and parodies of Taylor's ideas sprang from diverse sources, such as John Dos Passos's experimental novel, *The Big Money* (1936), and Charlie Chaplin's popular 1936 film, *Modern Times*.[12]

Clearly, Taylor's methods were not without their critics, and some experts in the field began proposing alternative approaches to science-based management—strategies that would allow and even encourage workers to retain their individual talents and input. Elton Mayo's Human Relations movement—perhaps the best known of these alternatives—centered on fostering a sense of belongingness in the workplace (generally a factory, in Mayo's writings) by giving individual workers the opportunity to express their thoughts and feelings, even if those thoughts were critical of management. Mayo, a professor of industrial research at Harvard University's Graduate School of Business Administration, focused on psychological strategies for allowing workers to "talk through" their problems, a process which would then, ostensibly, lead to solutions.[13] He also concluded that workers would be more effective if they were given opportunities for social connections with each other; he argued that a sense of shared goals and group belonging—rather than Taylorist advice on physical efficiency, which led to worker dissatisfaction and, ironically, to inefficiency—would increase worker loyalty and productivity. Therefore, much of his work provided guidance for managers on how to invite worker input and encourage workplace interactions. In *The Human Problems of an Industrial Civilization* (1933), Mayo recounts his industrial studies, which suggested that friendly managers who take an interest in workers' individual accomplishments and needs thereby contribute to workplace productivity, perhaps more than wage incentives do.[14] It is also important to note Mayo's contention that paying attention to the unique traits of individual workers means nothing unless it can be applied to management strategy. The key question asked by Human Relations is "how to advance beyond the mere revelation, how to develop from a knowledge-of-acquaintance of persons to a knowledge-about persons and a method of control" (Mayo 101). That said, Human Relations evinces a blend of control strategies; on the one hand, individuals are made to feel special as their unique talents and desires are addressed by supervisors, and on the other hand, a sense of group and community bonding is characterized as essential to any flourishing workplace.

Despite the apparent benevolence of Mayo's management strategies compared with Taylor's, some observers were not impressed with Human Relations theory. At least one writer even implied that management strategies meant to foster and coddle individuals actually had the same deleterious effect of Taylor's principles: the creation of mindless, interchangeable conformists. The main difference that William H. Whyte's *The Organization Man* (1956) draws between Taylor and Mayo is that in following Mayo's recommendations, the *managers* as well as the workers become conformists. Whyte argues that processes meant to humanize the monotonous, robotic workplace ironically make the workplace even more robotic, because the managers in charge of creating and enforcing workplace policy are themselves being turned into mindless yes-men. The individuality of managers is effaced, as they are constantly enjoined to behave according to certain conventions of friendliness, enthusiasm, and tact.

Perhaps best known for its chapters about the mind-numbing quality of American suburbia, *The Organization Man* is also a remarkably prescient commentary on selfhood and identity within corporate culture, touching upon issues later explored by Michel Foucault and Nikolas Rose. Whyte, who was an editor at *Fortune* magazine when he wrote this book, posits a sea change in American attitudes toward work. He describes a shift from the Protestant Ethic—focusing on individualism and personal success and salvation through industry, thrift, and competitive struggle—to the Social Ethic, which emphasizes following orders, respecting authority, and capitulating to collective opinions and needs rather than fulfilling individual goals. The main characteristic of the Social Ethic, according to Whyte, is "a belief in 'belongingness' as the ultimate need of the individual" (Whyte 1956, 7). He defines this belongingness as "deep emotional security that comes from total integration with the group" (32).

Though he admits that his remarks about the Protestant and Social Ethics are based in part on popular mythology, Whyte argues that these Ethics are nonetheless powerful forces in American society and that the Social Ethic primarily manifests itself through an increasingly common creature called the "Organization Man"—the mid-to-upper-level corporate worker. Whereas nineteenth-century corporations were developed and managed by rugged individualists who competed for profits in a harsh business environment, the collective nature of the corporation itself—the interconnection between workers and departments inherent in traditional corporate structure—led in the mid-twentieth century to the rise of the Organization Man: a manager highly skilled in the art of tactful human relations, but not much else.[15] Rather than focusing on entrepreneurship or on climbing the corporate ladder, the Organization Man is primarily concerned with managing other people's work and on fostering a sense of cooperation in the workplace. According to Whyte, the creative ideas and unique feelings of the Organization Man are squelched by corporate values and replaced by a desire to maintain a peaceful workplace environment at any cost. Thus, new ideas and conflicts are perceived by Organization Men and their supervisors as subversive, dangerous forces potentially undermining the serene status quo.

In one sense, Organization Man (who is, in this 1956 book, always a man—Whyte predictably relegates women to the chapters on suburban culture) may appear to be a favorable development; after all, workplace cooperation generally seems preferable to cutthroat competition between self-interested individuals. Whyte does not discuss competitiveness as a possible *danger* associated with increased individualism—an issue I will return to in Chapter 3 of this book—but instead posits individualism as a flawed but comparatively healthy attitude, preferable to the dangers of groupthink in the corporate context. Though Whyte admits that some aspects of organization life can be beneficial, he warns workers to resist the Social Ethic and to seek a middle ground between individualism and collectivism. Whyte challenges the apparent benevolence of qualities like cooperation and belonging and suggests that the community spirit advocated and perpetuated by Organization Men becomes a sinister form of governance:

> Every decision [a corporate worker] faces on the problem of the individual versus authority is something of a dilemma... For it is not the evils of organization life that puzzle him, *but its very beneficence.* He is imprisoned in brotherhood. Because his area of maneuver seems so small and because the trapping is so mundane, his fight lacks the heroic cast, but it is for all this as tough a fight as ever his predecessors had to fight. (Whyte 1956, 12, italics in original)

Again, workers as well as managers are prone to conformity, according to Whyte. For example, though Mayo's Human Relations techniques had obvious advantages over scientific management for workers, there were also serious problems, despite appearances to the contrary. Though Human Relations might have afforded workers the satisfaction of knowing their voices had been heard by management, the movement might not have afforded much else. Whyte worries that in Mayo's model, ultimately the worker is asked to adapt to the group's needs, rather than vice-versa: "The alternative of changing reality is hardly considered... While Mayo intended human relation to apply to the workers and managers both, the managers first seized on it as an excellent tool for manipulating the workers into a chronic contentment that would turn them away from the unions" (37–38).

An important point that Whyte does not develop, however, is that individualism should *also* be regarded with suspicion as a sinister form of governance.[16] In the next section of this chapter, I will discuss how this point plays out in the contemporary context.

The Organization Man was influential in its time, warning readers about conformity's dangers or at least informing them that one very worried writer was keeping tabs on corporate developments. But Whyte's was not the only voice cautioning Americans about the rise of conformity in the business world during the 1950s. One of American sociology's most famous books, David Riesman's *The Lonely Crowd: A Study of the Changing American Character* (1950), clearly inspired Whyte's arguments. Riesman describes a historical shift from the nineteenth-century preponderance of inner-directed people (who conform only to the demands of authority figures like parents, whose voices they have internalized) to the twentieth-century rise of other-directed people—people who, like Whyte's Organization Man, base their identities on the opinions and ideals of their peers. Riesman then links this development with a drastic change in the work world: the supplanting of manufacturing by the humanistic fields of marketing and management. While Riesman did not characterize other-directed people as inferior to inner-directeds, instead arguing that both modes of conformity were problematic but probably inevitable, the book was often misread as an anti-conformity call-to-arms.[17] Meanwhile, one of the best-selling novels of 1955 was seen as a direct challenge to the nefarious forces of conformity.[18] Sloan Wilson's *The Man in the Gray Flannel Suit,* later made into a film, features a protagonist who chafes at the chains of conformity in his office—a giant broadcasting company with a driven, workaholic CEO. For a while, Tom dutifully buttons up his suit, joins the sea of commuters on the local train, and capitulates to his supervisors' demands. His unhappiness grows:

> I was my own disappointment. I really don't know what I was looking for when I got back from the war, but it seemed as though all I could see was a lot of bright young men in gray flannel suits rushing around New York in a frantic parade to nowhere. They seemed to me to be pursuing neither ideals nor happiness—they were pursuing a routine. For a long while I thought I was on the side lines watching that parade, and it was quite a shock to glance down and see that I too was wearing a gray flannel suit.   (Wilson 1955, 300)

By the end of the novel, Tom triumphantly informs his boss that he refuses to let his life slip by while working overtime and declares his intention to spend more time with his family instead. Interestingly,

Tom's decision is not punished but rewarded; the CEO says that he understands Tom's desires and offers him a job with a more flexible schedule: "I guess we need a few men who keep a sense of proportion" (278). In the 1950s, readers of Wilson's novel may have been left with the impression that the supposedly stifling conformity of the American workplace need not be so stifling and could be changed by one rebellious man's voice saying, "No, thanks." In the decades that followed the publication of *The Organization Man* and *The Man in the Gray Flannel Suit,* management theory also picked up on the anti-conformity sentiment and directly began encouraging workers and managers to express their unique—and even rebellious—selves.[19]

SAME DIFFERENCE

As evidenced in the first paragraph of this chapter, corporate discourses valorizing difference actually tend to sound the same—similar to one another in both style and sentiment. There is an overwhelming sameness amongst the websites, management theories, and self-help books, which reiterate the point that the nonconformity and diversity of employees can be of great benefit for businesses. Whether or not corporate workers are or were ever coerced (or subtly enjoined) to conform, the Organization Man was for many years a prevailing image in commentary on corporate America—one that still persists to some extent today. However, changes in management theory in the 1960s and the 1970s pointed toward new images of business-people. Whereas Taylorist scientific management valued individuals exclusively for their measurable abilities to perform work tasks, and Human Relations theory utilized individual psyches to tailor tactics for bringing people into the fold of work-community, quality of working life (QWL) strategies emphasized both group solidarity *and* individualism. The success of QWL—which can be associated with the popular characterization of the 1970s as the "Me Decade"—relied on the idea that work and identity were inextricably linked. In QWL theory, work was reconfigured as creative self-actualization and group solidarity, rather than as alienating or repressive force.[20] Managers and employees "found themselves" at work—got to know their talents and interests while pursuing their callings. Later, management gurus further expanded this idea so that the expression of personal unique-ness became explicitly configured as an asset to both the worker *and* the organization.

Another way to begin considering the early stages of the shift in dominant imagery from the corporate conformist to the self-actualized manager is to examine parallel developments in the field of advertising. This field, of course, has strong ties with the manufacturing, service, and media industries—and the individualism advocated in business feeds from (and into) the individualism celebrated in commercials. While individualism discourses help to create certain types of workers—loyal, willing to provide input, et cetera—they may also create certain types of consumers: people who buy things to express their unique selves. In *The Conquest of Cool: Business Culture, Counterculture, and the Rise of Hip Consumerism* (1997), Thomas Frank traces the history of a significant change in American advertising during the second half of the twentieth century: an increasing emphasis on the value of individualism and uniqueness. Even just one hour spent watching today's commercial television confirms his thesis: ads, rather than advocating conformity and trust in old, well-established name brands as they did in the 1940s and the 1950s, today insist that consumers (and producers, for that matter) are unique individuals. Ads from the 1960s to today celebrate the expression of personal originality through the purchase of branded products; in television commercials from the past decade, country music superstar Garth Brooks reminded the Dr. Pepper drinker to "be you, do what you do"; shoppers for wireless service were told that "self expression is Cingular"; and Volkswagen congratulated Bug drivers on their bold tastes. Even the U.S. Army—surely not thought of as a hotbed of nonconformity—has utilized this tactic in its advertising slogans, from "Be All That You Can Be" to "An Army of One."

Frank argues that post-1960 advertising sets up a binary relationship between rebellious, hip consumers and boring conformists, frequently depicted as corporate bureaucrats—the very people paying for the advertising that lampoons them. But this binary is false, for even a cursory glance through the post-1960s publicity materials of corporate America reveals a celebration of uniqueness and even rebellion. Frank notes that long-standing stereotypes of corporate workers as conformists and yes-men, determined to succeed at the expense of expressing their true feelings or original insights, belie a trend in management theory and corporate PR: emphasis on the value of nonconformists for successful, profitable work organizations. Nonconformity—often called "thinking outside the box"—supposedly contributes to new and improved company practices and creates a workplace atmosphere where all workers feel comfortable expressing themselves. In television ads and in business discourses, the individual is king. What does this mean within the context of business, a field traditionally based on organizational hierarchy and teamwork?

This question can be answered by examining trends associated with the 1990s economic boom in the United States. One of these trends is the move toward nonhierarchical organizations—a move that began with the 1980s emulation of Japanese management styles, but soon developed a distinctly American twist. Tom Peters, a perennially popular business guru in the 1980s and the 1990s, devotes many pages of his 763-page tome, *Liberation Management: Necessary Disorganization for the Nanosecond Nineties* (1992), to the idea of horizontal management, wherein hierarchical relationships between workers and departments are flattened or abolished altogether. This organizational change necessitates a new definition of the successful worker: someone who is "liberated," that is, adaptable in the face of unfamiliar and changing work environments; unafraid to make independent decisions without direct managerial supervision; and willing to express and accept new, creative approaches. As Peters writes, both worker and corporate values must change with the tumultuous times (remember, this book was published at the start of the Internet boom): "It's up to you to take the initiative, start projects, seek out customers, build your own network. The marketplace has gone bonkers. Firms therefore must go bonkers to keep up. And so must you. Street rap replaces rigid marches to John Philip Sousa's predictable beat" (Peters 1992, 146). Individual workers must take responsibility for their projects and performance, rather than depending on management for guidance. Meanwhile, organizations, in Peters' view, must restructure (or, as he might put it, *de*structure) themselves to allow for increased employee autonomy.

Despite his dismissive attitude toward traditional business hierarchy, Peters implicitly concedes that *some* hierarchy is still necessary to success. The "liberation management" of his book's title is a form of management at a distance—corporate control relaying from a variety of points on a network, rather than emanating from one centralized location (the CEO, the head office, and such). Management regulations and surveillance are replaced by self-governing team- or project-based structures: "Project teams will neither quash individualism or blunt specialization... individual contributions will be more important than ever... you will be forced, routinely, to work/learn any job on the team" (Peters 1992, 154). Corporate governance occurs through peer reviews rather than supervisor evaluations; simply put, Peters suggests that teammates submit reports documenting one another's ability to work in teams. In Peters's model, the central roles of individual performance and input are clear; workers are relied upon to learn new skills, take risks, express their opinions to (and of) one another, and thereby reach profitable solutions.

Peters refers to failures only in passing as he quotes from Dick Liebhaber, then the head of operations at MCI: "We don't shoot people who make mistakes... we shoot people who don't take risks" (qtd. in Peters 1992, 145). Presumably, workers are not "shot" for expressing dissenting viewpoints, but they may well be fired if they don't fit the individualistic, nonconformist mold, or if they are reluctant to report on the performances of their coworkers/teammates. In a moment that stands out from the overwhelmingly upbeat, enthusiastic tone of *Liberation Management,* Peters himself forecasts doom for workers and managers unable to cope with today's innovative individualism: "Lean-and-mean structures, continuous education, self-generated projects, and ambiguity are in. The bad news: Brand-new definitions of careers and new shapes of organizations make the downside... onerous for those who don't get it" (146).

Contemporary business writers and management theorists—many of them clearly influenced by Peters—have developed similar ideas about the importance of individualism in the workplace. Some, for example, Ken Hultman and Frances Horibe, express sentiments similar to Peters's, but provide more specific advice to managers now coping with the "liberated" workplace. Horibe's 2001 book, *Creating the Innovation Culture: Leveraging Visionaries, Dissenters, and Other Useful Troublemakers in Your Organization,* offers tips for managing individualistic, nonconformist workers. Horibe acknowledges that these workers may be difficult and even unpopular, but insists that they are an essential part of any organization—contributing the valuable opinions and ideas that others might be afraid to express. Horibe also distinguishes between innovators and workers who go too far; she advocates management techniques for increasing workers' risk-taking tendencies, but advises managers to tell innovators—in advance—how long they have to work on projects, how much spending will be tolerated, and how decisions will ultimately be made. This balance between worker autonomy and management authority certainly seems reasonable, but also strongly suggests the role of individualism in contemporary versions of corporate governance: workers are "free" to make decisions and pursue risks for themselves and—in Horibe's scheme—are not punished for failed innovations. As suggested by Horibe's book title, however, these workers are simultaneously "leveraged" for corporate goals (and profits). Not an unexpected bottom line, perhaps, but one that demonstrates how individual identity now functions as yet another mode of control. Personality and creativity, like industry knowledge or negotiation skills, become corporate property.

Other management approaches stress the benefits of *compromise* with individualistic workers, rather than direct encouragement of dissent. In his discussion of organizational development (OD), a management theory introduced in the late 1960s and still used, in revamped form, today, Hultman argues for the importance of "balance" between workers' interests and corporate values. He traces the long history of conflict (and conflict resolution) between American workers and their employers, from the brutal conditions of factories at the turn of the last century and the unions founded to combat these conditions, to Mayo's humanistic approaches to management, to the work-as-self-actualization philosophy of the 1970s. The remainder of my discussion of contemporary manifestations of workplace individualism is based on Hultman's version of OD—specifically, his tenets for *aligning* worker and employer needs and desires. These tenets include fairness ("accepting and utilizing individual differences, trusting people"); choice ("viewing an individual as a whole person, willingness to risk"); and balancing autonomy and constraint ("using status for organizationally relevant purposes" only and "emphasizing collaboration") (Hultman 2002, 8). Reading these principles, I was struck by their obvious links with current trends in business policy—trends that emphasize and celebrate the individuality of workers: work-life balance, workplace freedom, and workplace diversity. While all of these trends—examined and analyzed in more detail in the sections below—sound like positive developments for workers, they also obfuscate serious problems in American business, such as extremely long (even boundless) work hours, the creation of "mommy tracks" preventing working women from getting the promotions they deserve, and the subtle enforcement of multitasking without adequate salary compensation.

PERSONALIZED SOLUTIONS FOR YOUR PERSONAL LIFE

The phrase "work-life balance" is common in contemporary corporate discourses, but its meaning is not always clear-cut. In human resources documents, work-life balance generally refers to a set of policies directed toward alleviating tension between employees' work hours and "personal" or "family" time. These policies may include part-time shifts; flextime schedules (compressed work hours); telecommuting options; generous maternity (and, sometimes, paternity) leave; leaves of absence; financial assistance for childcare or eldercare; onsite day care and schooling; and assistance with family travel arrangements for traveling executives. Some companies' work-life initiatives also include onsite health and fitness facilities, free or reduced-price admission to local cultural events and entertainment venues, and time off for community volunteer work. Through policies and initiatives like these, corporations of all sizes attempt to address the individual, unique needs and desires of their workers.

One way to illustrate the ubiquity of work-life concerns is through the policies and publicity materials of Ford Motor Company—a historic leader in one of America's most venerable industries. Though Ford (and the American auto industry as a whole) continues to face difficult times and controversies, the corporation, for many, remains synonymous with good old-fashioned corporate know-how. The name and exploits of its founder still appear in business textbooks. But the traditional, conservative Ford has changed in response to current management trends and has become more sensitive to employees' "non-work" obligations. The company's website boasts of the Ford Parenting Network—a "resource to the company on issues that affect working parents" (Ford 2002). The network promotes family-friendly policies to Ford management and provides parenting classes and seminars. On the website, Ford also describes its flextime policies; childcare consultation and referral; and "transitional work arrangements" (which allow employees to reduce their hours up to 90 percent, depending on need and management approval). In addition, Ford's "Safe-at-Home" program offers up to 80 percent of employees' childcare costs in emergency situations, as when a child is too sick to attend regular day care or when there are unexpected school closings. These are just a few of Ford's work-life policies; the long list of initiatives demonstrates that Ford will do just about anything to ensure that its workers avoid absenteeism. (What Ford does *not* publicize is the fact that many of its work-life initiatives were a response to pressure from the United Automobile Workers.) The website addresses all kinds of situations; there seems to be a program or policy in place for every possible individual need.

In the early twentieth century, Ford's attention to individual employees primarily entailed surveillance tactics; Henry Ford and his top managers regularly sent inspectors to workers' houses to check for certain standards of hygiene, health, and morality.[21] At that time, Ford was interested in workers' "personal" lives insofar as these affected work productivity; an unhygienic home could cause illness-related absences from work, or a supposedly immoral relationship could lead to distractions, which could in turn impair work performance. In a sense, the current vogue of work-life balance is not much different from Henry Ford's strategies; one aim of work-life policy is to eliminate distractions or ameliorate situations that could adversely affect worker performance. For example, Ford says that it now pays attention to work-life issues to "make [its] people as productive as possible" (Ford 2002). Similarly, Exxon Mobil states that its Flexible Workplace Program is meant to "address the diverse individual needs and expectations of employees" and "maximize employee productivity" (Exxon Mobil "Flexible Workplace Program" 2003). A testimonial from a Bank of America employee, found in the careers section of the company's website, attributes increased productivity and improved customer service to Bank of America's "My Work" program (Bank of America 2008).

Unsurprisingly, work-life programs, which can be expensive for employers to operate and maintain, exist in part because they benefit the companies that provide them. Extensive or thoughtfully designed work-life programming can foster worker loyalty ("My company respects and cares about me!") and aid in employee retention, thus reducing costs for recruitment, hiring, and training. Also, in a time when many Americans are hyperaware of scandal and greed in the business world, work-life programs can improve corporate image. Companies that provide services for their workers can seem sensitive, honest, ethical, and politically correct. And, of course, workers at such companies may feel increased levels of satisfaction. They may find it easier to care for their children or relatives. Those accustomed to constant business travel may be better able to spend time with their families and friends. They may not have to worry about finding babysitters or day care programs that can accommodate their busy schedules. As Jane Juffer writes,

> One might say that the domestic sphere has merely been co-opted in the interest of a better bottom line. To so argue, however, would take far too lightly… the everyday complexities of balancing work and childcare—realities that are more likely to change when women have the energy to address them and form networks of support than if women are so exhausted they can barely crawl into bed at the end of a 16-hour day. (Juffer 2005, 106)

The potential effects of work-life programs are closely linked to the sense of individualism assumed and reproduced in work-life discourses. For example, intensified attention to individual needs can lead to resentment and conflict. A *New York Times Magazine* article by Lisa Belkin reports on the bitterness of workers without dependents—people who feel they are being compelled to "pick up the slack" when their coworkers follow flextime schedules or take advantage of personal leave policies. In short, when attention to individual needs is overtly promoted, some people, perhaps inevitably, will feel that *their* needs are being neglected.[22] Meanwhile, workers who are tempted to utilize their employers' work-life policies are sometimes reluctant to do so. Women in particular may eschew offers of flextime or extended parental leave, for fear that they may be unfairly construed as weak or dependent or even for fear of losing their jobs. Corporate "mommy tracks," rather than providing women with the assistance and security they seem to promise, can harm women's careers by characterizing them as more focused on their families than their jobs. Also, as Doug Henwood's research indicates, jobs with flexible schedules tend statistically to have lower salaries than those with traditional schedules (Henwood 2003, 95). In this scenario, individualized attention from employers carries with it serious risk.

There is also a significant problem undergirding the very *concept* of work-life balance, one specifically connected with the version of worker individuality on which it depends. Work-life balance presupposes a division of the personal and the work-related, but this division, for many people, simply does not exist. These policies imply that workers, with their employers' benevolent assistance, can be flexible enough to devote their utmost attention to their jobs while taking care of their families and other supposedly "non-work" concerns. There is a proliferation of corporate policies pertaining to work-life balance, but no balance is possible, because the elements of work and life cannot be cleanly separated from each other. Work has become boundless—potentially, a 24/7 affair—and placeless—able to occur at any location. In the United States, the past decades' gradual extension of expected work hours has encroached upon—if not utterly overtaken, in some fields—the possibility of "private" time. As the 2002–2003 *Workplace Forecast* from the Society for Human Resources Management notes, "The hyper-competitiveness of a global economy and slim profit margins have created a culture where managerial and professional workers are expected to at least be available to work at any time … the pressure of work and family are raising stress levels and decreasing productivity" (Patel 2003, 9). The telecommuting options offered by many companies give people more time for their personal concerns, yet simultaneously open up the possibility of constant work—work at any time of the day or night, often without corresponding salary compensation. Republican legislation altering regulations for overtime salary speaks directly to this problem; the revised regulations challenge a rule set under the Fair Labor Standards Act of 1938:

employers must pay employees time-and-a-half for working more than 40 hours per week. Union representatives have argued that changes to this rule will negatively affect salaried, white-collar workers—many of them already victims of dot-com disasters, and many of them the very people most likely to work long hours due to the nature of their jobs. Some employers, meanwhile, have complained that the current rules impose old-fashioned "time clock standards" on industries where telecommuting and "virtual offices" have become the norm. In other words, because work can now happen anytime, these employers want to ensure that compensation does not expand in correlation with these absurdly long work hours.[23]

Of course, the work-life issue is also a gender and class issue, in ways both overt and subtle. As previously noted, many if not most work-life policies pertain to childcare, which is still primarily configured as women's work. Wendy Brown's ideas about liberalism's model of subjectivity imply that work-life initiatives perpetuate a notion of autonomous individuality (and a dichotomy between public and private) that is based on the continued exclusion and subordination of women. As Brown writes, "Gender and class converge here, as every middle- and upper-class woman knows who has purchased her liberty, personhood, and equality through child care and 'household help' provided by women earning a fraction of their boss's wage" (Brown 1995, 164–165). In other words, only *some* women can afford to play along with the corporate ideal of autonomous individuality—*at a cost*, to themselves and to other people. Brown also notes that women who are self-interested and ambitious, as encouraged by contemporary corporate discourses, are often sharply criticized. Similarly, Arlie Russell Hochschild, in her research on "the commercialization of intimate life," characterizes many current corporate work-life policies as stopgap measures that actually perpetuate the continued subordination of women, for example, the continued expectation that women should bear significantly more responsibility for childcare and household tasks than men do. Hochschild suggests that the current policies should be replaced with more ambitious and sweeping reforms following Sweden's model of "paid parental leave, sick-child leave, and other supports for working parents... We need to extend these reforms with a comprehensive program of job training and retraining for the economically dispossessed. Parental leave is of little use if we lack decently paid, secure jobs from which to take those leaves" (Hochschild 2003, 171).

Another, related way to look at the work-life problem is to consider what the term itself implies. "Work-life" policies strive to insert work into life, much like—as Rose argues—many twentieth-century management theories strove to seamlessly align work goals and personal goals (when linked with self-actualization processes, work becomes the aim and the purpose of life—one lives to work). We cannot "balance" work and life as if these were two entirely separate, unrelated elements, forever locked in conflict; for doing so only inserts work into life even more deeply. When such conflicts do surface in corporate policy or rhetoric, work is configured as the central, inevitable factor, while personal or family concerns must somehow be altered to accommodate work. As Stanley Deetz has argued, "The enemy is no longer the managers' expectations. The company is integrated into the self, leaving one's body and one's non-work relations as oppositional" (Deetz 1998, 166). Here is one telling example of this phenomenon: in the early 2000s, Ford's onsite childcare was provided by a company called Bright Horizons Family Solutions—as if a family were a problem in need of solving.[24] One cannot deny that some effects of work-life policies, like allowing people to keep their jobs, despite the kinds of personal priorities (e.g., family) that might once have led to dismissal or demotion, make workers feel grateful. But such policies also feed into the attitude that makes them seem beneficial in the first place: the attitude that work always takes precedence over all other activities and practices.

EXPRESS YOURSELF

Where William Whyte once envisioned a business world full of conformist zombies, today's business writers—and corporations themselves—are more likely to depict office environments as sanctuaries of individual expression, liberation, and creativity. The most immediately obvious example of worker self-expression might be the 1990s trend toward casual office dress codes and "dress down Fridays"—invitations for employees to put their unique fashion sense on display or to feel comfortable in their clothes rather than hemmed in by formal corporate standards.[25] But the notion of "free expression" in the workplace takes several non-sartorial forms. In line with this chapter's focus on worker individuality, I am particularly interested in contemporary corporate emphasis on employee self-expression through verbal or written input, independent decision making, and creative problem solving. Companies' focus on individual creativity, unique character, and expression in the workplace (evinced in corporate policies and publicity) accompanies a similar focus on these traits in business self-help books and management theory.

Even some of America's largest and oldest corporations have moved away from traditional management hierarchies and are encouraging individual workers to express their opinions and ideas about corporate decisions and policies. As noted earlier, vertical chains of command have been and are being replaced by "flattened" or horizontal structures, with fewer bureaucratic checkpoints. Probably inspired in part by the 1980s success of similar management strategies in Japan, many U.S. corporations have instituted team-based systems, where semiautonomous groups of employees become responsible for particular projects—seeing them through to completion without constantly relying on directives from supervisors. Direct communication between departments, managers, and employees has become common, making it easier for even entry-level workers to contribute their ideas. And managers encourage and expect them to do so. In an annual report, General Electric describes itself as "intolerant of bureaucracy" and asks its employees to "act in a boundaryless fashion... always search for and apply the best ideas regardless of their source" (General Electric 1999). Yahoo's corporate website highlights a quotation from the company's head of research: "The Research team at Yahoo! has the unique ability to work in a way that allows for freedom of big ideas... [We] have a mutual respect that encourages big thinking" (Yahoo "Life@Yahoo" 2008). Yahoo's "careers" website suggests that the company's workers are asked to provide their company with input, assume responsibility for projects, and complete them without babysitting from management. Similarly, Tom Peters, the perennially popular management guru discussed earlier, champions an individualist approach in *Liberation Management:* "Those who would survive, managers and non-managers alike, will simply 'have to make their own firm,' create their own projects" (12). But the work practices Peters describes do not sound "simple" at all; instead, in Peters's world, workers are expected to take on extra work, learn and train constantly, and assertively seek out more work at all times. The American entrepreneurial worker, a popular character type at least since the days of Horatio Alger, has taken on a new dimension: endless, limitless effort seems necessary for business success.

Many companies are explicitly looking for input from a certain *type* of worker; not just anyone can contribute the lucrative innovations that today's corporations crave. After all, what would "creative individuality" mean if anyone and everyone could possess it? No zombie conformists for Goldman Sachs or Yahoo—these corporations, like numerous others, tailor their human resources publicity materials to attract creative people. An investment banking and securities firm,

Goldman Sachs describes itself as "an opportunity, a journey and a passport to new adventures" and informs potential applicants that "working with [the company] can provide you with some of the most interesting challenges of your life" (Goldman Sachs 2008). Yahoo insists that it wants "creative minds that can take us new places… Big Thinkers who embody the fun, innovative, collaborative spirit that's uniquely Yahoo!" (Yahoo "Careers" 2008). Of course, much of this discourse begs a particular question, what corporation—in today's business environment *or* in the past—would proudly proclaim its dullness and its relentless devotion to the same old status quo? In other words, when corporations announce that they are looking for creativity and innovation and therefore looking for employees with—as Goldman Sachs puts it—a "zest for life," the revelation isn't exactly shocking.

Given the obvious, even trite, quality of this discourse, why might individual self-expression and creativity be heralded as such important values in business today? I can imagine several answers to this question. For one, management might—as William Whyte once suspected—want to cultivate worker cooperation and downplay the possibility of rebellion and dissent in the workplace. The logic at work here is simple: if employees are invited to speak their minds, they should therefore be less inclined to take their complaints to unions, lawyers, and other alleged enemies of corporate authority. Worker dissatisfaction is thus kept in-house, less likely to be subject to potentially damaging public or media scrutiny. But, given his firm belief in corporate groupthink, Whyte probably could not have anticipated a relatively recent development in this story: managers' active *fostering* of workplace dissent. In the turbulent wake of Enron, WorldCom, and other high profile scandals, some businesses in the early 2000s began reinstituting the bureaucratic checkpoints they had once dissolved, while others are strongly pushing individual workers to speak according to their consciences and to be unafraid of possible repercussions of "blowing the whistle" on unethical conduct.[26]

Despite corporate assurances, the encouragement of individual voice in the workplace—in terms of worker accountability and in other forms—has multiple effects rather than being, as corporations themselves suggest, uniformly beneficial for workers. For example, it is said that horizontal management structures can minimize workplace territorialism, allowing employees to expand their knowledge of skills and processes once relegated to different departments. Some workers feel that they thrive in such open environments and enjoy the learning opportunities. Others, however, feel themselves stretched thin by this "multitasking." The risk inherent in horizontal structures is that while one's individual contributions are valued, one's responsibilities can simultaneously accrue. Instead of jealously guarded boundaries between positions and departments, which keep certain responsibilities and risks confined to certain people and groups, new responsibilities may now land on the shoulders of individual workers. Tom Peters gleefully describes executive assistants who take on extra training in order to participate in the accounting or marketing departments of their firms, but what happens to workers who have neither the time nor the inclination to spend yet more hours and energy at work? Working toward career advancement is not a problem in and of itself, but now, it seems, the possibility exists that workers—many of whom already contribute far more hours than the once-usual 9-to-5—may be dismissed or overlooked for promotion for not making enough of an effort. Also, too few of these multitasking workers, with their multiple opportunities to contribute as well as their ever-growing responsibilities, are adequately compensated for their additional labor. In his research on the dot-com industry of the 1990s, Andrew Ross cites a report finding that new media workers in New York spent "as much as 13.5 hours of unpaid time per week" training themselves to keep up with rapid technological changes in their field (Ross 2003, 93). The Society for Human Resources Management warns that typical wage and benefits packages are inappropriate for today's multitasking workers, especially considering their nontraditional work hours: "A 24/7-work cycle will lead to a re-evaluation of compensation policies and greater use of pay-for-performance policies for many occupations... New reward systems will have to be created to keep employees engaged in their work and committed to their organizations" (Patel 2003, 27). While companies benefit from increased individual input, their emphasis on self-fulfillment or self-actualization through work allows for the simultaneous downplaying of monetary compensation. So, who wins?

Another reason for corporate emphasis on self-expression is the undeniable appeal of it for job applicants. As workplaces in the 1990s came to advertise themselves as casual, creative, and open to employee input, many of them also presented themselves as more "fun." Corporate rhetoric not only focuses on individual expression, but also on individual enjoyment; many companies and business writers insist that workers be both comfortable and happy. In the last 15 years or so, stories about new and unusual forms of office organization began to appear. Exchanged amongst exhilarated friends or breathlessly reported in the usually staid, gray pages of the

Wall Street Journal, these stories described conference rooms with Ping-Pong tables and pinball machines, web design firms where casually dressed employees could take afternoon siestas or bring their pets to work, and offices where mazes of drab cubicles were demolished and replaced with bright, airy, and "interactive" spaces. Though New Economy naysayers gloomily and accurately predicted that the fun (and the profits) would not last, discourse on corporate fun still emerges—sometimes from unexpected quarters.

Even after the dot-com bust, the high-tech computer industry still provides many examples of workplace fun (Yahoo has office foosball tournaments, Microsoft hosts frequent ethnic festivals complete with food and dance), but the good old Wal-Mart Corporation may boast the highest fun quotient. A workday at Wal-Mart, the number one corporation of the 2008 *Fortune* 500, begins with a cheer: an enthusiastic spelling of the corporate name, complete with "Hokey-Pokey"-like dance moves. Founder Sam Walton got the idea for the Wal-Mart cheer while visiting factories in Korea and brought it back to the United States to try with his own employees. His justification for this unorthodox decision was blunt: "Just because we work so hard, we don't have to go around with long faces all the time... It's sort of a 'whistle while you work' philosophy and we work better because of it" (Wal-Mart 2008). Walton then instituted a policy called "aggressive hospitality," enjoining his employees to be cheerful and ultra-friendly to customers, no matter what—an institutionally enforced positive attitude. Also, Walton included the following remarks as "Rule 6" on his list of successful management tactics:

> Celebrate your successes. Find some humor in your failures. Don't take yourself so seriously. Loosen up, and everybody around you will loosen up. Have fun. Show enthusiasm—always. When all else fails, put on a costume and sing a silly song. Then make everybody else sing with you... All of this is more important, and more fun, than you think, and it really fools the competition. "Why should we take those cornballs at Wal-Mart seriously?"   (Wal-Mart 2006)

This example strongly suggests that there is an ominous side to workplace fun, especially when it explicitly operates in the service of worker governance. Walton clearly wants to amuse and entertain his workers in an attempt to make his corporation more competitive. Fun companies, in his view, are less likely to get stuck in ruts and more likely to foster worker and customer loyalty. As he advises, "Constantly, day-by-day, think of new and more interesting ways to motivate and challenge your partners. Set high goals, encourage competition, and then keep score. Make bets with outrageous payoffs. If things get stale, cross-pollinate; have managers switch jobs with one another to stay challenged" (Wal-Mart 2006). But are fun activities and attitudes still fun when they're coerced? And even though store management may be trained to foster a fun environment for workers, other aspects of Wal-Mart's practices are sure to have the opposite effect. Barbara Ehrenreich's best seller, *Nickel and Dimed: On (Not) Getting By in America* (2001), features an account of her dismal experiences working "undercover" as a Wal-Mart sales associate—and there is barely a trace of "fun" as she describes the typical workday at Walton's company. Many pages of Ehrenreich's book are devoted to discussion of drug testing, particularly the personal humiliation and limiting of worker mobility it can entail. She describes management tactics that recall the heyday of Taylorist scientific management—most notably, conflicts over the right to bathroom breaks. Also, concerns about the optimal use of time on the job have taken a particularly virulent form at Wal-Mart, the corporation attempts to regulate what it calls "time theft," engaging in any activity not defined as "work" on company time. So, despite its rhetorical emphasis on community spirit and fun, "time theft" reduces camaraderie among workers—no non-work conversations are permitted—and encourages competitiveness and backstabbing. Even though Wal-Mart claims to care so deeply for individual worker fulfillment and enjoyment, there's not much fun happening for employees at America's most popular store.

DIFFERENT STROKES FOR DIFFERENT FOLKS

There are clear connections between workplace diversity and the issue of individuality. Much of today's corporate discourse about diversity amplifies and celebrates individual difference. Difference, corporations say, should be acknowledged, for it contributes to a creative atmosphere and enhances communication skills. Of course, as Wendy Brown argues, the concept of personal difference itself (in terms of gender, race, or class) provides the foundation for liberal notions of freedom and equality as well as—seemingly paradoxically—consensus. However, as Brown notes, for some people to fulfill the ideal of entre-preneurial individualism, others must be encumbered in some way. Like work-life policy, diversity management is a confrontation with this issue—an attempt to leverage difference to downplay tensions and optimize employee usefulness.[27]

The number of published books on the topic of diversity management is astounding. A keyword search for "diversity management" at Amazon.com yields 307 results; most of these were published in the 1990s, and, except for a small number on the management of diverse natural ecosystems, all pertain to the corporate context. Reading through the descriptions and reviews of these books reveals two main themes: the benefits of workplace diversity and the need for managers to learn techniques for communicating with "diverse" (read: usually non-white and/or non-male) types of workers. There are also books about gays and lesbians in corporate environments, generation gaps in the workforce, and workers with disabilities. The reason why there are so many business books on diversity management, it seems, goes well beyond a need to acknowledge the changing demographics of the United States. These books are not only about working with or tolerating inevitable changes in the American workforce, but also about leveraging those changes to full advantage.[28]

In corporate publicity materials, discourses about diversity bear a strong resemblance to discourses about creative, rebellious workers who think outside the box. According to these sources, the benefits of workplace diversity are largely the same as those of workplace dissent—as if being born non-white and/or non-male, for example, were some form of deliberate protest and challenge to the status quo. As did Frances Horibe in her book about dissenters, businesses emphasize the possibilities for innovation afforded by a diverse workforce. Accenture notes that "people from a wide range of cultural, educational and geographic backgrounds... are able to challenge conventional thought, offer unique perspectives and generate innovative ideas" (Accenture 2002). Risk management firm RCPL Forex argues that "having a diverse workforce encourages increased creativity and innovation... crucial to improved performance and continued business success" (RCPL Forex 2006). Ford goes several steps further, indicating in a website section titled "Diversity Proves Its Value" that "diverse work teams can outperform homogenous teams in quantity, creativity, and quality" and that "people who work, live and learn in integrated settings develop stronger interpersonal communications and negotiating skills" (Ford 2002).

These corporations give few indications of how workforce diversity automatically and inevitably leads to innovation and better communication, but AT&T provides one hint. One of many identity-based organizations within the company, Women of AT&T strives not only to provide social support to women workers but also to "promote awareness of AT&T in the community through active involvement in community-related activities" (AT&T 2004). Philip Morris discusses a similar strategy for reaching "minority" markets by organizing groups of workers based on their identities and sending them out into neighborhoods and communities. In short, like advertising did many years ago, corporations have discovered that individual identities can be constitutive of lucrative target markets and can also provide ideal vehicles for reaching those markets in an "authentic" and appropriate manner. There is an interesting tension here between a kind of group identity politics in the workplace ("Women of AT&T") and the corporate focus on individuality discussed throughout this chapter, but even when particular identity-based groups are celebrated, the center of that celebration tends to be *individual* difference and, more importantly, *individual* contributions. Accenture boasts that "the different points of view [workers from diverse backgrounds] bring lead to superior business solutions for us and our clients. Their individual experiences promote creativity and innovation and contribute to our success" (Accenture 2001). Similarly, Boeing claims to "value the skills, strengths and perspectives of our diverse team. We will foster a participatory workplace that enables people to get involved in making decisions about their work that advance our common business objectives" (Boeing 2002).

A suggestive passage found on IBM's website further complicates the notion of leveraging diversity.[29] In its attempt to recruit minority applicants, IBM also demonstrates one bottom line function of corporate diversity discourses: providing opportunities and methods for control. The passage in question is worth quoting at length:

> Racism, sexism, ageism, bias against people with disabilities, and homophobia are issues in our society. At IBM, we do not deny that they exist, but we will never let them come between us and our customers, or our obligations to our shareholders. Our goal is to keep them from influencing our workforce, our productivity, and our competitive edge. We must bring all issues back to how they relate to the marketplace and focus on one ism—consumerism.   (IBM 2002)

Here, identity is clearly corporate property. While IBM recognizes the social conditions that shape American culture, the company also insists that it can eradicate these forces through wise management of its diversity-friendly corporate culture, which is in turn rendered open minded and all-embracing through the magic of capitalism. The market loves individuals of all colors and creeds. The corporate celebration of difference serves to make differences more visible and thereby ever more vulnerable to market and corporate power. The more corporations know about you, the easier it is to mold you into an ideal worker and consumer. As Avery Gordon has noted, diversity management is "capitalist management; it is not democratic self-governance and it does not even offer group-based autonomy. At best it believes that differentially defined individuals may gain access to make decisions about new products... guided by the higher law of managerial direction towards successful global competition" (Gordon 1995, 18).

The issue of *inclusion* of difference in corporate settings may seem to contradict the business world's celebration of difference, but in fact operates according to similar principles. When difference is celebrated, it is included. When difference is included, it is made increasingly visible—and increasingly useful. This is one reason why, even with increasing and dramatic budget cutbacks for many companies, diversity programming is almost certain to continue into the future—perhaps in smaller-scale form. Indeed, the state of the U.S. economy is already affecting the various business policies, discourses, and attitudes I have described here: what happens to corporate individualism when layoffs are up and profits are down?

CORPORATE CULTURES, CORPORATE CULTS: THE RETURN OF CONFORMITY?

When William Whyte first diagnosed the problem of middle management conformity, he probably could not have foreseen the rise of the "lean and mean" horizontal corporation—the removal of administrative layers increasingly seen, in the 1980s and the 1990s, as so much bureaucratic dead weight. Also, it is difficult to guess how Whyte might have reacted to the more recent "return" of middle management, heralded by some business scholars as the answer to corporate America's ethical problems. *Business Week,* for example, describes and applauds a breed of middle managers primarily concerned with safeguarding ethics through increasing bureaucratic checkpoints for business decisions and thereby improving corporate credibility.[30] How will corporate individualism discourses fare within this climate of elevated corporate conscientiousness? After all, workplace individualism can carry with it certain problematic connotations, notably the possibility of self-interest trumping community spirit, but also the idea that workers can and should unilaterally make decisions without necessarily checking with the boss.

Suspicion of individualism also goes all the way to the top. The status of the charismatic CEO—that individualist par excellence—has suffered somewhat since Enron and other management scandals. The trend toward individualism I have described throughout this chapter might never have occurred without the encouragement and sponsorship of 1990s corporate founders and CEOs—many of them untraditional, publicity mongering, without formal business training, and surprisingly young. But public opinion about this breed of executives has significantly worsened, even though executive pay has remained steady or grown in the past decade.[31]

For example, many business experts have begun lamenting the corporate preference for charisma over honesty. *Newsday*'s Patricia Kitchen reports that executive search firms say, "In this post-Enron era of corporate greed, what's needed is a return to... old-fashioned concepts—character and integrity—so that everyone knows your motives when times get rough" (Kitchen 2002, D1). While integrity may not seem glamorous, corporate scandals have made the trait, or at least lip service to it, quite popular. Similarly, self-help books and autobiographies written by celebrity CEOs are not selling as well as they once did. In a column for the *New York Times,* Felicity Barringer reports, "With profits falling, unemployment rising, and Sophoclean tales of corporate fraud and greed still fresh in people's minds, executives—even well-known, successful ones—are no longer unquestioningly accepted as Saviors with Solutions" (Barringer 2003, 4). Business books continue to flood the market, but many of them gather dust on Barnes and Noble's shelves as readers think about high-profile corporate controversies and the volatility of the stock market. Many business writers condemn the tendency of corporations to recruit celebrity managers from outside their ranks, noting that the tactic is rarely successful. In his best-selling book, *Good to Great* (2001), Jim Collins argues that the most profitable and admired companies are rarely led by flashy, outlandish, self-help-book-writing CEOs; even those hyped celebrity executives specifically recruited to take companies to the next level of success usually fail. Instead, Collins writes, leaders who have taken their organizations from "good" to "great" tend to be humble, calm, and focused on their employees—not on their personal, individual fame. These "great" leaders are most certainly not the individualist renegades that were applauded only a decade ago by Tom Peters. Faced with emerging doubts and challenges like those expressed by Collins, it seems probable that corporate individualism discourses will begin to recede in favor of discourses about the new, community-minded "integrity."

While business writers question the corporate strategy of hiring charismatic CEOs, Dave Arnott cautions against companies actively recruiting certain personality types for employees at *all levels* of the organization. Arnott's shrill yet frequently persuasive book, *Corporate Cults: The Insidious Lure of the All-Consuming Organization* (2000), suggests that corporate individualism discourse has become so hyper-amplified that it has transformed into its opposite. Occasionally sounding like a contemporary version of William Whyte, Arnott uses examples from well-known companies to argue that corporate attention to individual needs and celebration of individual voices has paradoxically led to cult-like conformity and devotion to the workplace. He distinguishes between corporate cultures (defined, following Terrence Deal and Allan Kennedy, as "the way we do things around here") and corporate cults—organizations which, despite their benign or even fun appearance, inspire and/or coerce blind devotion in their employees. Arnott notes that many of *Fortune* magazine's so-called Best Companies to Work For display the three main aspects of religious cults: devotion, charismatic leadership, and separation from the community. These corporate cults, Arnott writes, thrive by recruiting candidates likely to fit into the culture, likely to feel that their individual attitudes and needs are being accepted and encouraged. He compares Southwest Airlines employees to Stepford Wives: "Employees were encouraged to express themselves... However, of the approximately fifty employees I saw that day, 100 percent of them were wearing the company shirt and either khaki shorts or blue jeans... organizational screeners [at job interviews] look for personality characteristics that allow candidates to join" (2000, 2).

In his analysis of the roots of the cult problem, Arnott discusses many of the same factors I have examined in this chapter, albeit from a dramatically different perspective. Central to his argument is the idea of work-life balance (or lack thereof); he writes that enculted workers have no lives whatsoever outside of work, because they have allowed themselves to be thoroughly absorbed by the organization. All non-work interests have fallen by the wayside. Arnott also acknowledges the role of fun in the workplace—enjoyable activities and events are used to seduce workers, who in turn decide that they don't need to "get a life" outside of work, because work itself is all the fun, friendship, and family they require. While I do not dispute that work-life balance and workplace fun have their uses and effects (as described in the sections above), the sharp dichotomy that Arnott draws between individual and organization fails to account for several key factors, including the fact that corporate individualism discourses—as I have described them throughout this chapter—may have helped to get us into this "corporate cult" mess in the first place. Arnott suggests that workers are constantly being duped into joining corporate cults, but neglects the idea that individuality, like conformity, has a price. He writes, "While [corporate] leadership certainly contributes to cultish behavior, the major part of the responsibility lies with the individual . . . You're in charge, and only you can allow the insidious lure of the all-consuming organization to take over your life" (ix). But, as suggested in my earlier discussion of Foucault and Rose, it's precisely this belief in the sovereignty of the individual—his/her powers, needs, and desires—that corporations utilize to their benefit.

Obviously, this is not to say that there are no conflicts between individual workers and the organizations for which they work. Describing challenges he faced while attempting to devise effective factory management tactics, Henry Ford once said that he hired people just to use their hands, but they kept bringing their minds with them. Even now that knowledge itself is considered a valuable commodity, Ford's words still neatly summarize a central problem for corporations: the confrontation between business needs and desires versus worker needs and desires. We can see the history of this problem played out across the twentieth century, from Taylor's attempts to optimize physical efficiency, to Mayo's suggestions for empowering workers through self-expression opportunities, to Whyte's warnings about the dangers of groupthink and need for increased worker autonomy, to Peters' ebullient tribute to horizontal, team-based organizations, where individuals can always contribute their ideas and pursue their personal interests (as long as these benefit the company). We can also see how contemporary trends in corporate discourse and management theory, including work-life balance, worker self-expression, and diversity, are responses to the individual versus organization problem. But both workplace conformity and workplace individualism have costs. As Ford's remark reminds us, corporate attempts to deal with workers who "keep bringing their minds with them" are not necessarily implemented with workers' best interests in mind—even when those interests are precisely what they are acknowledging, celebrating, and fulfilling. Rather, individualist discourses (and policies based on those discourses) comprise yet another opportunity to make those individuals optimally *useful*, including those personal traits that might ordinarily stand in the way of business progress.

As is the case with so many other aspects of business today, the future of individualism discourses and the policies that correspond to them is impossible to predict. Business writers have already pointed out the decline in certain individualist trends: charismatic CEOs, casual dress codes, and "fun" dot-com companies, to name a few.

Given budgetary constraints and downsized staffs in many fields and companies, work-life and diversity programming may fall out of favor. Worker self-expression might be less encouraged as the economy gets rockier and jobs are lost. People may mourn these changes, for all of these corporate tactics—recruitment of non-white employees, horizontal structures, open lines of communication, et cetera—can have productive effects, even while they bind people ever more tightly to their jobs and workplaces. But, as I have noted throughout this chapter, there is much to be suspicious of in corporate rhetoric of individualism, and it is ill advised to characterize some outcomes as constructive and other consequences as harmful, emphasizing the supposedly "good" over the supposedly "bad." We cannot choose some effects over others. It is crucially important always to keep in mind that these business policies and discourses are indeed *tactics*—and that such tactics have a *variety* of effects, inextricable from each other.

CHAPTER 3

SURVIVAL AT WORK: FLEXIBILITY
AND ADAPTABILITY IN AMERICAN
CORPORATE CULTURE

Don't forget this... it's the law of the universe that the strong shall survive and the weak must fall by the way, and I don't give a damn what idealistic plan is cooked up, nothing can change that.

—*Walt Disney*

Look, it's ridiculous to call this an industry... This is not. This is rat eat rat, dog eat dog. I'll kill 'em, and I'm going to kill 'em before they kill me. You're talking about the American way of survival of the fittest.

—*Ray Kroc*[1]

THE CORPORATE TAR PITS

"The giants of e-commerce, who walked among us, are culturally extinct now with a war on." So writes John Schwartz for the November 25, 2001, issue of the *New York Times* "Sunday Styles" section. In his rather gleeful description of the dramatic fall of the New Economy, "Dot-Com is Dot-Gone, and the Dream with It," Schwartz likens defunct e-commerce firms to dinosaur bones lodged in a kind of Silicon Valley Tar Pit. Just in case readers somehow manage to miss the point of the story, a Tyrannosaurus Rex skull, jaws agape against a purple plaid backdrop evocative of a computer screen saver, dominates one half of the "Sunday Styles" front page.

Schwartz points out that those "e-Decade" cheerleaders, who prematurely announced the rise of a brave new economic world, then began trying to sell memoirs about their own business failures. In short, he suggests, American corporate philosophy has turned away from New Economy discourses and toward more traditional—and perhaps more reliable—business practices. More importantly, Schwartz claims, firms that do not change with the cultural climate are destined for extinction.

The Darwinian imagery of Schwartz's narrative is nothing new. Businesspeople, financial writers, and management theorists have long been suggesting parallels between corporate policies and natural selection. What does change over time, however, is who plays the roles of hunter and hunted, who winds up a fossil, and who wins the "survival of the fittest" sweepstakes. Primarily through a discussion of popular business self-help books, which I will describe in more detail below, in this chapter I will trace a trend in business culture's use of Darwinian concepts: the increasing importance of two specific traits—flexibility and adaptability—to corporate "survival" in the 1980s, the 1990s, and today. I am also interested in how the term survival itself is deployed as well as some of the possible implications of that deployment. Ultimately, I will suggest that shifts in Darwinian discourse have changed what it means to be a good worker or a good manager, but not necessarily in productive or beneficial ways. As I see it, the focus on adaptability and flexibility has two especially troubling effects. First, individuals may be compelled to adapt ceaselessly. Second, the idea—central to contemporary corporate culture and business self-help—that one can survive through sheer will belies a truth central to the theory of natural selection, the same point that frightened so many of Darwin's contemporaries when *On the Origin of Species* was first published: when it comes to evolution, no one individual gets to *choose* to survive.

After an opening section that discusses historical examples of Darwinian language and imagery in American business, this chapter will engage with two 1980s versions thereof. Tom Peters and Robert Waterman's *In Search of Excellence: Lessons from America's Best-Run Companies, Publisher's Weekly's* number one nonfiction bestseller of 1983 and number one on *Forbes* magazine's "20 Most Influential Business Books" list, contrasts the traditional "rationality" and numbers crunching of industrial management with the more flexible, action-oriented, and instinct-based business strategies advocated by the authors. Peters and Waterman list eight attributes shared by the "excellent" companies they researched, particular qualities that allow

for what they call "managed evolution"—keeping a company optimally fit for marketplace conditions. Harvey Mackay's *Swim with the
Sharks without Being Eaten Alive: Outsell, Outmanage, Outmotivate,
and Outnegotiate Your Competition*—the number eight best seller
on the *Publisher's Weekly* business nonfiction list for 1988, alongside
books by such 1980s luminaries as Lee Iacocca and Donald Trump—
is a significant example of how corporate culture began in the 1980s
to move away from office-centric management and toward optimizing all aspects of individual adaptation for enhanced performance.[2]
Mackay's hesitant gestures toward less hierarchical, more flexible
work structures point the way toward policy developments to come,
as do his images of what it means to be fit for survival.

The chapter then examines more recent forays into Darwinian
corporate philosophy. Some of the most successful self-help business
books of the 1990s, including Spencer Johnson's *Who Moved My
Cheese?: An A-Mazing Way to Deal with Change in Your Work and in
Your Life* (1998), emphasize the idea of personal growth. Johnson,
whose book was on *Publisher's Weekly's* hardcover nonfiction best
seller list for more than 300 weeks, tells the story of individual evolution through self-actualization and provides readers with methods for
improving their ability to adapt at will. Kevin Kelly's *New Rules for
the New Economy: 10 Radical Strategies for a Connected World* (1999)
takes the notion of personal adaptation a step further, positing "intangibles" like "ideas, information, and relationships" as keys to success
for the individual worker, the company, and the market as a whole
(2). Kelly, a former editor-at-large for *Wired* magazine and a popular
management guru of the 1990s, compares businesses and markets to
ecosystems while retaining a sense that the fittest will survive a rapidly
changing economy. His is a kinder, gentler image of natural selection,
with an insistence on the interconnectedness of contemporary business. His image of office environments is likewise "friendlier," attuned
to employee creativity and playfulness, as well as flexibility, on the job.
Both Kelly and Johnson imply that flexibility—willingness to embrace
change—is central to survival in the corporate world. As I will suggest
in this chapter, however, this flexibility may not be as appealing for
workers as the self-help books seem to imply—particularly because it
entails potentially ceaseless effort.

While Michel Foucault's ideas of disciplinary power and technologies of the self are clearly appropriate choices of theoretical apparatus for a discussion of business self-help discourse, I have opted to
approach the topic from a different angle.[3] The seeming endlessness
of adaptation in corporate culture is central to Gilles Deleuze's study

of contemporary modes of power, "Postscript on Control Societies" (1990), which informs my own analysis throughout. Deleuze's control society concept, which builds upon (but does not supplant) Foucault's discipline model of power, is characterized by mechanisms for eternal training and assessment, such as continuing education, frequent training seminars for office workers, and competitive, flexible wage hierarchies based on performance. While the discipline model is often based within institutions (schools, militaries, workplaces) where the segmentation of time (through scheduling) and space (through office hierarchies or assembly lines, to provide a few examples) affects what people can potentially do, the control model accounts for what Deleuze calls the "breakdown" of many societal institutions by extending the presence of power in people's daily lives (178). Where discipline aimed to fix people in their positions, control embraces mobility, constant communication, and adaptability. Instead of working under (and responding to) the watchful eyes of managers and supervisors, workers are now held accountable for their performance through communication devices—e-mail, pager, or cell phone contact, for instance. Office space itself becomes part of the quest for constant communication; open meeting areas replace cubicles, optimizing possibilities for contact between coworkers and their supervisors. Meanwhile, the cybercommuter exemplifies how work's presence in daily life can increase exponentially in control society—instead of Fordism's segmented eight-hour workday, workers now have less structured yet potentially endless work time: "In control societies you never finish anything" (179).[4]

In this control model, workers' fitness for business success is in part based upon their constant availability, but mere availability is not enough to ensure survival in increasingly dog-eat-dog workplaces: "Businesses are constantly introducing an inexorable rivalry presented as healthy competition, a wonderful motivation that sets individuals against one another and sets itself up in each of them, dividing each within himself" (179). An intensified and constant attention to the betterment of the self is one important hallmark of Deleuze's control society concept. This betterment is clearly germane to the twentieth-century flowering of the self-help industry, both within and outside the business field. Power's workings are made increasingly efficient as individuals constantly strive to improve their lives through different types of training or adaptation (e.g., education, physical exercise, or attitude adjustment through therapy or self-help readings). These improvements can benefit individuals as well as their workplaces: "Many young people have a strange craving to be 'motivated,' they're always asking for special courses and continuing education; it's their job to discover whose ends these serve" (182).

That final point—the concluding moment of Deleuze's essay—resonates with ongoing discussions within cultural studies about the role of individual will as a concept in discourses of self-help and self-improvement. While the type of fitness they describe is first and foremost a physical fitness, Jeremy Howell and Alan Ingram's argument about developments in American health discourse suggests connections with the business self-help discourses I am examining here. Howell and Ingram describe a 1980s "cultural landscape" where Reagan and the New Right strategically promoted the traditional American value of self-reliance to deflect attention from their "draconian" social and economic policies (329). This promotion manifested itself in the impressive growth of the personal fitness industry, which instructed self-reliant individuals to take responsibility for themselves through discipline in diet and exercise. Howell and Ingram posit a simultaneous, parallel process in 1980s discourse about welfare and employment: any individual strong enough to take responsibility for him/herself could get and keep a job, without depending on government aid. Personal and financial responsibility are thus linked: "Illness, health care and unemployment were redefined as private issues of character—as a failure in individuals who refused to fight the good fight" (329). Like the business advice books I will discuss below, the personal fitness industry is part of a network of discursive forces that presume and reinforce the sovereignty of individual will by suggesting people can do whatever they commit effort to doing, regardless of social, physical, or economic circumstances.[5] The problem is that this prevailing self-help sentiment—that people can control every aspect of their lives—ignores the significant power of said circumstances, institutions, and discursive formations. Simply put, people cannot always choose to succeed, much less survive.

In their analysis, Howell and Ingram suggest that the discourse of all-American self-reliance was used to mask the nefarious workings of Reagan's policies and the "contradictions of capitalism" contained therein (330). I am unable to unmask, in similar fashion, any one prevailing "man behind the curtain" of Darwinian business self-help or any one particular way in which the discourse works. Rather, I am inclined to agree with David Carlone's analysis of the effects produced by business advice books such as Stephen Covey's *The Seven Habits of Highly Effective People* (1989): in various ways, these books help to shape what people can and cannot do. The recourse within business discourse to Darwinian imagery—most of which is oversimplified and perhaps even utterly misinterpreted for the purpose of making metaphors or parables—has the effect of naturalizing potentially harmful aspects of corporate life, for example, the potentially boundless injunction for workers to adapt to changing circumstances or the idea that failures (and successes, for that matter) are solely attributable to individual will.[6] I do not wish to suggest that we can simply look under the glossy surface of business self-help books and see how they function as tools benefiting the powers that be. Instead, I aim to examine what cultural work is accomplished through the valorization of adaptability and flexibility.

THE EVOLUTION OF "EVOLUTION"

Although the bulk of my discussion will focus on more or less contemporary American examples, the connection between evolution theory and business culture is much older and did not originate in the United States alone. The link was forged in the second half of the nineteenth century with the rise of social Darwinism, a set of beliefs initially espoused by two contemporaries of Darwin: English philosopher Herbert Spencer and Yale sociology professor William Graham Sumner.[7] In fact, credit for the phrase "survival of the fittest" belongs to Spencer, not Darwin.[8] Social Darwinism was a multifaceted movement, with sometimes-contradictory tenets, but its application to economics was fairly consistent. Spencer argued that laissez-faire, free market competition, without any government interference, was the natural way to ensure a community's economic health. Like the lions of the African savanna, businesses should have to compete with each other for resources, and those best adapted to survival will eventually eliminate their competition. Sumner further developed this idea, using it to attack socialism: "Let it be understood that we cannot go outside this alternative: liberty, inequality, survival of the fittest; not-liberty, equality, survival of the unfittest. The former carries society forward and favors all its best members; the latter carries society downward and favors all it [sic] worst members" (qtd. in Caudill 1997, 76).[9]

The tenets of social Darwinism were taken up in the twentieth century by some of America's best-known tycoons.[10] In his autobiography, Andrew Carnegie describes himself as a "disciple" and personal friend of Spencer—an unsurprising disclosure, given Carnegie's theories about business conduct (Carnegie 1920, 333). For example, Carnegie espouses a survival of the fittest philosophy not unlike the one endlessly rehearsed in the popular stories of Horatio Alger: in a free market, dedication and unflagging diligence, rather than class distinction, will lead individuals to business survival and, ultimately, success. For Carnegie—who, himself, rapidly rose through business ranks without the purported advantage of high society connections—the most significant and inspirational element of evolutionary theory was the idea that species progress toward optimum fitness: "I had found the truth of evolution. 'All is well since all grows better' became my motto... Man was not created with an instinct for his own degradation, but from the lower he had risen to the higher forms. Nor is there any conceivable end to his march for perfection" (339).[11] Clearly, this creative interpretation of natural selection corresponds well with Carnegie's Alger-like vision of business: through constant perseverance, workers will themselves to become increasingly fit and successful.

Similarly, Henry Ford, in *My Life and Work* (1922), distinguishes between two types of business competition: unproductive competition for material gain and monopoly versus healthy competition between workers and companies to be the best in their field. In this autobiographical account of his business ideas, he contends that Americans—as opposed to "foreigners," who "are content to stay as straw bosses" and remain satisfied with steady employment—continually strive for advancement by working (or thinking about how to improve their work) nonstop (100). Perhaps Ford's most noteworthy link with social Darwinist concepts, however, was his social welfare program. Inspired by the idea that low wage businesses are inherently unstable because workers become distracted by their struggle for subsistence, Ford devised a plan to share company profits with workers who fitted into certain defined categories, for example, married men "living with and taking good care of their families" and single men "who are of proved thrifty habits" (127). Ford employed 50 investigators, who observed workers at home and decided whether they fitted the plan's standards of "cleanliness and citizenship" and were therefore worthy of a share in the profits (128). In this way, Ford defined and enforced a certain type of fitness for his workers, not only for paternalistic reasons, but also for the benefit of the company's continued survival in an increasingly competitive market: "A man who is living aright will do his work aright" (128). In *My Life and Work,* Ford repeatedly insists that humans are inherently unequal in terms of fitness (abilities and talents) and that any society, government, or workplace endeavoring to foster equality is unnatural and therefore doomed to failure.

Mid-twentieth-century developments in organization theory also point toward the growing popularity of evolution imagery in business circles. Norbert Wiener's *Cybernetics* (1948), later considered a founding text for 1960s systems theory, characterized the regulatory apparatuses of animals as "information processing systems" (Shafritz and Ott 1987, 235). Wiener drew a parallel between these naturally occurring apparatuses and the problem-solving ability of human organizations. Like the respiratory or digestive system of an animal, an organizational or technological system detects environmental stimuli, scans for problems or changes, and then responds. The cybernetics model gained ground several decades after Wiener's book was published, when management theorists attempted to conceptualize the workings of computer systems. One can also see the influence of Wiener on more recent management gurus, particularly those who emphasize the importance of environmental factors, like Kevin Kelly and Seth Godin. But there is a significant difference between cybernetics and most other biology-based theories of business; for Wiener, environment is the key factor that dictates adaptation, while for other authors, humans (managers, employees) can and should take what many businesspeople call a "proactive" stance and make necessary or preemptive changes *before* the market—the "environment" factor in many Darwinian business philosophies—demands adaptation.

To highlight some striking examples of Darwinian discourse in American business culture from Wiener's time—examples that illustrate the preemptive/proactive stance described above—two of the most legendary and successful men in the history of commerce, Walt Disney and Ray Kroc, described the corporate world as an instance of natural selection. The epigraphs at the beginning of this chapter amply demonstrate how these founders of the Disney and McDonald's empires used Darwinian (and Spencerian) language, but their business policies are even more remarkable in this regard. Both men unabashedly attempted to destroy anything that hindered their progress toward market dominance. Challenges to their authority from competitors as well as from their own workers were squelched using an impressive variety of tactics. Disney fired employees who wanted to unionize and bought advertising space in *Variety* to accuse members of the Screen Cartoonists Guild of being Communists.[12] He demanded loyalty and diligence from his staff, which in turn would keep his studio at the top of the industry; Eric Schlosser writes that Disney once "made a speech to a group of employees, arguing that the solution to their problems rested not with a labor union, but with *a good day's work*" (2001, 37, italics in original). Similarly, Kroc, in an attempt to maximize profits by minimizing salaries, lobbied for a federal bill that would allow his company to pay teenaged workers less than the national minimum wage. McDonald's competitors fared no better than the restaurant chain's counter help. Kroc always tried to stay several steps ahead of other fast-food restaurants by lowering prices and by introducing menu and technological innovations. In doing so, he destroyed many smaller food service chains and independent diners.[13] While Darwin himself might never have recognized any connection between these business policies and his evolution theories, both Disney and Kroc envisioned themselves as survivors of the fittest kind.

The concept of personal survival has for several decades been a central theme in American popular culture as well as business, and the two realms have become increasingly intertwined with the popularity of business self-help. From Gloria Gaynor's "I Will Survive," to Survivor's "Eye of the Tiger," to Destiny's Child's "Survivor," song lyrics about getting through tough times have long dominated the American radio airwaves and *Billboard* sales charts. Book best seller lists abound with survival-related titles that fit neatly into the self-help genre, for example, Dave Pelzer's *A Child Called "It"* series or Iyanla Vanzant's *Yesterday, I Cried*. There are daily meetings for adult survivors of rape, incest, parental alcoholism, cancer... the list goes on, seemingly without end. Also, Nielsen ratings from the past decade demonstrate the faddish appeal of television shows like *Survivor* and *The Weakest Link*, programs in which contestants compete to win money by being the last person left standing. On both of these shows, however, it is very rarely the "best" player who survives (the one who is strong enough to withstand tests of strength and endurance on *Survivor* or on *The Weakest Link*, the one who is able to answer the most trivia questions correctly). Instead, survival takes a certain amount of strategizing: making oneself appear to be nonthreatening and mediocre until the last possible moment. The ultimate adaptation is neither physical strength nor intellectual prowess, but the ability to eliminate your competition before it eliminates you. Deleuze noted this phenomenon—and the connection to contemporary corporate culture—well before the debut of the aforementioned programs: "If the stupidest TV game shows are successful, it's because they're a perfect reflection of the way businesses are run" (179). As I will show in upcoming sections of this chapter, personal strategizing has become a key element of contemporary business self-help discourse about survival as well; again, constant efforts to adapt supposedly ensure success.

Greil Marcus has hypothesized that the high point of survivor discourse came in the 1970s. After the social turbulence of the 1960s in America, people who had escaped the decade relatively unscathed and, perhaps, relatively unchanged were survivors. As Marcus points out,

> Through the magic of ordinary language, "survival" and its twin, "survivor," wrote the 1960s out of history as a mistake and translated the 1970s performance of any act of personal or professional stability (holding a job, remaining married, staying out of a mental hospital, or simply not dying) into heroism. First corrupted as a reference to those "survivors" of "the sixties" who were now engaged in "real life," the word contained an implacable equation: survival was real life.[14]

In this 1970s model of survival, those who lived through periods of great change without changing *themselves* were considered to be survivors. Change, here, was something to live *through*, and this model evinces a nostalgic desire for an idealized past as well as anxiety about the precariousness of modern life. In the 1980s and 1990s, however, stasis and fear of change came to seem more like risks than assets. According to many popular business books from the 1990s, like Spencer Johnson's and Kevin Kelly's, global corporations and workforces, like human bodies adapting to infections, must finally *change* if they do not wish to suffer or perish. But, as Emily Martin notes, "can we simultaneously realize that the new flexible bodies are also highly constrained? They cannot stop moving, they cannot grow stiff and rigid, or they will fall off the 'tightrope' of life and die" (1994, 248). To bring the survival problem back to the corporate context, as Martin does, even those workers who seem most adapted to their surroundings are under constant pressure to keep up with the everchanging world. Those who stop moving with the times place themselves at risk. In short, flexibility itself may carry a steep price: the flexible worker must remain flexible *at all times* and must constantly train him/herself to become ever more flexible.

Martin argues that modern immunology, and specifically the prevalent notion that a flexible, adaptable body is a healthy, happy, and prosperous body, is a metaphor that extends into contemporary corporate and political philosophy as well as strategies for everyday living. She traces the genealogy of popular thought regarding the human immune system; her series of interviews with people from all walks of life, placed alongside analysis of popular science magazines, school health class materials, and films, reveals a trend moving from 1950s concepts of body-as-fortress (good hygiene acting as barrier against possible invasion by germs) to 1970s depictions of healthy bodies as well-oiled, Taylorized machines. In the 1980s and 1990s, increased attention to the AIDS pandemic resulted in increased attention to the immune system, including a reconceptualized vision of that system, when healthy, as flexible—adaptable to new and emerging situations or environments. Martin suggests that now and in the near future, "[what] will be forged is a conception of 'fitness' in which, just as surely as in nineteenth-century social Darwinism... some will survive and some will not" (xviii). This idea of fitness currently applies to getting by in the work world (where flexible specialization and openness to change are said to contribute to individual and company success) and to surviving a rapidly changing social realm (new demographic patterns, race relations, class structures, and globalization).

Today, worker flexibility takes a variety of forms, and the implications of emphasizing flexibility for survival are vast. Ulrich Beck has described worker flexibility in terms of work schedules ("flextime," compressed or part-time hours, temporary assignments, freelancing) and diverse work activities and skills—the popular resume phrase "multitasking." In *The Brave New World of Work* (2000), Beck shows how corporate emphasis on flexibility in an increasingly global marketplace works to disguise "a redistribution of risks away from the state and the economy toward the individual" (3). Simply put, flexibility can really signify job insecurity—"discursively 'sweetened'... by the rhetoric of independent entrepreneurial individualism" (4). In this way, the individual employee, never the employer or the economy, is to blame when downsizing occurs. Anyone who becomes part of the mass in a mass layoff did not train and adapt diligently enough. Beck and Martin's analyses suggest a possible problem with this picture: how much adaptation *is* enough? As Zygmunt Bauman argues, success at surviving "is always an 'until further notice' success; it is never final. It must be repeated over and over again... Survival is a lifelong task" (1992, 33).

Is survival of the fittest truly the American way, as Ray Kroc once suggested? The business truisms of the 1990s suggest as much. Since the terrorist attacks of September 11, 2001, American corporate culture has seemed to be moving toward the cutthroat competition once favored by Disney and Kroc. In part, this trend can be attributed to drastic changes in economic circumstances: dips in the stock market; lows in the consumer confidence index; massive hits to certain industries (air travel, national and international tourism); ethical scandals; and impatience with so-called e-commerce firms that have no net profits.[15] The U.S. unemployment level has increased, and competition for available jobs is fierce. In this tense climate, business culture's emphasis on self-help, individual adaptation, and flexibility persists and is perhaps stronger than ever. After all, advice on equipping oneself to handle change in the workplace seems particularly appropriate as workers get downsized, and firms remain unsure of their fate.

MANAGED EVOLUTION

Popular business guru Tom Peters, whose *Liberation Management* is discussed in Chapter 2, is often described as a maverick and a trendsetter in the business management field.[16] Many of his quirky phrases, including "Brand You" and "managing by wandering around" (MBWA), have entered the lexicon of corporate language. His first best-selling book, *In Search of Excellence* (cowritten with Robert Waterman), introduces management concepts that continue to be put into practice today, a full two decades after its initial publication. The link between corporate practice and evolution emphasized throughout *In Search of Excellence*—particularly, the idea of flexibility and adaptation as a *strategy*—anticipates and sets the stage for contemporary Darwinian business discourses.

In their 1982 book, Peters and Waterman position themselves as innovative and even rebellious by critiquing certain long-standing business truisms: always strive for growth (because bigger is better), ensure efficient communication and decision making through a strong chain of command, and consult "the numbers" before approving any action. Ultimately, Peters and Waterman call on managers, who want their companies to thrive in an ever-changing business environment, to cast aside what they learned in business school and instead embrace two kinds of flexibility: flexible organization and flexible thinking. Inflexibility can doom corporations, especially large ones: "If companies do not stay fit and relevant, they do not survive... Most of today's *Fortune* 500 were not there fifty years ago... Ten years ago our automobile giants seemed invincible. Today we wonder whether more than one will survive" (Peters and Waterman 1982, 109).

Despite the foreboding expressed in the lines just quoted, at the time of its publication, *In Search of Excellence* was characterized as a refreshing burst of optimism in an uncertain business world. As *Business Week* reporter John A. Byrne wrote of the book's early 1980s context, "Many believed entire industries were vulnerable to the Japanese onslaught. *[In Search of Excellence]* attacked the management-by-the-numbers mindset and sent a positive message that there were many American companies that had got it right" (2001). Though the book's assessment of many U.S. corporations is indeed upbeat (too upbeat, as we shall see), the predominantly cheery tone is belied by Peters and Waterman's repeated "survival of the fittest" refrain—if American companies don't evolve, they're heading for certain extinction. The reader can easily envision the traditionally structured corporation slowly sinking in the tar pit as Peters and Waterman list the problems caused by traditional management wisdom:

> *For one, the numerative, analytical component has an in-built conservative bias. Cost reduction becomes priority number one and revenue enhancement takes a back seat.* This leads to obsession with cost, not quality and value; to patching up old products rather than fooling with untidy new product or business development; and to fixing productivity through investment rather than revitalization of the work force. (1982, 44, italics in original)

Peters and Waterman therefore challenge the megacorporations to reconsider their organizational strategy. They advocate "chunking"—the creation of small, ad hoc worker task forces that can quickly respond to company and marketplace needs, rather than relatively rigid hierarchies that tend, in the authors' view, to slow down production and stifle innovation: "We see [chunking] as a vehicle for enhanced efficiency as well as a vehicle to foster adaptation and survival" (113). More importantly, Peters and Waterman also recommend that corporate managers shift from "rational" thinking to creative problem solving. Traditional business rationality, they argue, is dangerously inflexible because it discourages and even punishes risk-taking behaviors in workers and managers. But risks—called "blind adaptations" or "mutations" in the authors' Darwinian lingo—are integral to a company's continued success. Through chunking, "a corporation encourages a high volume of rapid action... it makes mistakes, it finds unanticipated success—and new strategic direction inexorably emerges" (114).

Peters and Waterman's evolution metaphors, which they favorably contrast with industrial management's frequent use of military symbolism, exemplify the tendency within business discourses to characterize adaptation as something that can be *willed*. While the authors do not go so far as to claim that controlling the environment—or marketplace—is possible, they do describe corporate evolution as a strategy for success; companies that respond to the marketplace *not* by anticipating fluctuations and trends (as in older management models), but by constantly inventing and implementing new ideas, will be survivors:

> Indeed, we believe that the truly adaptive organization evolves in a very Darwinian way. The company is trying lots of things, experimenting, making the right sorts of mistakes; that is to say, it is fostering its own mutations. The adaptive corporation has learned quickly to kill off the dumb mutations and invest heavily in the ones that work.   (114)

This passage is troubling, though, in that the process described within it more closely resembles eugenics than natural selection. Thanks to the implicit belief in evolution-as-willed—the idea that a corporation can simply make the "right sorts" of errors or that it can easily decide to slough off experiments that don't work—Peters and Waterman's language takes on a disturbing tone. In short, the dark side of adaptation through experimentation becomes clear: dumb mutations— projects that don't appear to work right away and, perhaps, the jobs of the people who develop and advocate them—are "killed off." In his close reading of Peters's work, Christopher Newfield argues that Peters "omits a vision of employees steering products and markets, for products and markets steer people, who can choose only their own efforts of adaptation. The employee is tyrannized as before" (1995, 36). Along these same lines, it is worth noting that Peters and Waterman unabashedly, uncritically celebrate corporate risk taking, but make no mention of possible consequences: who pays for failed mutations?

Critical commentary on *In Search of Excellence* may supply some answers to that question. Although, as noted earlier, the book has been highly influential in both business publishing (through the proliferation of similar books) and business itself (through the widespread integration of recommended management strategies), Peters and Waterman's groundbreaking work has been called into question on more than one occasion. In 1984, *Business Week* published a cover story titled "Oops!" that pointed out the failures of many of the companies called "excellent" by Peters and Waterman. Some of the so-called excellent companies, such as Amdahl and Data General, "fell on hard times soon after [the book's publication]" (Byrne 2001). The book's overall accuracy and academic rigor came under close scrutiny, particularly Peters and Waterman's glowing reviews of such ill-starred firms as Atari and Wang—apparently, the abundant risk taking and mistake making did not pay off for everyone.

The criticism got louder when, in a 2001 article for the magazine *Fast Company*, Peters himself admitted that he and Waterman "faked the data" (78). Peters has since claimed that *Fast Company* editor Alan M. Webber concocted that phrase and used it for an aggressive headline—an allegation that Webber does not deny: "It was hyperbole. It's in service of a bigger point, which is to trust your gut" (qtd. in Byrne 2001). Regardless of the truth about Peters and Waterman's research protocol, Peters's reputation suffered, and Waterman is "sad" about what happened because "it's Tom being Tom again. He loves to be outrageous... we [already] got criticized after the book was published for being flippant" (qtd. in Byrne 2001). In this case, Peters may have jeopardized himself by taking risks and nearly become one of his "dumb mutations" in danger of being destroyed while the fittest survive.[17]

THE BOOT CAMP FOR NATURAL SELECTION

In a famous scene from Oliver Stone's 1987 movie, *Wall Street,* high roller Gordon Gekko (played by Michael Douglas) addresses a roomful of Teldar Paper shareholders. Assembled Teldar representatives look on, with facial expressions ranging from mild disgust to absolute horror, as Gekko grabs a microphone and tells the crowd, "The new rule of evolution in corporate America seems to be survival of the unfittest. In my book you do it right or you get eliminated." He then proclaims that the era of bloated, bureaucratic management must end, points out the ludicrously large number of vice presidents onstage at the meeting, and suggests that the company's top personnel spend all day pushing papers back and forth. The crowd bursts into applause, now convinced, perhaps, by Gekko's sleek and deadly efficient version of corporate organization—in short, his justification for destroying Teldar. Following Gekko's evolution logic, bureaucracy-heavy companies are like dinosaurs, seemingly powerful but ultimately destined for extinction. In contrast, companies that are better able to adapt to new environments are like the speedy and resourceful small mammals that thrived when the giant reptiles perished.

Whether or not Gekko's description of corporate evolution can be extended to real-world aspects of American business culture, the account of fitness described above—provided, ironically, by *Wall Street's* "bad guy"—seems apt and perhaps even prophetic, especially when viewed in light of 1990s and early twenty-first-century business best sellers. More than two decades have passed since the cinematic release of Oliver Stone's heavy-handed critique of high finance, but the evolution imagery so gleefully used in Gekko's notorious "Greed is Good" speech persists. In fact, it seems that the tendency to describe business and economic phenomena in Darwinian terms has become more pervasive than ever. More importantly, Gekko's speech captures a volatile moment in the business world and enacts a conflict, in corporate philosophy, between what Raymond Williams might call "dominant" and "emergent" formations. Teldar Paper's top-heavy management model—with upper-level personnel responsible for painstakingly documenting their business decisions and an emphasis on methodical, perhaps even slow, strategizing for the future—was dominant in much of twentieth-century American commerce. In *Wall Street*, Gekko is the mouthpiece for an up-and-coming approach to business practices—an advocate of making companies "lighter," more intense, more efficient, and above all more focused on creating value for shareholders rather than worrying about in-house development.[18] Although Stone's film depicts Gekko as unscrupulous and even utterly heartless, there is no denying that Gekko's vision of the future has its advantages; like those who share his philosophy years later, he is portrayed as one of the wealthiest and most powerful men in the world of finance. Also, his claim that bloated bureaucracy is destined for extinction reverberates with Kevin Kelly's warning more than a decade later: "Today, if your company is like GM, it's in deep trouble" (1999, 2).

Published one year after the American theatrical release of *Wall Street*, Harvey Mackay's business self-help book, *Swim with the Sharks without Being Eaten Alive* (1988), similarly captures a moment on the cusp between older business models and "lighter," more flexible versions thereof. *Swim with the Sharks* was a phenomenal best seller in the late 1980s and early 1990s, and its title, alongside the violently physical language used throughout the book, suggests a survival of the fittest theme writ large. Such chapters as "Smile and Say No until Your Tongue Bleeds"; "Make Decisions with Your Heart, and What You'll End Up with is Heart Disease"; and "The Best Way to Chew Someone Out," offer no-nonsense advice for managers—and repeatedly indicate that corporate competition is an example of natural selection. To survive that selection process unscathed, one must cultivate the proper attitude: "Who says you're not tougher, smarter, better, harder-working, more able than your competition?" Mackay—CEO of Mackay Envelope Corporation—asks. "It doesn't matter if *they* say you can't do it. What matters, the only thing that matters, is if *you* say it" (80). If you have confidence in yourself, those marauding lions will go after another zebra in the herd. Furthermore, in Mackay's vision, one must always try to fill the lion's part oneself by constantly remaining several steps ahead of all competitors. Like Carnegie more than half a century earlier, Mackay insists that individual will can ensure survival in often inhospitable business environments. Mackay's book implies a sinister connection between adapting to changes in one's workplace and keeping one's job; his recommendation of constant training—"just keep on learning"—is unabashedly linked with job security and natural selection throughout *Swim with the Sharks*.

In a saturated market, Mackay advocates doing the best one can and waiting for the competition to slack off and/or die off: "Position yourself as Number Two to every prospect on your list... there are going to be Number Ones that retire or die or lose their territories for a hundred other reasons and succumb to the Law of Large Numbers" (65). This kind of coldly competitive strategy, he argues, is only natural; the envelope business, for example, is increasingly challenged by modern communication technologies, so, for the company to remain profitable and their jobs to remain secure, Mackay's employees must fight to take someone else's customers. Since there is no more room for territorial expansion, companies must deepen their market share instead. The way to accomplish this task is through constant, unrelenting effort. Therefore, Mackay's number one enemy in *Swim with the Sharks* is useless activity: "With all of the Anonymous Groups we have for dealing with human imperfection, why is it we haven't organized to combat the most dangerous, expensive, and self-destructive habit of all: wasting time?" (74). Since Time Wasters Anonymous has not yet been invented, Mackay provides a set of tips for optimizing one's "down time," for example, traveling with a tape recorder to jot down notes, keeping that same tape recorder on one's bedside table for nighttime note taking, and listening to business advice cassettes during commutes (a handy piece of self-promotion, perhaps, given the availability of audio versions of *Swim with the Sharks*).

Mackay is also straightforward, if not blunt, in his equation of attitude improvement with human evolution. In one of the many inspirational stories sprinkled throughout *Swim with the Sharks*, he notes that for many years, no one believed that any runner could break the four-minute mile record. Then, in the year after Roger Bannister accomplished this supposedly unattainable goal, 37 other runners followed suit: "What happened? There were no great breakthroughs in training. Human bone structure didn't suddenly improve. But human attitudes did" (80). This point is the book's central focus, one that has been explored by many self-help authors before and after Mackay: with self-confidence (or even arrogance), anything is possible; training yourself to be self-confident is training yourself to be fit. But there is an important difference between Mackay's advice and many earlier versions of otherwise similar business counsel. Unfortunately for those who might endeavor to follow Mackay's advice, survival Mackay-style requires constant commitment to one's work—placing salesmanship, for example, over and above all other aspects of life. Witness his hiring policy, tellingly titled "Mackay's Boot Camp for Natural Selection" (200). All Mackay Envelope job candidates are subject to a lengthy human resources process: nine in-person interviews with upper-level staff members, one phone interview with Mackay, a series of reference checks, an interview with Mackay in the candidate's *home* ("I want to see the candidate's personal values at work in the most revealing setting. It's also a great integrity test"), a social event ("How does this person act in a social setting? It's especially important for salespeople because that's when they need to be their most skillful and persuasive"), and an appointment with an industrial psychologist (200).[19] Mackay also sends applicants to meet two or three of his peers—fellow businesspeople considered to be masters in the sales field.[20] And, while these hiring practices may seem downright bizarre on paper, they are actually not so unusual in terms of business practices—he merely describes extreme versions of policies and strategies, such as elaborate personality testing and multiple interviews, used by many firms today.

The expanding emphasis on individual performance described in Deleuze's control society essay is apparent in these hiring policies and throughout *Swim with the Sharks*. Mackay wants to know what his employees are like when they are out of the office, at home, or at social events. He wants to know how they spend their weekends, because, as he suggests, workers and managers alike (himself included) must *constantly* strive toward self-improvement: "You have to keep changing and keep learning… adding a few new songs to your program every chance you get. If you don't, the world will pass you by" (253). It follows that the workers who are most diligent in their constant self-improvement are also those most likely to keep their jobs. Mackay does not explicitly make this connection; in fact, his calls for employee and manager self-improvement are couched in typical self-help language: *you should do what is best for you*. Control mechanisms are effective for precisely this reason: what's good for your workplace is also, it seems, what's good for you. I will say more about the double-edged relationship between self-help discourses and business practices in the next section of this chapter, but it is worth noting here that the promotional materials for a more recent Mackay book, *Pushing the Envelope: All the Way to the Top* (2000), highlighted several ideas that suggest further movement toward mechanisms of

Deleuzian control, especially the emphasis on endless worker self-improvement as beneficial to corporate organizations. According to Mackay's official website, "pushing the envelope" means "pushing the boundaries and pushing yourself to better maximize your advantage—to be better, faster, and smarter and to get the results you want, in business and in life" (Mackay 2000). Chapters are devoted to keeping up with younger competitors (by mastering new technologies) and taking speed reading courses if your ability to retain information is slowing down with age. In short, the undercurrents of natural selection language remain strong here, but Mackay seems to be swimming upstream.[21]

"Move with the Cheese and Enjoy It"

Spencer Johnson's *Who Moved My Cheese?* strongly suggests that adaptation and flexibility training are indeed endless. This phenomenally successful self-help book, full of advice geared toward workplace issues as well as personal relationships and family dynamics, posits flexibility as something that can be willed and developed through individual dedication. The book is divided into three main parts. The first section describes a group of friends at a high school reunion, talking about how their lives have changed since graduation. One of the friends offers to tell a story that inspired him to deal with life changes in a healthy way. Part two of the book is that story: a tale of two mice (named "Sniff" and "Scurry") and two "littlepeople" (named "Hem" and "Haw") who live in a maze. The mice, as rodents are wont to do, run through the maze in search of food to eat each day. The littlepeople, however, "used their brains, filled with many beliefs and emotions, to search for a very different kind of Cheese—with a capital C—which they believed would make them happy and successful" (26). Hem and Haw eventually fall into a routine, going to the same place each day, where Cheese always awaits them. Finally, one day, they are shocked to discover that the Cheese is gone. Fear and resentment paralyze them as they wait in vain for the Cheese to return. Finally, when they find themselves on the brink of starvation, Haw decides to take action and bravely ventures forth into the maze in search of new Cheese. As he travels, he writes affirmations and guidance on the walls: "If You Do Not Change, You Can Become Extinct" (46), and "The Quicker You Let Go Of Old Cheese, The Sooner You Can Enjoy New Cheese" (60). In the end, he learns to laugh at his predicament, finds new and improved Cheese, and learns to enjoy life again. Hem never reappears, but the end of the tale suggests that he is on his way to meet the now-enlightened Haw.

The third part of *Who Moved My Cheese?* returns to the friends at their reunion. They discuss the story and, in case its larger meaning is not already obvious, slowly spell out how the parable relates to their lives. They compare themselves to the different characters in the story: are they more like the mice, who instinctively knew to move forward when their cheese disappeared? Or, are they like Hem, who was so blinded by rage that he could not move on with his life?[22] The reunion attendees also make connections between the story and their work situations: "Hem reminds me of a friend of mine... His department was closing down, but he didn't want to see it... We all tried to talk to him about the many other opportunities that existed in the company for those who wanted to be flexible, but he didn't think he had to change" (79). One attendee believes that Hem eventually decided to embrace change and find new Cheese, but another disagrees: "Some people never change and they pay a price for it. I see people like Hem in my medical practice. They feel entitled to their 'Cheese.' They feel like victims when it's taken away and blame others. They get sicker than people who let go and move on" (83).[23] Essentially, in this last passage, people who are sick and frightened must empower themselves instead of becoming resentful about the painful changes in their lives.

Johnson's version of survival of the fittest is fairly straightforward: personal reluctance toward change is a potentially fatal flaw, but everyone has the capacity to learn how to adapt to new situations. It is difficult to discuss this book without resorting to disgusted critique. After all, as Thomas Frank points out, the book rather shamelessly justifies corporate downsizing: "[Haw] sets off through the maze again, running the rat race, but finding along the way that job insecurity is good for his soul... Those who had been fired learned to relish their new situation ('there was New Cheese out there just waiting to be found!') and those who were permitted to stay stopped complaining and bowed to management's new scheme" (2000, 250). While Frank's argument is persuasive, his analysis of the upshot to *Who Moved My Cheese?* is perhaps more productive: "Will the time ever come, Americans might well ask, when *we* get to move *management's* cheese?... 'Change,' like the American corporation itself, is the product of argument and social conflict. We have as much a role in it as the 'change agents' on high, whether they ask our opinion or 'listen' or not" (250). A book like Johnson's is not simply and solely harmful to readers, for it can also be used to justify *employee* desires for change, rather than just management whims. Also, in a time of economic uncertainty, if a book can help people to feel better about the unpleasant and often unavoidable changes in their lives, so be it. But for Johnson, change is avoidable or, if not, at least agreeable: for example, through individual flexibility training, he suggests, workers can probably prevent themselves from being downsized before it even happens. Then, if it happens anyway, well-adapted workers are already equipped to adjust to their changed circumstances. It's a highly disturbing "win-win" scenario.

In his *New Rules for the New Economy: 10 Radical Strategies for a Connected World* (1999), former *Wired* editor-at-large, Kevin Kelly, broadens and intensifies the version of individual adaptability found in Johnson's work by showing how it connects with the evolution and survival of companies and even entire economies. Like Johnson, Kelly depicts evolution in a way that naturalizes employee downsizing as well as firm takeovers and bankruptcies: "No balance exists in nature; rather, as evolution proceeds, there is perpetual disruption as new species displace old, as natural biomes shift in their makeup, and as organisms and environments transform each other" (108). Like organisms and species in nature, workers, companies, and industries come and go. As such, Kelly espouses the philosophy, "No Harmony, All Flux." He amplifies other business writers' emphasis on adapting to change by claiming that flux is the way of the corporate world, just as it has always been in the natural world. Change is old fashioned because it is linear and causal, whereas flux is an unpredictable network of interconnected changes, "like the Hindu god Shiva, a creative force of destruction and genesis... This dynamic state might be thought of as 'compounded rebirth.' And its genesis hovers on the edge of chaos" (109). Kelly advises companies to embrace flux by cultivating "sustainable disequilibrium"—natural harmony is fleeting, and therefore, corporate harmony must be a stagnating, life-threatening force. Kelly even advocates *devolution* for "stuck," maximally adapted organisms/companies. Oddly, despite these descriptions of a business ecosystem marked by unpredictability, Kelly's faith in individual human will remains: he assures readers that they can choose to evolve or devolve as they see fit. His empowering take on chaos clearly does not correspond well with elements of chaos theory, upon which it appears to be loosely based. The kind of determinism implicitly championed in *New Rules for the New Economy*—the idea that people can teach themselves to (d)evolve with the predictable result of business success—contradicts chaos theory's emphasis on the unpredictability of the universe.

While most of *New Rules for the New Economy* eschews the comforting self-help conventions of Johnson, Kelly's discussion of devolution makes sympathetic gestures toward readers intimidated by flux. He writes, "Organizations, like human beings, are hardwired to optimize what they know—to cultivate success, not to throw it away" (85–86). He acknowledges that it is easy in business to stick with what's comfortable, with what works. As is the case with *Who Moved My Cheese?*, however, situations that seem easy and comfortable can suddenly become menacing. Even though doing so may seem counterintuitive, temporarily devolving, without the "Hem and Haw" of delay, is sometimes what's best for you and your workplace. Like Emily Martin's image of flexible bodies forever struggling to remain balanced on a tightrope, workers and companies, in the schema put forth by Kelly and Johnson, must always be aware of (and prepared for) flux. Given these images, it seems that this endless adaptation for survival—with its accompanying, constant paranoia about what lurks in the future—is almost more painful than not surviving at all.

Other than his account of "the dark side of flux" (110)—the ever-looming possibility of extinction for those who don't embrace disequilibrium—Kelly's description of the New Economy seems lively and freeing in many ways.[24] He dismisses the Taylorist principle of optimal efficiency as counterproductive and naïve; efficiency is for machines and robots, while opportunities are for humans, who should "demand flexibility, exploration, guesswork, curiosity" and other fun aspects of New Economy work (147). Also, he insists that the brave new version of American corporate capitalism is available to anyone who chooses to retain an open mind: "A persistent, invisible swell pushes the entire econosphere forward, slowly thickening the surface of the earth with more things, more interactions, and more opportunities. And that tide is accelerating, expanding a little faster each year" (141). Whereas Harvey Mackay acts as a doomsayer about capitalist change, arguing that "no matter how bright you are or how good you are at what you do… Capitalism constantly devours its own creation and gives birth to new ones" (Mackay 1988, 256), Kelly celebrates "the remarkable ability of evolution to create a bit more, on average, than it destroys" (141).

Was Kelly still celebratory after 9/11, when more and more e-commerce companies started heading for the Chapter 11 Tar Pits? The answer is yes. John Schwartz, after comparing the U.S. recession's dot-com casualties to fossilized dinosaurs in a newspaper article, refers to Kelly's opinions about business in late 2001:

Kevin Kelly, who... helped create the heroic ethos surrounding dot-com entrepreneurs, acknowledged "it came tumbling down with the towers." But Mr. Kelly insisted that these people would rise again. The generation of tyro executives who crashed and burned "got better business education than they could if they had gotten a Harvard M.B.A.," he said. "They didn't set out to learn, but, boy, they are much smarter now." He predicts that the last decade has been the "layup" for a true cultural revolution to come—he could not be specific, and his words may strike many as more dot-com hyperbole.[25]

And so, the dot-commers who lost jobs or businesses gained valuable knowledge from their experiences and would therefore be stronger and even better equipped for survival when they began to rebound. Regardless of whether Kelly was right or wrong in his prediction, his hopeful take on the future of e-commerce again depicts survival as something that can be guaranteed, or at least made much likelier, through adaptation and flexibility.

WHERE THERE'S A WILL?

Seth Godin's provocatively titled business advice book, *Survival is Not Enough: Zooming, Evolution, and the Future of Your Company* (2002), contains one noteworthy surprise within its pages. While much of the book traffics in ideas quite similar to those described earlier in this chapter, unlike other writers Godin insists on the importance of environment as a determining factor in corporate success and challenges the popular assumption that evolution can be willed and strategized. In the silly imagery of the following passage, the start of a new direction for Darwinian business discourse can perhaps be seen:

> Penguins don't evolve on purpose. They don't have meetings about evolution. They don't debate the most effective routes for their future... Instead, evolution is built into their daily lives and is embodied in their reproductive cycle... The difference between a penguin and your company is simple: While you both evolved to the point where you could succeed, the penguin continues to evolve and your company tries desperately not to... *Your organization, unlike the penguin, is built on the fiction that someone is in charge, that the world is stable, that you get to choose what happens next*... Alas, change is unceasing and unyielding, so the best strategy is to embrace it and evolve.   (Godin 2002, 44–45, italics mine)

But, despite the proclamation that stability and will are "fiction," Godin returns to the idea of evolution as a voluntary action ("the best strategy is to embrace it and evolve"). Elsewhere in his book, he contends that organizations can be *trained* to evolve at regular intervals with minimal trauma to the workers and managers involved in the changes. Also, he argues that to evolve successfully "is to win. Every time" (45). Still, his penguin comparison is somewhat refreshing, in that the central role of individual will is at least briefly diminished—a highly unusual sentiment to find in a business self-help book. As Mary Parker Follett pointed out over half a century ago, in 1933, management theorists are especially invested in the notion of individual will and control: "I believe in the individual not trusting to face or chance or inheritance or environment, but learning how to control his own life. And nowhere do I see such a complete acceptance of this as in business thinking, the thinking of more progressive business men" ("Mary Parker Follett" 2005). This aspect of business philosophy has never changed much, even though corporate structures, strategies, and cultures look a lot different from how they looked last century or even last decade.

As I have suggested throughout this chapter, business culture's depictions of endless flexibility and adaptability as survival tactics tend to focus on individuals rather than companies or economies. In terms of their natural selection metaphors, one aspect of Darwinian theory that these depictions neglect is the significance of population (rather than single organism) survival in the evolutionary process. Future business philosophy and self-help literature might work differently if survival (and its corporate analogue, success) were not portrayed as something that individuals can always determine entirely for themselves. While it might seem counterintuitive for self-help books to de-emphasize the power of the individual, it also seems appropriate—especially given today's unpredictable economy—to stick closer to Darwin's theories when Darwinian imagery is used, to acknowledge the inconsequential nature of individual agency within evolution and, by extension, in business. Kelly's work gestures in this direction; in the passage I cite here, he contradicts his belief that people can prepare themselves for flux: "One day, along the beach, tiny red algae suddenly blooms into a vast red tide. A few weeks later, just when the red mat seems indelible, it vanishes... The same biological forces that multiply populations can decimate them" (33). No one individual cell in the red tide is accountable for the decimation of this population, and no one individual worker is fully responsible for the failure or success of his/her workplace. This idea is easily lost or forgotten in the face of injunctions to adapt and remain flexible ceaselessly.

Unfortunately, Kelly does not devote much space to identifying those crucially important "biological forces"—and, by extension, those forces in the business world—to which he briefly refers. In nature, those forces might include climate, environment, or predation, and in business, the forces are social and economic circumstances, other institutions, and discursive formations. Also, in business as in nature, the combination of factors affecting organization or population survival is unpredictable. The story of Enron—once seemingly invulnerable like Kelly's red tide, now a scandalous embarrassment—provides a dramatic example that illustrates the significance of these factors and forces. Some former employees of Enron attribute the company's 2001 collapse to its extremely competitive workplace culture. In "Victims and Champions of a Darwinian Enron," *New York Times* business writer David Barboza interviews ex-Enronites, who recall the self-interested "kill-and-eat culture" at their office: "People tried to take work away from you," recalls Brandon Rigney, who once operated Enron's official website, "There was a Darwinism for ideas, for projects" (C5). While many factors contributed to Enron's downfall, the type of workplace strategizing advocated by business self-help gurus like Mackay and Johnson seems to have had the opposite of its intended effect: rather than insuring individual success and shielding workers from downsizing, it helped to destabilize an entire company and led to mass layoffs and bankruptcy. In short, the kind of corporate culture encouraged in the books I have described here helped to foster an environment of rampant ethical abuses, which in turn undermined chances for workers' success and the corporation's staying power.

Barboza learns from his ex-Enron interviewees that competition between workers and departments "undermined the company's health ... For example, it is widely believed that compensation for the people who negotiated deals with other companies was based on the size of the transactions rather than their long-term effect on the bottom line" (C5). Also, the endless adaptations favored within Enron during its most successful years in the late 1990s—constant pressure to find new ways to make profits, like trading electricity rights and introducing the concept of water rights—may have distracted workers from paying attention to bottom-line issues, particularly the importance of ethical conduct. According to *Business Week,* increasing post-Enron concern about the ethics of corporate executives has prompted many companies to increase their ranks of managers, in the hope of providing checkpoints for business decision-making processes (Byrne, Lavelle, Byrnes, Vickers, and Borrus 2002).

Business schools scrambled to make room for required ethics classes in their lists of course offerings (Singer 2002, 11). As instances of "creative bookkeeping" were uncovered seemingly every day, ethical conduct—paying attention to the circumstances and forces in which all organizations are embedded—became a success strategy in business. And, in the wake of the Enron disaster, the business world became somewhat more vigilant about an issue outlined by Deleuze, in his descriptions of control society: who benefits from certain business policies and decisions, and does the answer to that question need to change?

Given the dismal fate of Enron and other now-notorious companies, it is clear that survival is not something that can be willed or chosen and that the notion of individual will cannot account for which businesses will succeed and which will go bankrupt. Perhaps the focus on *personal* survival and self-interest—found in self-help best sellers, popular television shows, and pop singles—is part of how contemporary versions of corporate capitalism have strengthened their hold on American culture. With media vultures circling over dying companies felled by scandal and error, a move away from the individual—including the individual's power to ceaselessly adapt and to be flexible—might not only help to salvage the reputation of American corporate culture, but, much more importantly, might benefit the workers who keep that culture running.

CHAPTER 4

TAKING CARE OF BUSINESS: CORPORATE PERFORMANCE, SELF-CARE, AND THE HEALTHY WORKPLACE

JOGGING ON THE JOB

In 1995, I worked at a small and unglamorous trade magazine publishing firm in downtown New York. The firm was located in a nondescript building, in a waterfront neighborhood better known for its colorful nineteenth-century history of gang warfare than for its desperately dull business district. From my department's office on the twentieth floor, I could see across King Street to the tasteful chrome and marble offices of one of the few power companies to build its headquarters in the area: the slick advertising agency Saatchi and Saatchi. Throughout my brief tenure at the trade publisher, I was grateful for Saatchi's presence nearby, for the company unwittingly provided me with hours of entertainment. Watching the joggers circle Saatchi's state-of-the-art rooftop athletic track helped me to get through many a tiresome afternoon at work. I counted how many times a certain person or pair passed by my windows. I observed Saatchi executives' attempts to conduct business meetings while running in place. I admired the flashy spandex of expensive running suits and the gleaming leather of brand-new Nikes. Before seeing Saatchi's office building, I was unaware that physical fitness had entered the workplace—my first job out of college was a traditional coffee, donuts, and cigarette breaks kind of scenario. Since that time, however, I have found that physical health—in terms of exercise, diet, and even sleep habits—has become an integral part of many corporate cultures. Both physical and psychological health have long been factors in management theory and corporate practice, but the presence of health-related discourses in the American workplace has dramatically intensified. This chapter will examine some manifestations of workplace health policy and will analyze the links between health practices, ideals of corporate performance and productivity, and worker governance. A section about workplace diet and fitness looks at corporate health policies and practices, while two sections about worker sleep habits discuss how the proliferation of health-positive ideas from self-help writers and business consultants has entered the realm of management strategy.

The chapter will also examine a link between self-care discourses and corporate governance: the phenomenon of medicalization. Today, the human body's activities and functions are increasingly subject to the ministrations of medical science; symptoms are identified and categorized, creating new disorders and syndromes, which are then remedied or relieved through treatment regimens. I see a parallel between the increased medicalization of the human body and enhanced possibilities for the constant, far-reaching management of workers.[1] Discourses of self-help, medicine, and corporate management all depend in part upon appeals to individual self-improvement; people are constantly compelled to monitor and micromanage all aspects of their lives. As Jeremy Howell and Alan Ingram rightly point out, "The corporate edifice of health will be built on the lifestyle action of individual bricks" (2001, 342).

After a detour through the work of Michel Foucault and Gilles Deleuze, whose work suggests how the notion of self-improvement can contribute to the efficiency of management strategies, I will return to examining how health is configured by corporate, self-help, and medical writers, and the links between these configurations. I am not so much concerned about the idea that consultants, self-help writers, and corporations themselves may use health promotion as a profit-making tactic, as this point is immediately obvious. Rather, what concerns me in this investigation is the growing number and diversity of possibilities for management; workers can be governed—and learn to govern themselves—through diet and exercise habits and even through the very basic, mundane bodily phenomenon of sleep.

POWER, CONTROL, TRAINING

Michel Foucault's later work is especially helpful for examining how discourses of self-care create ways of living in the world and allow relations of power to circulate. In "Technologies of the Self" (1982), Foucault defines his title phrase as strategies "which permit individuals to effect by their own means, or with the help of others, a certain number of operations on their own bodies and souls, thoughts, conduct, and way of being, so as to transform themselves in order to attain a certain state of happiness, purity, wisdom, perfection, or immortality" (225). In short, people learn to govern their daily habits and activities, and this self-governance is undertaken to benefit themselves as well as the groups and organizations to which they belong: countries, families, schools, workplaces, et cetera.[2] From a Foucauldian perspective, in the business context, a person's work ethic is not solely focused on helping the company for which the individual works, but also focused on bettering the self (through career advancement, higher wages, personal satisfaction, and the like).

Foucault posits a complex relationship between self-care and care for others. He traces a historical shift from Greek to Christian traditions, wherein the commandment to "take care of yourself" was gradually eclipsed by the injunction to "know yourself." While Greek society embraced self-care as a productive and positive activity, correcting errors in daily practice, Christian versions of self-care entailed self-renunciation: recognizing and publicly acknowledging one's flaws and sinful desires. The movement toward Christian principles may explain why many people "are more inclined to see taking care of ourselves as an immorality, as a means of escape from all possible rules" (228). Indeed, self-care was and still is sometimes characterized as self-indulgence, but in the twentieth century—particularly with the rise of the social sciences, including psychology—the Christian inclination toward self-care as self-renunciation seems to have all but vanished.[3] Accepting the idea of "taking care of oneself" is certainly central to the contemporary success of the self-help industry in all of its many forms, such as therapy, support groups, or best-selling books such as *Chicken Soup for the Soul*. Newspapers, magazines, pop psychology, medicine, and Hollywood cinema all repeatedly recommend or even insist that we take care of certain aspects of our selves, our lives, by enjoining us to talk about our everyday problems and thus move toward monitoring and correcting them. As Foucault writes, "The techniques of verbalization have been reinserted in a different context... in order to use them without renunciation of the self but to constitute, positively, a new self" (249). Even self-training that seems primarily physical in nature is frequently posited as simultaneously attitude training; when one's body is in better shape, so are one's moods and one's ability to think clearly. Also, as Mike Featherstone has noted, physical training and bodily improvement are often conceived as a kind of self-marketing: trying to advertise one's best self and demonstrate one's willpower and ability to handle discipline (1991, 171). In short, self-care is no longer selfish, but responsible—and a wise strategy.

To situate this theoretical apparatus in the contemporary context of American business, the intersection between "technologies of the self" and the governance of corporate and medical authorities may produce particular sets of habits and practices in individual workers. Guided by corporate health programs, self-help books (many of them written by medical or business professionals), consultants, and a sense of self-interest or drive toward improvement, individuals may work to change their diet, exercise, and sleep habits, make them healthier. This is one example of how "technologies of the self" have made corporate management so efficient—the process seems to be good for everyone involved. Personal and job-related goals seem to be smoothly aligned, while other priorities (e.g., familial bonds and friendships) are often omitted from the equation; as Stanley Deetz writes in his Foucauldian interpretation of organization theory, "The enemy is no longer the managers' expectations. The company is integrated into the self, leaving one's body and one's non-work relations as oppositional" (1998, 166).

An individual drive toward improvement can certainly benefit the person who feels it, whether the improvement in question is represented as physical, intellectual, financial, or emotional.[4] But, as Gilles Deleuze notes, other possible benefactors also exist: "Many young people have a strange craving to be 'motivated'; they're always asking for special courses and continuing education; it's their job to discover whose ends these serve" (1990, 182). As discussed in Chapter 3, Deleuze's "Postscript on Control Societies"(1990) reminds readers that despite what he posits as a contemporary breakdown of social institutions (such as family, school, church, and workplace), the presence of formerly institutional authorities is more pervasive than ever before; people's time may be thoroughly colonized by concerns about work and self-improvement. If employees want to make themselves optimally efficient and educated, if they want more authority and higher wages, they can train themselves and possibly attain those goals. But, as Deleuze argues, the ends they are serving are not solely their own. And, unlike in earlier work organization models where training might start and end within workplace walls, control society can be characterized by a collapse of the distinction between work and life. The potential endlessness of training—one can feel compelled to work toward self-improvement anywhere and at any time—suggests constant possibilities for judgment, which in turn may lead to constant competition between workers. Given the pervasiveness of management in control society, it is no wonder that physical fitness and even sleep—which could be considered one of the most private and personal of human activities—are now part of corporate strategy and are figuring prominently in self-help regimens.

THE BODY CORPORATE: WORKPLACE FITNESS PROGRAMS

In the early 1900s, when industrial management became an established element of the American business landscape, concerns about worker health were common. Frederick Taylor and his followers carefully analyzed the physical activities and abilities of laborers to optimize factory efficiency. During World Wars I and II, production speedups led to increased fitness monitoring and the continued medicalization of worker energy, fatigue, and motivation; one prevailing sentiment of the era was that "lost time in work steals a part of the nation's capital" (Rabinbach 1990, 291). Physical health remained a significant factor in business management after World War II—despite the gradual mid-century shift toward office-based, less physical work and the corresponding emphasis on workers' *psychological* health (Human Relations strategies, personality testing/screening, and the like). With the rise of sports medicine and kinesiology in the 1950s and 1960s came numerous research findings about the beneficial effects of regular exercise on human strength, energy level, and mood. By the mid-1970s, many large corporations, including Xerox, Exxon, and Mobil, latched onto the fitness trend and created workplace exercise programs (Howell and Ingram 2001, 331).

Today, corporate fitness policies and practices are quite common and are far more intricate than simple encouragement to use the company weight room or to participate in a firm-wide weight loss contest. Many companies have onsite, full service gyms; running tracks; or weekly Weight Watchers meetings. Others offer discounts or reimbursements for gym memberships or reduced insurance co-payments for employees who can provide documentation of their exercise regimens. Some firms, for example, the pharmaceutical manufacturer Wyeth, offer their employees money for diet pills and even gastric bypass surgery (Derer 2003). Many corporations have also made fitness-friendly changes to their office buildings, by moving parking decks further away from headquarters, encouraging workers to take the stairs by deliberately installing slow elevators, and stocking vending machines with inexpensive, low-fat snacks. Hewitt Associates, a consulting firm, found in 2003 that 95 percent of almost 1,000 surveyed employers had a health promotion program in place (Vandewater 2003). Meanwhile, according to studies conducted by StayWell Health Management, "17 percent of companies with 500 or more employees offer incentives to encourage participation in their workplace wellness programs, and 23 percent of companies with 20,000 or more employees use incentives" (Terry 2008).[5]

I see two main forces driving the current popularity of workplace fitness. One of them, while unsurprising, is worth at least a brief mention: the rising cost of health insurance. The Henry J. Kaiser Family Foundation—a nonprofit research organization—found that health insurance premium costs increased by 13.9 percent on an average from spring 2002 to spring 2003 (Henry J. Kaiser Family Foundation 2003, 1).[6] And it is no secret that some workers are more expensive to insure than others. *USA Today* reports on two studies that attempted to quantify the total cost of health care, insurance, and sick leave for obese workers at American companies; one study (by the *American Journal of Health Promotion*) estimated $12.7 billion, while another (by *Health Affairs*) estimated over $30 billion (Derer 2003). To help ameliorate skyrocketing costs, many corporations are encouraging use of fitness programs by "offering lower copays and richer benefits to employees who renounce their unhealthy ways" (Vandewater 2003). Union Pacific calculated that it could save $1.7 million by reducing by one point its percentage of overweight employees—54 percent of 48,000 people—and therefore launched an aggressive program to improve worker fitness and diet (Zernike 2003). Alarming statistics about the price of health care and insurance—and optimistic reports about the cost effectiveness of corporate health programs—encourage companies to protect the bottom line by instituting health-friendly policies and practices. Also, as Mike Featherstone points out, corporations are latching onto the popular idea that physical fitness is a financially sound strategy for individuals, their workplaces, and even *American society as whole*; to state the case bluntly, according to this logic, healthier people are less of a "public burden"—illness is, after all, expensive (Featherstone 170). Fitness is not only responsible, but also patriotic.

The second reason guiding the corporate implementation of fitness programs is the belief that physical health improves work performance and productivity. This idea has a long history in business discourse. American Taylorists, and the late nineteenth-century European "science of work" researchers from whom they drew inspiration, posited diet as a predictor of worker energy and productivity. Physiologists of the late 1800s championed the frequent consumption of fats, meats, starches, and sugars for optimal energy levels. Comparative studies from that era examined the typical diets of workers from different nations and ethnic backgrounds; for instance, researchers claimed that the diet of French railroad workers (vegetables and soup) was less nutritional and satisfying than that of English railroad workers (roast beef)—thus explaining the "inferior" quality of the Frenchmen's work (Rabinbach 1990, 216). The food preferences of the typical American worker (and the foods available in the United States) drew high marks from researchers, and these preferences, in turn, created "more favorable conditions for the expansion of [the American worker's] productive force" (Rabinbach 216). But the concern about worker health was not confined to diet alone. In 1862, the French industrial hygienist Apollinaire Bourchardat argued that the expenditure of energy at work required "a 'recuperation' of energy through adequate nutrition, rest, and sleep" (Rabinbach 36). The idea that energy and productivity are renewable resources gained ground in the United States in the early twentieth century, fitting into the context of increasing popular interest in many relatively new—and sometimes half-baked—scientific and science-based ideas: Freudian psychology, neurology, scientific management, Fletcherism, and eugenics, to provide a few examples.[7]

It appears that the link between fitness and productivity has entered the realm of everyday common sense; as Knight Ridder reporter Judith Vandewater neatly summarizes, "A healthy employee is a productive employee" (2003). The managing editor of *Employee Benefit News*, Craig Gunsauley, claims "employers know that healthy employees make less [*sic*] health care claims and are more productive" (Derer 2003). But common sense and "just knowing" alone will not necessarily convince corporations to implement fitness promotion programs—is there more specific evidence that worker fitness levels affect productivity levels? The answer is a wishy-washy "yes, and no." At smaller companies, the effects of sick days or disability leave on overall productivity is easy to see. As David Hunnicutt, president of the nonprofit organization Wellness Council of America, puts it, "If a *Fortune* 500 company has 150 people a day out sick, there are still thousands of workers to cover for them... But if you're a small company with six employees, and two are out, you've just lost 33% of your workforce" (qtd. in Harper 2004). For larger companies, however, statements on productivity loss due to health-related absenteeism or low worker energy levels are remarkably vague. The American Productivity and Quality Center and MEDSTAT (a nonprofit research group and a health care market information company, respectively) simply say that "Research and outcomes projects are set up to demonstrate the link between productivity and health... A corporate consensus exists that improving the quality of work life will improve productivity and costs savings will result" (Substance Abuse and Mental Health Services Administration 1998). Other researchers and organizations study the links between productivity gains and losses—Towers Perrin health care consultant Jay Savan claims that "roughly half the cost of a medical episode is lost productivity," and *Health and Productivity Management,* a publication devoted to the topic, claims that workplace fitness programs can increase productivity—but it is not entirely clear how productivity is measured (qtd. in Vandewater 2003; Fabius et al 2008).

In short, "productivity" itself is a problem. The concept is used to justify corporate practices—not only health promotion, but also downsizing, speedups, outsourcing, and offshoring—but data on productivity is imprecise and easily manipulated. In *After the New Economy* (2003), Doug Henwood comments on the viability of various economic indicators and is especially concerned about the so-called productivity burst of the 1990s, which he characterizes as a possible "statistical illusion" caused in part by the difficulty of defining what "output" and "real monetary value"—two concepts upon which "productivity" is based—mean (Henwood 25, 42–43). Also, rather than being attributable to management strategies like work-life balance or health promotion, as the researchers cited in the paragraphs above would have it, Henwood persuasively argues that productivity increases, if indeed they exist, are linked with much less worker-friendly practices:

> It may be that very unglamorous things—the cheapening of labor through outsourcing, the movement of much of production to low-wage countries, continued unwillingness of firms to share their good fortune with employees, and what the people at *Labor Notes* call "management by stress" (pushing human workers and work arrangements to their breaking point and maybe a little beyond)—are the real underlying mechanisms. It may also be that people are actually logging lots more hours on the job than get recorded in the official statistics. (25)[8]

So, given the vagueness, the unclear causes, and the possible inaccuracy of statistical information about productivity, why do so many employers accept the adage that healthy employees are productive employees—and strategize accordingly? After all, health promotion programs, even if cheaper than insurance costs, do come with a financial price. One possible reason is that the popular emphasis on self-motivation and morale downplays the fact that the nature of work in the United States in the 2000s is *partially responsible* for Americans' poor health (and poor health habits). Many researchers and writers have argued that our high-tech society encourages people to remain sedentary; Eric Finkelstein, author of *The Fattening of America,* specifically points to career choice as one factor contributing to obesity rates (Barrett 2007). Office work—much of which involves sitting in front of a computer terminal for at least eight hours per day—certainly qualifies as sedentary. Work's role in the less-than-ideal dietary and fitness habits of Americans should not be denied, and yet the emphasis in health-related corporate discourse is on "management" of the problems rather than on significant changes in the nature of work: the long hours, the common expectation that lunch breaks will be taken quickly or at one's desk, the sitting still for hours on end, the stress.[9] It therefore makes sense that corporations, while helping to encourage worker fitness, are also emphasizing individual responsibility: each worker is responsible for making him/herself the best s/he can be—and the corporation brings opportunities for fitness within office walls, rather than fostering a less stressful environment or shortening hours so that workers have time to engage in their athletic activities of choice. If you aren't physically fit, it's your fault—you should work harder. Meanwhile, companies enjoy the good publicity that accompanies announcements about their worker-friendly policies—the deals on insurance and the aerobics classes in the boardroom.

It is also likely, though, that many corporate managers are looking at productivity from a less technical standpoint than the one discussed by Henwood—they are thinking of the concept in general terms by envisioning related concepts: efficiency, energy, or morale, to name a few. This phenomenon would help to explain the vagueness of corporate and business press statements on the topic of productivity. It would also suggest another way in which the two reasons for corporate health promotion discussed above—bottom-line insurance costs and a desire to improve productivity—can be connected with the governance-through-self-improvement tactic described in the previous section of this chapter. As insurance premiums rise and employers seek cost-cutting strategies, discourses celebrating individual responsibility and self-motivation enter wide circulation. For example, in the "Healthy People 2000" report issued by the U.S. Department of Health and Human Services, then secretary of health Dr. Louis Sullivan "emphasized the importance of each and every American being responsible for improving the health of the Nation through personal action" (Howell and Ingram 2001, 326). In line with popular discourses celebrating the initiative and discipline of the physically fit individual, companies are linking individual motivation, responsibility, and self-improvement to workplace culture and morale and therefore incorporating fitness into overall work training. This phenomenon—the expansion of corporate training into aspects of life that do not seem directly related to work—will be explored much more in the next section of this chapter, in a discussion of business and self-help discourses about sleep and individual performance.

POWER NAPPING

The official website for the National Sleep Foundation (NSF) heavily emphasizes information that could prove intriguing to corporate CEOs: a 15–20 minute daily nap for all employees can improve productivity, make workers healthier and less accident prone, and function as a "value-added employee benefit" to aid in the retention of talented staff members (NSF 2000). The publicity materials for Alertness Solutions, a California-based consulting firm, describe how fatigue adversely affects job performance and workplace safety and suggest ways to counteract the problems caused by sleep deprivation. Meanwhile, Tom DeLuca, a hypnotist and showman known for his popular college campus performances, offers a workshop called "Power Napping® for Less Stress" that, according to an online advertisement, can provide "the best solution for exhaustion in this demanding business environment" (DeLuca Enterprises 2000). DeLuca also promises that corporate workshop attendees can decrease their stress and increase their focus. His impressive client roster includes such *Fortune* 500 companies as American Express, Ford, and AT&T Network Systems.

Discourse regarding the health benefits of sleep—and the dangers of sleep deprivation—is common and is nothing new. What *is* relatively new, however, is the connection between corporate policy, management strategy, and sleep-related medical and self-help advice. In line with contemporary management trends that many companies describe as "humancentric"—flextime programs to improve the work-life balance of parents, free onsite gyms or yoga classes to encourage daily exercise and stress reduction for full-time employees, or increased attention to diversity recruitment programs—some U.S. corporations promote workplace napping. Some companies invite consultants or therapists to speak to workers, organize workshops about nap strategies, or recommend self-help books with sleep tips. Others even incorporate their emphasis on naptime into office design, providing sleep rooms or tents for employees. While the number of corporations with official napping policies is much smaller than the number with fitness promotion programming—comprising about 1 percent of 754 companies surveyed by the Society for Human Resource Management (SHRM) in 2001, and the number has not since increased—sleep-related self-help books, articles, and websites are plentiful and are often tailored for corporate audiences.[10]

Increased attention to the issue of sleep is one example of how the emerging relationship between corporate policy, self-help discourses, and the findings of medical science is fraught with complexities and contradictions. Referring to medical experts for justification and credibility, corporations, consultants, and writers encourage healthy habits in workers. Getting enough sleep—one of these healthy habits—is portrayed as a boost to productivity. Simultaneously, however, the American business world often demands long work hours that would necessarily preclude eight to ten hours of sleep. Workers can benefit from corporate cultures that emphasize individual health, but even as companies boast of their humancentric or worker-friendly cultures, they use them to a wide variety of ends, including increased profits, improved efficiency, employee retention, and the attraction of new and talented applicants. Adding to the complexity of this issue is the inconsistent nature of the medical findings upon which self-help and business discourses are often based. Despite corporate and self-help recourse to medical authorities to justify claims about sleep, medical research regarding sleep's benefits for human performance, and the potential health hazards of sleep deprivation, is by no means conclusive.

Sleep may seem a poor fit within American corporate culture. After all, the idea of a tireless work ethic—a significant if frequently stereotyped aspect of Puritan and American immigrant cultures—is a long-standing American tradition. Also, in the United States, work hours have significantly increased over the past decade, thus cutting into possible sleep time.[11] But, sleep's emerging significance within business discourse suggests just how ubiquitous contemporary corporate training has become; even a basic bodily need is now deployed for the objective of improving performance and productivity.[12] While sleep promotion has yet to become a major factor within workplace policy, it has nonetheless entered into the corporate realm, through two main conduits: business consultants and self-help writers. There is some overlap between these categories, for example, writers who also lead corporate training seminars. They also have a theme in common: self-improvement through micromanaging bodily habits, which can occur anytime and anywhere. Advice about how to improve or alter one's sleep regimen, made convincing through recourse to medical authorities and often made to seem crucially important through references to job success, is ultimately aimed toward optimizing individual performance, and work habits in particular.

Of course, the overwhelming emphasis on performance and productivity found in publicity materials from sleep-related business consultants makes sense from a marketing standpoint. Most likely, it would be difficult to convince corporations to hire sleep consultants (or to buy their books) if the usefulness of such consultants were not expressed in terms of profit; consulting firms make money by purporting to make more productive employees and, in turn, more lucrative and efficient companies. In an interview for a nationally syndicated newspaper article, sleep researcher and business consultant Dr. Mark Rosekind helpfully quantifies this issue:

> "You want me to pay these people to sleep?" [corporate clients] ask. "My response is, 'Right now, you're paying them to have their head nod and to drool from 3 to 4 o'clock in the afternoon. What would you spend for a 5 percent improvement in someone's performance on the job? (qtd. in Stevens 2C)

Dr. Rosekind, who runs the Alertness Solutions consulting firm, is one of many professionals taking part in the growth of the sleep industry in the United States. Many of these professionals, sometimes self-described as sleep promoters, bear a strong resemblance to other types of corporate consultants. They work to institute corporate policies meant to increase employee productivity—in essence, getting more bang for the employer's buck, getting that "5 percent improvement" mentioned by Rosekind. Sleep promotion makes particular sense for companies where drowsiness may cause physical harm to employees and clients or customers; for example, Dr. Rosekind began his sleep research at NASA, where he found that pilots who were allowed a 40-minute nap during long flights performed better than those who were not allowed to nap. Several airlines and railway companies have since instituted a policy known as the "NASA Nap," in the hopes that more sleep will lead to fewer employee errors and risk behaviors—and fewer accidents. Employer-sanctioned naptime plays out differently in office environments, however. One way to illustrate this difference is a newspaper interview with Art and Ray, two workers at a Fort Worth energy company who disagree on the subject of napping at work. Art says that he shuts his office door and takes a 15-minute nap once a day. "I'm just doing what I need to do to do what I do," he states (qtd. in Stevens 2C). While Art hopes that his employer will someday officially allow napping on the job, his coworker Ray prefers this alternative: "I'd rather go home 15 minutes early" (qtd. in Stevens 2C). Thus, Ray would rather his time not be explicitly devoted to the betterment of company productivity, whereas Art's napping, according to his own description of it, allows him to continue performing job tasks. Art describes the naptime as a necessity—something he needs to function at work.

Art's response fits neatly into popular discourses about sleep. The bottom line of these discourses is that adults require a certain amount of sleep for "optimum performance" (Hellmich 2001, 1D).[13] Ray focuses on a personal or bodily desire to leave work and go home, but Art remains committed in his interview responses to Rosekind's model, also echoed by Dr. Don Weaver of the Sleep Medicine Associates of Texas: "People erroneously believe that they have to burn the midnight oil to succeed... Their motto is 'The best never rest' and the truth is, the best rest" (qtd. in Stevens 2C). Art says that he naps because he feels he must do so to keep performing for his employer. Art, Rosekind, and Weaver are not alone; March 3 to 9, 2008, marked the observance of the ninth annual National Sleep Awareness Week. Workers across America were encouraged to nap at the office, in the name of improved performance.[14] The National Sleep Awareness Week events program for 2002, organized by the NSF, featured a suggestive slogan: "Sleep for Success" (NSF 2002). The NSF does prioritize other elements of sleep, for example, treatments for disorders such as chronic insomnia, sleep apnea, and restless legs syndrome, but also heavily emphasizes how sleep deprivation may affect people's careers and companies' profits.

Like the NSF, Rosekind's Alertness Solutions firm assists companies where employee sleepiness might lead to injury, but also offers assistance to any companies desiring sleep-related consulting. Alertness Solutions promises to utilize "tailored strategies and comprehensive approaches that reduce fatigue-related human error and performance decrements" (Alertness Solutions 2000). These approaches may include a combination of workshops, seminars, presentations, brochures, and training to deal with issues ranging from shift scheduling to executive jet lag to legal counseling after fatigue-related accidents in the workplace. Interestingly, even the Alertness Solutions publicity material most directly focusing on individual wellness accentuates the bottom line of profit; a section of the firm's website describes how sleep disorders may contribute to high blood pressure and heart disease, but suggests that these ailments primarily matter because they pertain to corporate insurance costs. With the help of Alertness Solutions, workers might train themselves not only to perform more efficiently, but also to avoiding draining company resources.

Other sleep consultants focus more exclusively on napping in the workplace as a boost to employee performance. Two of the best-known nap promoters in the United States—William and Camille Anthony, authors of *The Art of Napping at Work: The No-Cost, Natural Way to Increase Productivity and Satisfaction* (1999) and proprietors of The Napping Company, Inc.—argue that employer-sanctioned naptime is an effective strategy for improving corporate efficiency. To advocate workplace napping, they offer a variety of services and products (books, T-shirts, and $5.95 five-packs of doorknob signs that announce "Working Nap in Progress"). William Anthony, a professor of psychology at Boston University, and Camille Anthony, a financial consultant and politician, advertise their presentations and workshops on how napping at work can boost performance and overall company morale. As they put it, "Everyone knows a good nap does wonders for your productivity" (Anthony and Anthony 1998). As I will demonstrate in the next section of this chapter, the corporate-friendly ideas espoused by the Anthonys and other sleep consultants, despite frequent references to medical authorities, often seem more based on this kind of "everyone knows" common sense than on the findings of medical research.

Dr. William C. Dement and Dr. James B. Maas, two self-help writers who actively promote sleep, repeatedly mention their medical credentials in their books. After all, they must assure readers that some of their more controversial ideas—for example, the advocacy of daily naptime in the workplace or the assertion that humans perform best with ten hours of sleep rather than the usual suggestion of eight—are worth following. Dement and Maas explicitly emphasize and target corporate employees and managers as a reading audience, tailoring their discussion of the science of sleep toward people who want to improve aspects of their lives through changes to their health regimens.[15] Given what I have already suggested about the sleep promotion industry's methods for strategically targeting corporate audiences, it should come as no surprise that Dement and Maas forcefully argue for a link between sleep and performance, even when other medical authorities seem reluctant to do so. Dement and Maas repeatedly acknowledge and thereby further strengthen the link between health and human performance and then connect the performance issue to the work world. And, even though they are both doctors, their top priority does not always seem to be human health. Even Dement, who characterizes American culture's disdain for healthy sleep habits as a state of emergency, considers worker productivity to be a crucially important problem facing the United States today. In *The Promise of Sleep: A Pioneer in Sleep Medicine Explores the Vital Connection Between Health, Happiness, and a Good Night's Sleep* (1999) he writes, "I am left with a feeling of how the conventional schedules, sleep debt, and clock-dependent alerting deprive... employers or cheat them from getting their money's worth" (87).

One of the review blurbs for Maas's *Power Sleep: The Revolutionary Program That Prepares Your Mind for Peak Performance* (1998) resonates with Dement's observation and nicely encapsulates the overall message of Maas's book. Sol M. Linowitz, former U.S. ambassador to the Organization of American States and former chairman of the board for Xerox, comments that Maas "makes the convincing argument that the best way to stay awake is to get more sleep" (qtd. in Maas 1998, 1). This seeming contradiction demonstrates the values espoused by Maas: sleep is a strategy, which can be used to optimize personal efficiency and productivity without drastically altering one's work habits. Maas argues that there simply are not enough hours in a day for busy executives who want to "succeed in all aspects of life... sleep has a low priority in their active schedules" (xvii). So, he suggests a compromise: most of the day may be taken up by work activities, but executives can optimize the use of all of their hours by prioritizing sleep whenever possible. Any office napping policies should be utilized, and where those policies do not exist, employees should lobby for them. Sleep should be a significant part of any available "free time." Basically, Maas recommends ways to achieve a compromise between work needs and bodily needs, without questioning whether those work needs are actually needs in the first place. In *Power Sleep*, long work hours are taken as a given fact of life, so sleep (and, presumably, other personal needs and habits) must be micromanaged around those hours.

The key difference between Maas and Dement—and between Dement and the sleep promotion consultants described earlier—is that rather than suggesting power naps in the workplace and scheduling sleep around the demands of work, Dement advocates an overall cut-back in wakeful hours, including work hours. In *The Promise of Sleep*, Dement, who researches sleep at Stanford University and describes himself as a founder of sleep medicine in the United States, laments that "societal pressures to work more and at odd hours—evenings, weekends, the night shift, round-the-clock—have reduced our sleep time over the past century by about 20 percent" (218). He goes on to point out that contemporary American work schedules are cer-tainly to blame for sleep deprivation, but that other types of cultural injunctions, for example, the popular motto "Work hard, play hard," are also culpable. Whereas in centuries past, people had to confine their work and play to daytime hours, the widespread availability of electric light, Dement notes, now allows most Americans to utilize every moment of available time, if they so desire. Dement gravely and repeatedly pronounces that the prevalence of sleep deprivation is a nationwide medical crisis and suggests healthy alternatives for people who want to be as productive as possible. Rather than simply proposing naps as a quick solution to the sleep deprivation problem, Dement notes that the inflation of work hours may well be the root of the "tiredness at work" issue in the first place: an idea that corporate consultants and other self-help writers pointedly ignore.

SLEEP MEDICINE AND MEDICALIZATION: WHAT DO THE DOCTORS ORDER?

Given the prevalence of sleep-positive discourses—such as self-help books, magazine articles, timeworn adages, and health class lessons—about how proper sleep habits can enrich life, the lack of empirical evidence linking sleep and performance is surprising. For example, the search engine of the National Library of Medicine, PubMed, yields few scholarly articles that explicitly and definitively demonstrate how sleep patterns affect human cognition and behavior, two components of overall performance.[16] Consultants and self-help writers often imply that their recommendations for improved work performance are based on medical science, but existing medical findings, while suggestive, are frequently inconclusive.[17] These inconclusive find-ings, however, have not slowed the ongoing medicalization of sleep or the development of pharmaceutical options for patients with sleep problems. Later in this section, I will discuss a sleep disorder drug, Provigil, which may have particularly disturbing implications if used, like self-help tips or consultants' advice, in the business world. The Provigil example provides a clear illustration of the link between medicalization and management; aspects of mundane activities (like sleep) are characterized as symptoms and disorders to be treated and are simultaneously configured as possible areas where people can manage their behavior, focus, and other performance-related components of their everyday lives.

A sample of articles from the *Journal of Sleep Research* and other medical journals indicates that while researchers seem to agree that sleep (or lack thereof) has effects on human performance, those effects are quite difficult to define or to quantify.[18] Within the selection of articles I surveyed, the strongest statement of particular effects brought about by lack of sleep comes from Dean W. Beebe and David Gozal, whose work focuses on a specific sleep disorder, obstructive sleep apnea (OSA). The sleep disruption and blood gas abnormalities caused by OSA "prevent sleep-related restorative processes, and further induce chemical and structural central nervous system [CNS] cellular injury" (Beebe and Gozal 2002, 1). This CNS injury, in turn, affects daytime behavior and cognitive abilities. When OSA and other documented disorders are not factors in research, however, medical researchers seem markedly less likely to confirm specific effects of sleep or sleeplessness. Another article reports that sleep fragmentation may cause a broad decrease in attention span, but "did not significantly increase objective daytime sleepiness or lower cognitive performance on a battery of cognitive function tests" (Kingshott, Cosway, Deary, and Douglas 2000, 353). One article even notes an *increase* in responsiveness and verbal and mathematical learning ability following total sleep deprivation (TSD), claiming that "the brain may be more plastic during cognitive performance following TSD than previously thought" (Drummond, Gillin, and Brown 2001, 85). Self-reported sleep disturbances and night shift schedules were two predictors of accidental death at work, but researchers were unable to corroborate self-reports of early morning and late day absentmindedness in experimental subjects (Åkerstedt, Fredlund, Gillberg, and Jansson 2002; Manly, Lewis, Robertson, Watson, and Dattaa 2002).

Even when testing the links between sleep and performance in fellow medical professionals, researchers seem unwilling to state definitively that sleep deprivation may affect cognition or behavior on the job. In a review article published in *JAMA*, Matthew B. Weinger, M.D., and Sonia Ancoli-Israel, Ph.D., describe proposed congressional legislation that advocates the limitation and regulation of medical residents' work hours. State governments and groups of lobbyists from medical schools and training hospitals cite the adverse effects of sleep deprivation on residents' job performance, particularly in emergency situations requiring quick decisions and steady hands. Whereas public safety risks have already led to work hour regulation in the commercial aviation industry, medical work hours have heretofore remained unregulated. Yet, the present legislation is considered controversial, because, as Weinger and Ancoli-Israel note, medical researchers still disagree about the "magnitude and significance of the clinical impairment resulting from work schedules that aggravate sleep deprivation" (2002, 955).

As members of the medical field continue to study sleep's effects on human performance, researchers are also testing the performance effects of a drug called Modafinil (hereafter referred to by its commercial name, Provigil), which is indicated to help users maintain a state of wakeful alertness during daytime. Whereas the business consultants and self-help writers I discussed in the previous section posit sleep as productivity-boosting and therefore productive in itself, early advocates of Provigil implicitly figured sleep as a problem in need of a solution. This drug, which may allow users to remain awake and productive for several days, is seen by some as a revolutionary way to boost human work productivity through sleep deprivation and time conservation, without significant side effects. When first tested on rats in the early 1980s, Provigil caused wakefulness, but not hyperactivity— one of the key problems with otherwise effective pharmaceutical stimulants like Dexedrine. Early tests revealed other advantages of Provigil as well; pharmacologist Matthew Miller, interviewed by Jerome Groopman for the *New Yorker*, explains that the drug aids the functioning of the two physical components of wakefulness: vigilance (being alert to threats) and attentiveness (being able to "focus on cognitive tasks") (qtd. in Groopman 2001, 53). Tests on military personnel have shown that Provigil can be helpful in wartime situations, for example, when soldiers must guard a base overnight or fly halfway across the world without stopping. One can also imagine similar possibilities for Provigil within the business world. For example, workers using Provigil might be better able to cope with the long work hours so often demanded by corporate America.

Provigil, developed by the pharmaceutical company Cephalon, has been approved by the U.S. Food and Drug Administration and is now being marketed as a treatment for a specific syndrome, excessive daytime sleepiness (EDS). According to Cephalon's online patient and physician guide to Provigil, EDS was originally noticed in narcolepsy patients. The key symptom of EDS is patients' inability to stay awake when they want to or should do so. EDS patients often fall asleep during business meetings or school classes, while driving, or while sitting still in one place for an extended period of time (e.g., at a film or a play). Cephalon's online guide indicates that EDS is almost always linked with narcolepsy and other documented sleep disorders, such as sleep apnea and restless legs syndrome, but medical sources suggest otherwise. The Center for Narcolepsy, Sleep and Health Research (CNSHR) at the University of Illinois at Chicago notes that "among the general population the most frequent reason for EDS is inadequate nighttime sleep (or in the case of shift workers, inadequate extended sleep)" (CNSHR 2002). According to Dr. Mark W. Mahowald from the University of Minnesota Medical School, "The most common cause of excessive daytime sleepiness in modern society is chronic sleep deprivation" (Mahowald 2000).

Like Dement in *The Promise of Sleep,* Mahowald also argues that chronic sleep deprivation is usually "driven by social or economic factors" (Mahowald 2000). He describes the sleep problems of shift workers in industrialized countries and the chronic disruption of sleep by the 24-hour availability of e-mail, Internet, and other technologies. Thanks to Provigil, however, there is a pharmaceutical solution to this deprivation. The medicalization of EDS may allow and encourage the quick fix of extended wakefulness; certainly, it won't encourage companies to reduce work hours or challenge today's growing corporate demands on workers' time. Provigil thus has potentially sinister "side effects" when imagined in a corporate context; now that the drug is readily available to the general public, will workers be encouraged to use it and thus contribute even longer work hours without rest?[19] Groopman worries that the drug could allow workers to overcome bodily limitations in the name of business success: "In the corporate world... to be able to get by on five hours of sleep or less is a badge of honor, a mark of the Olympian executive who can straddle time zones, bridging the Nasdaq and the Nikkei" (2001, 54). As in the case of wellness or work-life benefits provided through corporate policies, workers using Provigil might "benefit" from the sleep deprivation possibilities it provides, in terms of improved wages or accelerated career advancement. But, as Deleuze might note, the worker is not the only benefactor of the decision to take Provigil, a drug for which the potential long-term effects remain unknown.[20] The more time a worker can stay awake, the more time s/he can spend contributing to her/his business organization. In turn, that increased contribution—with Provigil, unencumbered by the lack of focus and logic that sleepiness and older types of stimulants may cause—will make that worker's employer more competitive. Some people might choose to improve themselves as workers by taking the drug, thus extending their availability for work tasks without sacrificing efficiency or productivity. These are clear motivations for businesses to encourage its widespread use; as Dement writes in *The Promise of Sleep*, "If no one had to sleep, my guess is that society would only find more work for us to do" (260). Dement's comment and the Provigil example itself suggest how sleep deprivation as well as sleep promotion can be used in the service of corporate governance—a governance which, rather than working through company policy or regulations directly enforced by management, operates within the seemingly personal realm of human health.

FIT FOR WORK, FIT FOR LIFE

What is the future of workplace health practices and policies, especially given cuts to medical benefits at struggling companies in today's less-than-stable economy? One issue that has been appearing with increasing frequency in corporate medical discourse is the possibility of health-based discrimination. As noted earlier, many workplace fitness programs are particularly concerned with lowering obesity rates—but might this concern constitute a "scapegoating" of overweight employees? Corporations with health programs avoid potential lawsuits by focusing on rewards for participation rather than punishments for lack thereof. In short, while discrimination is illegal, providing incentives for health program participation (lower co-pays, better deals on insurance, rewards from a plaque to a gift certificate to a paid vacation) is not. Companies cannot require obese employees to pay more for insurance, because doing so would discriminate against employees with medical conditions that cause obesity.[21] But a gray area remains: since so many workplace health policies and practices emphasize how good health habits improve worker productivity, is there any underlying assumption that overweight workers are less productive than thinner ones? If so, clearly the opportunity for discrimination—in hiring or promotion processes, for example—persists. So does the opportunity for governance—the corporate preference for certain body types over others, in the hiring process and in the workplace, may perpetuate assumptions about physical appearance and "train" people to shape themselves accordingly.

Also, with the widespread availability of improved genetic testing technologies, a workplace legal issue has arisen, genetic discrimination. Much as industrial/organizational psychologists were once tasked with administering personality tests to screen out job applicants who were "bad fits" with a company's values, doctors may be asked to disclose and analyze job applicants' genetic predisposition for certain diseases—conditions for which employers would rather not shoulder the health costs.[22] This phenomenon may sound like something from a science fiction film, but a 1997 survey by the American Management Association revealed that 6–10 percent of U.S. employers were conducting some form of genetic testing at that time (American Management Association 2004). Meanwhile, the American Medical Association reports that "hundreds of cases have been documented of people... who have lost jobs or insurance coverage based on reported genetic 'abnormalities'" (American Medical Association 2004). Several worker and human rights organizations have expressed concerns on this issue and lobbied for policy changes. The American Civil Liberties Union (ACLU) has already called on Congress to pass legislation barring such discrimination, on the grounds that people should not be penalized for conditions beyond their control. The ACLU also argues that the genetic testing has not been proven wholly accurate and that people might begin avoiding health care because they fear their test results will jeopardize their employment chances. Indeed, while corporations claim to be concerned about worker health, some of their health-related policies may be putting workers' health at risk. Clearly, this is an example of the expansion of Deleuzian control into new and surprising realms.

It seems likely that the issues described in this chapter will continue into the future, barring a sea change in the way corporations configure productivity and training and the way many Americans prioritize aspects of their lives. As Stanley Deetz notes,

> The formation of routine practices leaves alternative practices overlooked; the concept of "private" removes concerns with child rearing from the workplace; or "cold medications" suppress the intrusion of the body's self-defenses into the work effort. If not suppressed, each of these tensions could lead to significant change, learning, and creative solutions... The body is medicated (with caffeine, cold and stomach medications) to mask the symptoms of stress and fatigue, and the heart and home are replaced with consumption and hope of what "we" will have. (1998, 165–166)

In short, the solutions on offer for dealing with work-life balance, including health aspects thereof, are merely bandages attempting to cover a gaping wound. Provigil does nothing to alter the fact that many employees' work hours are unreasonably long. Worker fitness programs—while they may help employees to get more exercise or follow a more nutritional diet—do not change the fact that long, sedentary workdays are common and can contribute to health problems.

The intersection between medicine, self-help, and the corporate realm is a complex one. Certainly, workers can improve aspects of their lives by following medical or self-help advice, whether or not that advice is mediated through, influenced by, or reinforced by corporate values. Employers and businesses can also benefit from the decisions and practices of workers, however. The question is whether or not the balance between self-care and care for others is too dangerous a compromise. A next step in exploring this nexus could be an investigation of examples other than fitness and sleep, for example, advice related to assertiveness or self-esteem or corporate retreats tailored to encourage team building or interpersonal trust. Another idea might be to study other instances where medicalization and management meet, for example, discourses about workers with attention deficit disorder (ADD), including the possible benefits of ADD within corporate culture.[23] In all of these examples, training for corporate work has expanded well beyond traditional management theory, business school wisdom, and the development of technical expertise and is now encompassing more of people's daily lives and habits. And now, as I have demonstrated, diet, exercise, and sleep—things that may seem personal and intimate—are yet more possible components of corporate management and training. Even in the extreme case of Provigil, the issue is essentially about training: what steps can people take to manage their lives? How can people's daily habits be made to fit—and benefit—corporate practices and values? In coming years, it is to be hoped that we may find the medical field interrogating its deepening connections with corporate America and examining precisely how corporate interests utilize both medical findings and pharmacological breakthroughs. I think it is more likely, however, that we will find that the possibilities for corporate training have become virtually endless.

CHAPTER 5

EVERYTHING TO GAIN: THE INTENSIFICATION OF CORPORATE PROGRESS, PRESENCE, AND RISK

She studies the simple formula: a pound of fat makes two pounds of soap, one of which will trade for the next pound of fat. A simple enough thing, and nothing can keep it from covering the earth.

—*Richard Powers, Gain*[1]

THE PRICE OF PROGRESS

So far in this book, I have emphasized the strengthening of corporate influence in (and on) American culture, especially the way business values may exponentially expand the presence of work in people's daily lives. The following have been noted in earlier chapters:

- The business world's celebration of worker individuality and "freedom" operates in the service of corporate governance by leveraging aspects of employees' identities, encouraging loyalty and creativity, and reducing possibilities for tension in the workplace.
- The value that corporations place on adaptability and flexibility means that work-related training can become boundless and constant.
- Companies' interest in their workers' physical health contributes to a process whereby people are groomed to be ideal employees: optimally productive, diligent, and free of non-work distractions.

While corporate discourse and practice will remain a central topic in this chapter as well, I will examine it from a somewhat different angle here. Rather than investigating how corporate culture is tailored to specifically shape or govern how workers live, this chapter will scrutinize how corporate notions of "progress" constitute a movement toward an ever-increasing ubiquity of business values and interests outside of the workplace, outside of workers' homes, out in the world at large. Advertisements have entered home computers, elementary schools, and the bathroom stalls at the local bar. Employee training has become embedded in people's daily activities. Business ideals such as flexibility and entrepreneurial individualism permeate American society, help to dictate who succeeds and who fails, and decide what's hot and what's not. Meanwhile, the by-products of corporate manufacturing and distribution fill the air we breathe and the water we drink, and companies also provide the medicines used to cure or alleviate the effects of this poisoning on the human body—another kind of ubiquity. This is the new progress: a network of linked processes (and consequences) that intensify corporate presence to the point where corporations themselves become invisible forces, paradoxically everywhere and nowhere.

Developments in the meaning of progress are important, because while it is often tempting to blame particular companies or industries for particular societal problems (fast-food chains for obesity, Wal-Mart for suburban sprawl, oil companies for wars in the Middle East), such problems arise not only from specific corporations, but also from a specific model of corporate capitalism wherein ownership and management are broadly dispersed, and the assumption that the market demands speed and constant innovation is widespread. The "progress" ideal functions as a conduit for the spread of business influence and values in a world where corporate authority and responsibility are increasingly difficult to pin down. This is not to excuse or downplay individual companies' responsibilities for certain problems. Rather, it seems that a productive discussion about the possibility of societal change—if indeed there is such a possibility—must take into account the effects of more general business values like "progress" and must examine how such values get circulated.

Through a discussion of two "case studies"—the American megacorporation Procter & Gamble (P&G) and Clare International, novelist Richard Powers's thinly disguised fictional version of P&G (and similar companies, such as Colgate and Lever)—I will illustrate how the contemporary version of progress functions, examine some of its many effects, and analyze one of its end results: intensified business presence.[2] I will characterize progress as an ideal that simultaneously widens and deepens business presence and imposes corporate logic wherever it goes. I am less interested in the actual harvesting and utilization of resources—so integral to progress as we know it—than I am in the forward-looking, risk-ignoring, and acquisitive mind-set that *transforms* humans and their environment into "resources." Utilization and optimization practices encourage an outlook, which can be detected at least as far back as the Italian Renaissance, but seems especially vigorous now, wherein all human effort must be configured as "useful" to be pursued further or taken seriously. These "useful" efforts are often accompanied by dangers and risks that are downplayed and widely distributed. Ultimately, I will argue that today's corporate progress and presence are becoming boundless despite the risks involved and may, one day, even be unfettered by the human hands that once kept the process moving steadily, perhaps inexorably, forward. Upcoming chapter sections will investigate various aspects of (or stages in) the intensification of progress and presence, including the optimization of natural and human resources, the cycle of consumer "need" creation and fulfillment, and the distribution of risks.

First, a brief overview of the P&G case study, to suggest the particularly strong connections between this specific company and the progress issues just described. In *Soap Opera* (1993), her history and exposé of P&G, *Wall Street Journal* reporter Alecia Swasy describes P&G's attitude toward the ideals of innovation and progress. From the company's 1837 founding as a small manufacturer of soap and candles, to its late nineteenth-century heyday as a pioneer in the fields of marketing and product development, to its current status as one of the largest, best-known, and most profitable businesses in the United States, P&G's name has been associated with modernization and novelty. P&G, the makers of Tide laundry detergent, Ivory soap, Pampers diapers, and many other famous brands, brings consumers worldwide new products every year and provides the world of professional business with creative management and advertising ideas. Given its long-standing reputation for innovation, one might think that today's P&G would have a particularly robust approach to research and other such engines of ingenuity. Swasy argues, however, that this is not the case; her interviews with P&G employees indicate that the pressure for "short-term returns" allowing the corporation to remain competitive "has replaced the traditional long-term view that allowed scientists to work unquestioned for years" (Swasy 1993, 75). Despite what this short-term thinking seems to indicate, P&G envisions a long future full of its products and its influence; as the company's official website informs prospective job applicants, "There's no limit to the potential for growth" (P&G "U.S. Jobs" 2003). In short, progress is still the goal, but P&G emphasizes immediate profits over future successes, and Swasy notes throughout her book that it steadfastly seeks out lucrative avenues for quick, continued expansion despite the possibility of costs or risks.

This attitude is not at all unusual among American companies. General Electric's familiar slogan, "Progress is Our Most Important Product," is a telling example of how U.S. corporations tend to define and characterize the concept of progress. It would be easy to say that for many American businesses, like P&G, progress simply signifies expansion—the ongoing enlargement of the company's physical territories, its product line or number of services, and, most importantly, its market share and revenues. This "manifest destiny" model of progress no longer seems wholly accurate, however, now that the presence of corporate business in the everyday life of the average American has deepened and intensified to such an astonishing degree. There is another, emerging kind of corporate progress, one that goes beyond the drive for physical or even financial expansion, one that could be more appropriately categorized as a move toward *ubiquity*. As the General Electric slogan suggests, progress itself is not only the means (for growth, for higher profits) but also a kind of end. Progress is an engine for more progress, more corporate presence.

Indeed, the "progress engine" has run roughshod over obstacles in its path—as Swasy and other corporate watchdogs have demonstrated. One particularly unnerving example is P&G's response to the 1980 death of 25-year-old Pat Kehm, who succumbed to toxic shock syndrome (TSS) allegedly (almost certainly, according to Swasy's sources) caused by the P&G product Rely Tampons. Despite numerous complaints about the product's safety, P&G moved forward with its Rely marketing blitz while refusing to place a warning label on the tampon packaging (Swasy 1993, 137). Through a generous grant program, P&G, which never accepted responsibility for the product's potential dangers, pressured medical researchers to announce and publish findings in favor of the company, findings that would call into question the connection between Rely and TSS (Swasy 142). Meanwhile, people who tried to speak out against the company, including Kehm family attorney Tom Riley, found many of their speaking engagements and television and radio appearances mysteriously cancelled (148). The Rely brand was discontinued fairly soon after the crisis, but not soon enough to prevent more women from becoming seriously ill.[3]

In another disquieting case, conflicts between P&G and anticorporate protesters allegedly became violent in Perry, Florida, which was once home to one of P&G's Buckeye Pulp Mills. The company came to town in 1947, having used the promise of jobs to pressure the state legislature into classifying Perry's Fenholloway River as "industrial class-five," which means that manufacturing concerns can legally dump toxic wastes and sewage into the water (208). Decades of unregulated dumping into the Fenholloway ensued, as did widespread environmental contamination and significant increases in local cancer rates. One local woman, who joined a group protesting the mill's effects on local fish populations, was beaten, raped, and left for dead by an assailant allegedly under P&G's employ (222). Yet, P&G is still a multimillion dollar company that regularly wins corporate citizenship awards. The extent of P&G's presence and influence in the above examples—and the stark difference between the heavily advertised public face of the company and some of its policies regarding consumers, workers, and the environment—give the age-old question "What price progress?" disturbing new shades of meaning. This chapter will investigate what progress has now come to entail—how the business practice of "making things useful" (which does not necessarily equal "making useful things") can affect our everyday lives and how the progress ideal tends to crowd out other ideals, so that risks are downplayed and corporate growth seems out of control.

A Note about Sources

My discussion of P&G integrates information and ideas from several sources. One of these is Swasy's *Soap Opera,* which combines elements of straightforward historical inquiry and journalistic muckraking. Swasy uses testimonies from many informants, some of them anonymous, to corroborate her claims about P&G, which, in her estimation, is a particularly nefarious corporation that persecutes workers, intimidates its critics, places consumers in grave danger, and destroys the environment. While *Soap Opera* is just as dramatic as its title implies, the book is also a helpful reference (providing insights from P&G executives, entry-level employees, and anti-P&G activists) and a courageous, mostly persuasive, argument. (Swasy's status as a *Wall Street Journal* reporter also strengthens her credibility.) Another of my reference points is Oscar Schisgall's *Eyes on Tomorrow* (1981), which provides a historical account quite different from Swasy's—a celebration of P&G as epitome of the glories of free enterprise. Charlie Decker's business advice book, *Winning with the P&G 99* (1998), is similarly celebratory, suggesting how readers looking for success can utilize P&G's unusual management and marketing tactics.

In addition to these book sources, I draw on publicity materials from P&G itself: press releases, job applicant information, executive speeches, and corporate reports. Because the practices and effects of large corporations like P&G are diverse in and of themselves, consulting an eclectic collection of sources is necessary.

At first glance, Richard Powers's 1998 novel, *Gain*, may seem like an incongruous reference point for this chapter. After all, this book thus far has focused on business communication, self-help, journalism, and other ostensibly nonfiction materials. But the novel, which was named one of the "Business Books of the Year" by *Business Week* in 1998, encapsulates and explores a thought-provoking history of progress as a problematic ideal that drives business practices and decisions. *Gain* intertwines two narratives. One narrative strand is an anecdotal history of Clare, an American company that, just like P&G, was founded in the nineteenth century as a small family-run firm making soap and candles. By the 1990s, Clare becomes a giant corporation with an impressive variety of products and interests, from household products to agricultural chemicals to pharmaceuticals. Powers describes how the company weathers crises and competition, how the founders and their successors change their business practices over time, and how the organization incorporates, diversifies, and becomes phenomenally successful—even ubiquitous. The other narrative strand is about Laura Bodey, a woman who learns that she has ovarian cancer. *Gain* traces the rapid, terrible progression of her disease. As Laura becomes increasingly ill, she discovers that many people in her hometown also have cancer and that, like her, many of them have no previous family tendency toward the disease and no other significant risk factors besides their physical proximity to Clare headquarters. Powers deftly meshes his two plot lines, showing how corporations expand and deepen their presence and how this intensified presence affects people's lives. In short, Powers shows how incorporation can even eventually lead to "decorporation" for Laura and other unwitting victims of business "progress."

By examining P&G and *Gain*'s Clare side by side, we can see Powers's novel as a productive response not only to corporate practices, but also to the positivist, "expert" discourses that corporations like P&G would find authoritative, such as financial statistics, marketing reports, or corporate PR statements. The novel constantly questions and undercuts the various "voices" through which Clare expresses itself, including advertisements, press releases, and the products themselves. Powers asks, who or what can be trusted? What effects are produced by these particular modes of communication?

A company like P&G most likely would not take seriously these challenges from a work of fiction, but Powers's testimony illustrates one kind of response to the progress ideal and reflects and reproduces the debate between different "authoritative" sources (between Swasy and Schisgall, to cite one pertinent example). My approach to literature in this chapter—briefly summarized above—has precedents in cultural studies scholarship. For example, in *Outside Literature* (1992), Tony Bennett challenges the dependence on aesthetic considerations in literary studies (considerations often used to distinguish literature as a "special" or privileged mode of discourse) and argues instead that literature is a specific type of communication, which, like other types of communication, has particular, characteristic traits. Bennett distances himself from the common assumption that "nonfictional" endeavors such as economics or history are somehow more concrete or real than the supposedly superstructural category of culture, which is often dismissed as mere manipulation or false consciousness. He also advocates Foucault's idea that we should not seek meanings hidden behind statements, but instead look more closely at what is said, and at the discursive field in which it is said (Bennett 1992, 74). This "closer look" can suggest how truths and ideals are constructed and distributed. With these ideas in mind, I will look at Powers's *Gain* not as a privileged insight into the workings of corporate America or as a symptom of how corporations have become a social problem, but as a provocation—and as part of a network of linked discourses about business practice and progress. As Powers himself said in an interview when asked about his goals when writing *Gain*, "I could have done tobacco. But what do you reveal when you preach to the converted? You've actually reduced what we might finally come to know about the way the world works. And my sense is that a novel is one of the places where you can actually open things up, and bring them to their full complexity" (qtd. in Tortorello 1998). Before discussing the novel and the story of P&G in more detail, I want to take a closer look at some of the theoretical ideas that inform this chapter's examination of the "full complexity" of progress.

THEORIES OF PROGRESS, PRESENCE, AND RISK

My characterization of progress as an ideal that intensifies business presence is partially inspired by *Empire* (2000), Michael Hardt and Antonio Negri's sprawling diagnosis of contemporary capitalism. While *Empire* does not frequently use the term "progress" itself, it loosely traces an illuminating history of the concept of use value—a concept central to my thinking on progress in this chapter. Using examples from the Renaissance era, including the work of Sir Francis Bacon and Galileo Galilei, Hardt and Negri argue that in the "origins of modernity... knowledge shifted from the transcendent plane to the immanent, and consequently, that human knowledge became a doing, a practice of transforming nature" (72). Powers formerly reserved for and attributed to divine forces were now seemingly in human hands, as people learned more about how to manipulate and utilize their environment: "Modernity... develops knowledge and action as scientific experimentation and defines a tendency toward a democratic politics, posing humanity and desire at the center of history" (74). Suggestive of Hegelian dialectics, this humancentric approach to encountering the world means that people appropriate, absorb, and use otherness (natural resources, in the Bacon and Galileo examples, but labor resources—and human talents and efforts—would also apply) for their own purposes (to further scientific knowledge and to make a profit).

Hardt and Negri show that this concept of use value is central to the intensification of corporate capitalism. The mind-set that drives forward the utilization of natural resources is a template for the transformation of human efforts and talents into "resources" as well. Working primarily with ideas introduced by Gilles Deleuze and Félix Guattari in *A Thousand Plateaus* and by Michel Foucault in *Discipline and Punish*, *Empire* describes a shift from extensive to intensive capitalism. Extensive capitalism, as its name suggests, primarily depends upon expansion (of property, market share, etc.). Hardt and Negri associate extensive capitalism with Foucault's discipline model of power, which entails ordering individuals and keeping them in their place. For example, students are arranged in classrooms according to measured intelligence, soldiers are arranged in regiments according to their roles in warfare, and workers are arranged in factories according to their assigned tasks in the assembly line. These acts of arrangement become an efficient way to define and control individual actions. According to Hardt and Negri, discipline "fixed individuals within institutions but did not succeed in consuming them completely in the rhythm of productive practices and productive socialization; it did not reach the point of permeating entirely the consciousnesses and bodies of individuals" (24). Some readers might not agree with this characterization of discipline (though his descriptions of power are initially based in institutional sites, like schools, factories, and prisons, Foucault argues that governance does indeed permeate social networks in that it affects what particular bodies can do). However, the basic premise of Hardt and Negri's argument—that "productivity," usefulness, and similar values have become increasingly important and influential—cannot easily be disputed.

Hardt and Negri define *intensive* capitalism as "a control that extends throughout the depths of the consciousnesses and bodies of the population—and at the same time across the entirety of social relations" (24). Business practices and values are unconfined by office and factory walls; they are out in the world, affecting daily life, and becoming increasingly naturalized. They are everywhere, but also nowhere—rendered invisible through sheer ubiquity. Intensive capitalism is also a self-perpetuating cycle; as Hardt and Negri note, "The great industrial and financial powers... produce needs, social relations, bodies, and minds—which is to say, they produce producers" (32). When this intensive version of capitalism takes hold, people are made into ideal workers and consumers—in other words, made useful.

The concept of intensive capitalism is also explored by Deleuze and Guattari in *A Thousand Plateaus: Capitalism and Schizophrenia* (1980). This book provides useful language for describing contemporary corporate progress, intensity, and ubiquity and is clearly a strong influence on Hardt and Negri's ideas.[4] Deleuze and Guattari claim that the intensification of capitalism can be seen in certain late nineteenth-century socioeconomic trends, including the first stirrings of scientific management in factories and the development of an elaborate wage system that explicitly linked salary with worker productivity. These two trends, among others, contributed to a mind-set wherein labor became an abstract value—labor itself, rather than specific skills and talents, was now configured as a useful commodity. Anything and everything could fit under the rubric of "work"; individual abilities and efforts were all brought into the ever-expanding realm of the useful. Business values "impose the Work-model upon every activity," Deleuze and Guattari write, "translate every act into possible of virtual work, discipline free action, or else (which amounts to the same thing) relegate it to 'leisure,' which exists only in reference to work" (Deleuze and Guattari 1980, 490). In modern times, they note, even seemingly "useless" activities, like watching television, work in the service of capital; the couch potato viewer takes in at least 20 minutes' worth of corporate advertising per hour, thus functioning as a test audience, and his/her program choices are registered and studied by marketers. Seemingly anticipating lingo that is now frequently used in the marketing field,

Deleuze and Guattari characterize such a TV viewer as a "user," who thus can "tend to become an employee" (492). Literally everyone is "employed" in some way by corporate interests—in this intensive (Deleuze and Guattari use "integrated" or "integrating") capitalism, "the destiny of human beings is recast" (492). In the remainder of this chapter, I will show how *Gain* explores this twist in human destiny and how P&G exemplifies it.

Many contemporary critics, including Ulrich Beck and François Ewald, have expressed serious concerns about this destiny, about the effects of intensive capitalism on human life. In *Risk Society* (1986), Beck claims that one of contemporary society's most pressing problems is how to manage risks—how to mitigate or reduce dangers and how to make the personal, environmental, health-related, and economic hazards of everyday life seem negligible or natural ("you win some, you lose some" or "that's just the way things go"). In an era when ideal solutions to widespread socioeconomic and environmental problems seem impossible to find, and corporate decision makers are increasingly dispersed, the concept of risk management becomes especially important. Risk management, which works in part through shifting risks away from groups (like corporations and governments) and onto individuals, is central to many organizations, including insurance agencies, government bodies or committees, and medical research groups. According to Beck, risk management is deemed crucial because without it not only would everyday life be more dangerous, but also, future scientific, technological, and economic "progress" might be impeded.

To run a pertinent example through Beck's ideas on progress and risk, if American consumers (some, not all—many people wouldn't care in the first place) were informed about the water contamination caused by paper mills like P&G's Buckeye facility in Florida, they might take it upon themselves to protect their health, their families, and their communities. Such protective strategies could range from personal decisions (installing a home water filter system, avoiding the consumption of fish caught in rivers near paper mills) to broader actions (publicizing the issue in newsletters, lobbying politicians, organizing protests). All of these strategies require some diligence and effort from individuals—but, except in rare circumstances where bad publicity trumps concerns about expenditure, corporations like P&G do not have to spend time, money, or energy to change their ways. Instead, the people affected by companies' risky practices must make the effort to find out about the risks and try to counteract or avoid them.

Of course, paper mills do not inherently have to dump toxic waste into waterways, and if consumers were fully informed that the environmental risks of manufacturing might well outweigh the benefits of mass paper production, some might demand changes in corporate practice, which might in turn create new costs for corporations. The new manufacturing costs in this scenario are precisely the type of impediment that risk management seeks to avoid or downplay; citizens (living near paper mills and elsewhere) may have to suffer the consequences of paper manufacturing, but the manufacturers themselves will be spared having to outlay additional capital for redesign of facilities or development of environmentally friendly processes. While the constant downplaying and management of risks contribute to consumer apathy, risks become more global and ubiquitous—for instance, even countries with the greatest commitment to reducing pollution are affected by the lax environmental policies of other countries—and the responsibility for handling risks is increasingly shifted from governing bodies and corporations to individuals. *You* have to make sure that the local factory isn't dumping toxic waste into your town's waterways, *you* have to research which products are detrimental to your family's health, *you* have to be prepared for biological warfare, *you* have to keep emergency savings available in case you get downsized at work. As the examples of P&G and Clare International demonstrate, the marshalling and use of "resources," the creation and satisfaction of consumer needs, and the growing ubiquity of business values all carry significant risks—and it seems that consumers rather than corporate entities are paying the price.

The Use of Use

Gain, Powers's novel, begins in a tranquil garden, where Laura Bodey, a real estate agent and divorced mother of two, enjoys a typical suburban morning in her hometown of Lacewood, Illinois. She admires the blooms in her beloved garden, where she "coaxes up leaves, gets them to catch a teacupful of the two calories per cubic centimeter that the sun, in its improvident abundance, spills forever on the earth for no good reason except that it knew we were coming" (7). In this uneventful opening scene, Powers sets up one of the main themes of his novel and foreshadows another. The sun exists precisely to be made useful for humans; even though plants are the benefactors of its radiant energy at the particular moment Powers describes here, the "we" in "it knew we were coming" clearly does not refer to the plants. Powers's use of the word "improvident" also suggests that the sun would not necessarily be useful without human will, without the expenditure of effort; instead of allowing solar power to "go to waste," people have found ways to improve and develop the world by harnessing what the sun provides. Like a farmer, Laura coaxes the leaves to do what's good for them, thus ensuring that her plants will grow. But, as Laura is about to discover, dangers lurk within this process of utilizing and optimizing nature. After she is diagnosed with ovarian cancer, Laura searches for reasons why she might have gotten sick. During painful chemotherapy sessions and trips to the hospital, she remembers her garden... the chemical pesticides and fertilizing agents that she used there may be what triggered the disease. While *Gain* never definitively pinpoints the cause of Laura's cancer, the novel *strongly* suggests that these gardening products, developed and manufactured in Clare International's Lacewood headquarters, are to blame. It seems that optimizing our natural resources can be hazardous to our health.

The garden scene illustrates one aspect or phase of business progress, which is the effort to make all available resources optimally useful. Natural materials, workers' labor, human talents, energy, and ideas... in business, these are all generally characterized as resources and must be marshaled, consumed, and exploited for the purpose of making profit and expanding corporate presence. Even profit itself—seemingly the end of the line—works in the service of expansion and intensification; as the stories of P&G and Clare suggest, profit is constantly reinvested to bring about future profit and progress. In short, the real point of progress is to drive more progress. In his fictional account of Clare's history, Powers illustrates this shift from corporate manifest destiny—described as "a carefully worked-out theory that American business could work once and only once, with a blank continent in front of it to dispose of" (337)—to contemporary corporate intensification; even when it seems that large businesses cannot grow any larger, they can still deepen their presence. Specifically, business values and ideals can permeate everyday life through a variety of conduits, including advertisements, sponsorships, products and services themselves, and lobby groups that help to ensure government cooperation with corporate desires. Meanwhile, business presence also manifests itself in the environmental damage that corporate production and manufacturing can cause and, as *Gain* suggests, in the illnesses caused or worsened by that environmental damage.

The optimization of natural resources is one phase of the intensification of corporate presence. Even before Clare arrives in Laura Bodey's hometown, altering and optimizing nature is central to

Lacewood's development: "At first, the town subsisted on the overhauled earth. Wild prairie weeds gave way to grain, a single strain of edible grass, grown on a scale that made even grass pay" (Powers 1998, 3). The town's agricultural efforts become more and more successful over time, as people find improved ways to cultivate the soil: "Growth from bone meal and bat guano. Nourishment from shale. Breakthroughs followed one upon the other, as surely as May followed April" (4). These lines hint at the inevitable, inexorable quality of progress—as May follows April, new ideas are hatched and applied, farming improves, and someone or something may have to "pay" for human successes—for example, for the risks ignored or downplayed in the name of the progress ideal.

As Hardt and Negri note, "All of nature has become capital, or at least has become subject to capital" (2000, 272). The optimization of natural resources, however, is merely a precursor to another phase in the intensified contemporary version of progress. Central to the philosophy of *Gain*'s Clare and to P&G, even more so than the utilization of nature, is the notion that all human efforts (talents, ideas, energies) can and should be configured as potentially profitable, as useful. Activities and abilities are pursued and judged according to their use value. One example of this phenomenon is P&G's philosophy of "sustainable development"; Paul Polman, the president of the company's Western Europe division, once remarked that corporate environmentalism would only maintain its current momentum as a trend if businesses were repeatedly made to see the usefulness—the potential profitability—of social responsibility and eco-efficiency (Polman 2002). In this model, taking responsibility for the welfare of the natural environment (whether by developing fuel-efficient manufacturing processes or just by recycling office paper) is not a useful activity in and of itself—not until it is configured as potentially money making or money saving. P&G has evinced a similar attitude about research (as noted in the first section of this chapter) and about employee relations strategies (as discussed in Chapter 2, many companies leverage "work-life" policy to their best advantage—and P&G is no exception).[5]

Like P&G and other corporations, Clare International assesses people, their talents, and their activities according to their "usefulness." In *Gain*, the conflict between Benjamin Clare and his older brothers, Resolve and Samuel, functions as a parable of usefulness and the progress mind-set. Benjamin is a Harvard-trained botanist uninterested in his brothers' soap and candle manufacturing company. Disgusted by what he calls "the perversity of economics"—the fact that selling frivolous goods assures greater profits than selling necessities does and that it is better to manufacture "needs" than to manufacture necessities—he hopes to avoid joining the family business. So, he leaves Boston and joins a research expedition to Antarctica in the hope of discovering new plant species, but instead finds himself saddened by the prevailing attitude of his fellow sailors: research is performed only when it promises to yield something useful. Unsurprisingly, the funding for the expedition is based on the same premise: "So long as research's goal fell in sea-lanes so full of shrimp and fish, commerce was a great believer in research" (Powers 1998, 53). Confronted with the vast nothingness of the Antarctic continent and, later in the journey, with the distinctly alien value system of Tongan tribespeople, Benjamin begins to question the traditional Western notion of progress. He asks a Tongan man about an engraved tribal war club:

> The New Englander shrank from this irrational richness of carving while simultaneously thrilling to the appalling waste. Surely, he asked an island warrior, there must be a more economical manner with which to propel a canoe or bash in a head. More economical, the native conceded. But not as convincing… This handiwork bore some fuller utility to it than Clare's eye could discern… use supped more broadly in the islands than it did in the land of measure. A war club more elaborate than a railroad locomotive, taking more time to make… What, in the final face of things, was the use of use? (57)

Stunned by his new realizations, Benjamin begins to criticize the Western practice of teaching "native" people "useful" things—a process he comes to associate with taming, docility, and the ultimate extinction of ideas, values, objects, and people that do not seem sufficiently pragmatic. As it turns out, he isn't too far off the mark; when the research expedition's boat capsizes, most of the crew's collected specimens are destroyed, but Benjamin's maps of previously uncharted territory survive: "With them, fabled locales fell into fact, hurrying the world toward a society of universal trade" (61). Despite his reluctance, Benjamin cannot help but be swept along in the forward motion of progress.

Upon his return to Boston, Benjamin asks his brothers for money so that he may continue his scientific inquiries, but Resolve refuses, "Knowledge. Your pearl of great price. We only sent you to university in the first place in the mistaken belief that the cost of your edification would someday cease to be a drain and begin to return something to the family's current account" (71). Benjamin's attempts to remind his brothers of Christian doctrine—"Wasn't knowledge of God's creation the reason why we store up riches here at all?"—are swiftly struck down as Resolve insists that Benjamin make himself useful by joining the firm: "What does life ever propose that one do, but come work?" (71). This scene neatly encapsulates what business progress is about: knowledge is only pursued when it is immediately useful and potentially profitable, and usefulness and profit become little more than the means for *more* profit, *more work*.[6] Benjamin's eventual capitulation to his brothers' demands becomes yet another commentary on usefulness; he gives Resolve a surviving specimen from his travels, which, aided by a racist slogan ("The red man never worried about his skin... Why should you?"), is later used as the appealing "mystery ingredient" that makes a new Clare soap a popular brand. Benjamin and his research finally become profitable for Clare, and the non-Western "red man" is tamed, reworked, and made useful for Western business. Natural and human "resources" become raw materials for manufacture and commerce.

Like Benjamin, the Clare company itself, despite some reluctance on the part of its founders, gets swept along in progress. *Gain* traces the development of American capitalism's highly competitive "grow or die" mentality.[7] Philosophical debates between the Clare brothers surround all important business decisions; Samuel insists on keeping product quality high despite the significant financial costs of doing so, while Resolve realizes that the firm will go bankrupt if it follows Samuel's ethical lead. Resolve finds "that progress demanded the destruction of much that had once been considered wealth" (105), while Samuel continually resists the shift from family-run partnership to incorporated firm. After much deliberation, the brothers discover that "survival offered Clare no alternative but incorporation... As with other creatures in upper food ranges, its search for more fuel was intermittent but continual" (155–156). Like the Clare brothers (especially the forward-looking Resolve), P&G founder Cooper Procter also characterized business progress—incorporation and expansion—as an inevitable necessity. He "foresaw growth opportunities for P&G that would necessitate additional plants, new equipment, the development and introduction of new products—in short, a need for capital expenditures that would extend beyond the financial means of the partnership" (Schisgall 1981, 51). Obviously, the partnership did incorporate (in 1890), and soon after this momentous occasion, P&G began to expand as if there were no choice in the matter. When Lever, a Canadian company, began competing for P&G's market share, Procter and his colleagues found that building a Canadian plant "seemed the *only logical means* to meet the Lever challenge" (80, italics mine). The seeming inevitability of the progress ideal becomes clear here; despite misgivings, early P&G executives felt forced to expand the company, because the market and the prevalent values of the business world seem to demand expansion.

Procter's resigned, yet ultimately enthusiastic, response to incorporation and expansion intensified later in P&G's history, when the "grow or die" mentality found expression in a competitive corporate culture that encouraged heated rivalries not only with other companies, but also *within* P&G itself. In the 1930s, P&G developed an unusual approach to marketing that pitted different brands (and the people responsible for them) against each other; later, this approach was also introduced in P&G's advertising department. In this model, management encourages (or coerces) innovation by rewarding strong brands and letting seemingly weaker brands fall by the wayside. Employees are under constant pressure to improve brand performance: "Internal competition is one of the biggest motivators. Brand managers treat competing brands down the hall like their most bitter enemies at Unilever and Colgate... P&G overhires for [brand manager] jobs and weeds out those who don't make the cut" (Swasy 1993, 11).[8] Here, issues of use value—particularly, the idea that humans are ultimately business resources—again emerge; as former CEO Richard R. Deupree put it, "The brands would vie with one another like brothers in a race, not like enemies. Internal competition... would bring into play every talent, every ability, every tool possessed by brand managers" (qtd. in Schisgall 1981, 162). The next question is, what exactly do these useful "human resources" bring into being? What happens when businesses insist on innovation at any cost, and what are the effects of these innovations?

NOT-YET-HUMAN DESIRES

As Powers shows in *Gain,* and as the history of P&G's expansion and incorporation indicates, the "grow or die" mentality leads to a version of progress wherein all available human effort is directed toward corporate expansion and intensified presence—people are configured as resources. I have already discussed the reconfiguration of natural "resources" and human knowledge as use value, but P&G and Clare International also point toward another, strongly related aspect of the "human resources" issue: workers' ingenuity directed toward the creation and satisfaction of *needs*, activities which, in turn, intensify corporate presence through the proliferation of products, services, and advertising messages. This aspect of business progress is cyclical: to keep growing, corporations attempt to create new needs (or, more accurately, desires) through advertising and publicity and then create products to fill those needs. When those new products prove inadequate (or are characterized as such through advertising), newer, improved products are developed and publicized. This constant regeneration of consumer needs not only heightens corporate profits, but also intensifies corporate presence: as *Gain*'s protagonist Laura Bodey realizes, Clare and other companies live in every room of her house, lurking in the most unexpected places through products of all varieties: "The weather stripping, the grout between the quarry tiles, the nonstick in the nonstick pan, the light coat of deterrent she spreads on her garden. These and other incarnations play about her house, all but invisible" (Powers 1998, 7). As Swasy, Schisgall, and Decker all note, P&G's presence within the average American household is likewise so ubiquitous as to be rendered invisible: people wake up in the morning with the help of Folgers Coffee, brush their teeth with Crest, and launder yesterday's clothes with Tide—all P&G products. So, even if consumers wanted to remove all traces of P&G from their homes, actually doing so would be seriously difficult. And the prevalence of business values and ideals makes the boycott unlikely, anyway—as I will discuss in the next section of this chapter. I will return to the idea of corporate presence in a later section of this chapter, but will first address the relationship between progress and the typical business cycle of need creation and fulfillment.

As mentioned earlier, P&G is justifiably famous for its product innovation and for its advertising. P&G's interest in consumer desires—while always significant—really solidified in 1923, when the company hired Dr. D. Paul Smelser, an economist, to anticipate fluctuations in commodities markets. Instead of examining purely economic factors alone, Smelser asked questions about consumer behavior. How do people use the products they buy? What kinds of people buy particular items, how often, when, and why? P&G historian Oscar Schisgall claims that Smelser invented market research as we know it today. By mid-twentieth century, P&G was famous for its in-depth consumer surveys and door-to-door research strategies. For example, both Swasy and Decker report that P&G's researchers in the 1950s watched people wash their hair to see how shampoos were used and asked people questions about their toilet paper habits: did they crumple the paper or fold it into neat squares? This intensified approach to marketing, coupled with P&G's 1921 founding and subsequent expansion of an independent research and development division, made P&G a leader in the creation of new "needs." The company's leadership in this area continues in the 2000s; materials from its human resources department explain that the consumer and market knowledge division is "Procter & Gamble's best 'secret weapon'... the organization that builds the company's renowned gut-level understanding of 'what consumers think and what they want.'" (P&G "Consumer Market Knowledge" 2003). Indeed, when Decker praises P&G's often uncanny ability to anticipate market trends, he may not realize that the corporation, in his description, sounds like it is engaging in sinister surveillance, a la an Orwellian Big Brother: "P&G looks beyond what consumers say they want. P&G digs into consumers' attitudes and behaviors for any hints that might reveal a 'problem' that the consumer doesn't know she has or an opportunity to make her life easier or more pleasant" (Decker 1998, 19).

Tide detergent is one example of progress configured as the creation of "needs"; as Decker points out, as of 1998, Tide's ingredients and packaging had been improved over 70 times (39). One innovation leads to another—the invention of washing machines initially galvanized the P&G manufacturing apparatus at the beginning of the twentieth century: "With the expectation that mass production of such equipment, plus the spreading electrification of U.S. homes, would change laundering methods, Procter & Gamble accelerated its research to develop a general purpose flaked soap for machines" (Schisgall 1981,100). Once a basic detergent formula was established, the process of product specialization (and proliferation) began, with plenty of advertisements to remind consumers of needs they never knew they had. P&G introduced detergents with whiteners, bleaches, enzymes, faster-working enzymes, even whiter whiteners... and when P&G flooded the market with possibilities, its competitors felt compelled to do the same, to "grow or die." The story of Tide epitomizes how corporate processes can speed up, amplify, and intensify; mere expansion of market share is not enough for giant corporations in direct competition with each other. In short, the creation of more stuff leads to the creation of more stuff, and this creation process contributes to corporate ubiquity; through detergents and other products, businesses enter homes, schools, hospitals, and wherever else there is a "need" to be filled. This process, because it is so often rewarded by consumers and shareholders, is endlessly repeated. Former P&G board chairman Ed Harness once remarked,

> In this era of what is called consumerism, the critics of American business are quick to say that all products are alike, that advertising

is a snare and a delusion, and that the government ought to be given responsibility for guiding consumer wants. [P&G's]... business seems to give the lie to much of this. Not a single one of the major forward steps we have taken here has been based on anything but the proven ability to offer the public better products than those previously available.   (qtd. in Schisgall 1981, 219)

Over time, P&G has justified many of its more controversial policy decisions by appealing to the corporate mission of progress that Harness describes. In the 1970s, when research scientists hypothesized that the phosphates in household laundry detergents were destroying American lake ecosystems, many companies, in response to local and state bans and consumer demands, quickly removed their phosphate products from the market. P&G, however, claimed that the removal of phosphates would significantly decrease the cleaning action of detergents and justified its refusal to switch to more eco-friendly ingredients by saying that it did not want to sell any inferior products. The controversy culminated in a lawsuit, wherein P&G charged that the city of Chicago's 1972 ban on detergents containing phosphates—driven by a desire to protect Lake Michigan and the Illinois Waterway from nuisance algae—was unconstitutional because it hindered interstate commerce. A decision in favor of P&G's claim was later reversed in a court of appeals. Despite the lawsuit's outcome and widespread criticism from consumers and researchers, P&G and its apologists still defend the decision to continue selling phosphate detergents, saying that the public had been misled by incomplete or incorrect scientific findings: "P&G refused to pander to the consumer hysteria" (Decker 1998, 108). Similarly, despite the glorification of consumer desires in its advertisements and PR statements, P&G is no friend of consumer advocacy groups like the ones that lobbied for non-phosphate detergents and has repeatedly characterized such groups as anti-American, dangerous, and apt to undermine the country's laissez-faire approach to business. In 1979, then vice chairman Brad Butler said, "In the American democratic system... the very concept of an agency for consumer advocacy is wrong because it is based on a philosophy that there is one national consumer interest. In fact, there are countless consumer interests based on each of our personal needs and wants" (qtd. in Schisgall 1981, 273).[9] There are interesting contradictions in Butler's statement. Obviously, P&G, like most companies, defines and tries to meet consumer needs in order to enhance its profits, but—as evidenced in the examples above—actual consumer feedback is not always welcomed by the company. This suggests that other forces are at work, including, perhaps, market trends, budget concerns, or pressure from shareholders. Also important, I'd suggest, is a philosophical force: P&G's desire to stay true to its much-vaunted progress ideal. In other words, even though the development of new, non-phosphate detergents would have provided P&G with an opportunity for innovation, the removal of the "miracle ingredient" of phosphate, at least in the short term, would have seemed like the opposite of progress—a move backward. And the company characterized phosphate removal as such when it claimed that non-phosphate detergents were inferior products.

Like P&G, Powers's Clare International describes its mission as an obligation to satisfy the consumer: "Clare has a charter to make whatever people want and need... We will find out each niche where we can compete, and apply our proven methods to make our contribution" (Powers 1998, 328). The fictional corporation learns that "progress" can entail constant product innovation and that advertising can foster new consumer needs and desires. More importantly, Clare, in its advertisements, publicity, and executive speeches, justifies its constant intensification of innovation (and, as we shall see in a moment, the costs of that intensification) by defining it as a lofty goal. When Clare develops an all-synthetic soap, Powers encapsulates the company's triumph: "The tower-blown, spray-dried, immaculate molecules truly consummated an ancient aspiration: Resolve's reverie, Benjamin's dream... A race that could make everything from scratch would be beholden to no one... Life would be at nothing's mercy" (324).[10] By the novel's end, Clare has come a long way from Benjamin's early, disgusted realization that the creation of desires is the strategy of the successful capitalist. The disgust and disbelief have long been replaced by a romanticized, noble-sounding version of the same idea—a dedication to serving the customer above all else. But customers may also pay a steep price for such business practices as rapid expansion, sped-up product development and proliferation, and the emphasis on "progress" above all other values.

ACCEPTABLE RISKS

Even when the business world depicts consumers as the ultimate arbiters of a company's success, those same consumers often fall victim to the risks that emerge when the process of progress intensifies. As Ulrich Beck's work suggests, the discourse of business progress makes those risks seem more palatable. P&G CEO A. G. Lafley neatly sums up the notion of progress as noble mission: "P&G is leading innovation. P&G is taking the initiative to make everyday life better" (Lafley 2002). I see at least three strands within P&G's rhetoric of progress; certainly, one is the aforementioned drive to serve consumers and to satisfy them more with each improved product. Another is the related drive to enrich the world of business: "The fact that one company's activities always compel competitors to devise their own improved products" (Schisgall 1981, 226). But, more generally, P&G sees progress as benefiting society as a whole—this is the third strand of the rhetoric: P&G products can purportedly give people the good, safe, and healthy life. It is easy to feel suspicious about such a claim, and in fact, P&G—even while wrapping its activities and risks in the stirring imagery of "making life better"—sometimes shows its cynical, pragmatic side. John Pepper (P&G CEO, 1995–1999), in a sustainability report coauthored by Chad Holliday, CEO of DuPont, offers a synopsis of the bottom-line benefits of this betterment:

> Market choices allow us the freedom to decide how best to use our own resources to enhance quality of life... For example, dental health and hygiene is still poorly developed in many parts of the world. P&G has partnered with national organizations in many countries to raise awareness, through advertising, of the importance of dental health... In the process, consumers are informed about a public health issue, and we lay the foundation for a new market [for P&G's Crest toothpaste brand] where one did not previously exist. (Holliday and Pepper 2001)

Pepper's honest assessment of progress is refreshing in a way, because we can clearly see the guiding force behind making life better: opening new markets and making more profits. This guiding force is by no means surprising, but is worth underscoring simply because the word "progress" is so bound up in rhetorical appeals: idealism, patriotism, et cetera. In *Gain*, Powers explores this rift between the rhetoric of progress and the effects of business practices. Resolve Clare's wife, Julia, is the mouthpiece for a romantic, noble, nineteenth-century discourse of progress that becomes inextricably bound with the Clare company's mission. A journalist who publishes political opinions under a pseudonym (so that her gender does not endanger her writing career), Julia wholeheartedly subscribes to the idea of American manifest destiny through the glories of democracy, technology, and commerce: "From this spinning globe would flow beneficence such as only lunatics and prophets had heretofore imagined" (Powers 1998, 93). When Resolve dies and Julia becomes involved in managing Clare, she brings her forward-looking philosophy to bear on the company. Under her leadership, Clare expands, diversifies, and enjoys booming profits—all the while celebrating progress and ignoring the possible *price* of the business's rapid development. For example, one of the company's founders dies in an industrial accident during a wartime production speedup, and factory practices cause "a rising tide of coal tar treacle that threatened to drown the nation in advancement's sewage" (145). Meanwhile, Benjamin Clare, with a romanticism similar to Julia's, embraces the era's scientific progress: "Clean at least, and released from pain, humanity could rise and fill the day. No deeds would be denied the race" (146). Despite the circumspect worldview he demonstrated in earlier arguments with his brothers about capitalism, Benjamin does not foresee the horrors that science will help bring into being in just a few short decades.[11]

By the mid-twentieth century, the risks inherent in Clare's scientific, commercial, and financial progress become so serious and widespread that they cannot be ignored; the rhetoric of "making life better" through consumer satisfaction, business enrichment, and societal improvement helps to downplay the dangers, but cannot make risks disappear. Like P&G, Clare finds itself at the center of a controversy when its Awe detergent, full of phosphates, is blamed for "dying" lake environments. Interestingly, the effects of Awe on freshwater ecosystems sound quite a lot like the effects of P&G and other corporations on American commerce: "The natural process had somehow begun to accelerate... Some supernutrient fed the aquatic plants, speeding up the lake and choking it on its own growth" (335). Progress—in plant growth and in human society—becomes quicker and deadlier; growth itself becomes potentially fatal. In its depiction of Clare's destructiveness—particularly as epitomized in the story of Laura Bodey's cancer—*Gain* repeatedly asks how these circumstances developed, what their effects on the average person might be, and what (if anything) can be done to counteract the risks and dangers brought to us in part by corporate practices. The "gain" of the novel's title is, at best, a problematic gain. For example, Laura is confronted at a supermarket by a 55-year-old grocery bagger who asks one of today's most pressing questions, paper or plastic? Laura considers the decision:

> What is she supposed to say? Liberty or death? Right or wrong? Good or evil? Paper or plastic? The one kills trees but is one hundred percent natural and recyclable. The other releases insidious fumes if burned but requires less energy to make, can be turned into picnic tables and vinyl siding, has handles, and won't disintegrate when the frozen yogurt melts. (27)

Clearly, neither choice is ideal—all aspects of consumerism come with a cost. (The age of the grocery bagger subtly suggests yet another cost of intensive capitalism—people needing to work at entry-level or minimum wage jobs well into their adulthood.) *Gain* demonstrates one possible response to this costliness: the continual sloughing of corporate responsibilities onto individuals.[12] As early as the nineteenth century, risk management was already a presence on the American landscape. When Benjamin returns from his research expedition in Antarctica, he is disgusted to learn about a new-fangled method for instrumentalizing and naturalizing the risks of everyday life, the insurance industry. Benjamin also witnesses the growth and spread of business risk through the rise of "incorporated" business structures, which, while giving corporations the legal rights and status of human individuals, simultaneously disperse risk and responsibility amongst increasing numbers of people: managers, shareholders, and the public. Also, he sees the sacrifice of human lives to the gods of "progress": "He could not keep track of the accelerating factory explosions in Brooklyn and Baltimore. He only noted that the industrialists always managed to escape prosecution on the grounds that their works had done more cumulative work than harm" (68).[13] As noted earlier in the discussion of progress rhetoric, this idea of "cumulative work" or progress outweighing risks makes it easy to downplay or ignore said risks, but the story of Laura Bodey—her last name implies an "everywoman" quality, but the intricate details of the narrative give her tragedy a specific, human face—brings the effects of progress to the forefront. In a sense, Powers rewrites the story that so many corporations want to tell us about their "cumulative" work improving society.

Corporations like Clare do have an answer to the risk conundrum— an answer, unsurprisingly, that provides even more profit for them. In short, they not only fulfill needs they have created, but also produce and distribute *products responding to the damage caused by the production and distribution of their products*. For example, *Gain* suggests that Clare products caused Laura Bodey's cancer and also notes that Clare manufactured Laura's chemotherapy medications. This is another aspect of business "progress" and its link to the intensification of corporate presence. Companies—and the system of which they are a central part—cause or worsen environmental or social problems and then try to provide the means for "solving" or ameliorating those problems, a neat cycle. A moment toward the beginning of *Gain* foreshadows this phenomenon; the Clare brothers, arguing about business policy in the early nineteenth century, decide that "importing taxed soap made as little sense as bottling spring water or charging a fee for air" (20). Of course, today there are plenty of corporations that make an impressive profit by bottling spring water and quite a few that charge for fresh oxygen: companies that sell HEPA filtration units for homes and businesses or offer air circulation technologies or manage oxygen bars in stylish gyms and spas. Now that corporate businesses have contributed so much to the destruction of "natural resources" as basic as water and air, they're able to turn around and charge consumers for "clean" versions of the things they've destroyed. In a more general sense, many corporations have also profited by publicizing themselves as eco-friendly or socially conscious—another way in which progress (and the intensified corporate presence that accompanies it) comes to resemble a network of linked processes: corporations contribute to problems and then purport to "fix" them.

It would be too easy, however, to blame one or two specific corporations for particular social problems and to accuse only these corporations of profiting from people's suffering. Though she eventually joins a lawsuit accusing Clare of exposing Lacewood's citizens to carcinogens, Laura resists the urge to hold Clare alone responsible. Powers, too, resists that urge; a seemingly incongruous passage at the end of *Gain* reveals the widespread dissemination of blame, risk, and profit—the global sweep of production and distribution. After Laura dies, a nurse finds a disposable camera left in a drawer in the empty hospital room. Powers enumerates the multiple steps involved in producing a camera like this one: pulping timber for cardboard and paper packaging, molding plastic for both camera and film, manufacturing the device itself via mechanized assembly line, sealing cartons with powdered glue, and decorating packaging sleeves with colorful dyes. Powers calls the disposable camera a "true multinational," with components derived from Canada, Korea, Australia, Jamaica, Guinea, and the Gulf of Mexico, all stamped "Made in China": "Labor, materials, assembly, shipping, sales markups and overheads, insurance, international tariffs—the whole prodigious creation costs less than ten dollars. The world sells it to us at a loss, until we learn to afford it" (348). Indeed, countless people in many countries are gaining and losing, complicit in a production process where they may never even see the final product—a product that eventually becomes landfill.

Gain also acknowledges how consumers—who are, after all, a crucial part of the system just described—become complicit in the progress mind-set that drives innovations and the deepening of corporate presence.[14] As Laura, in her hospital bed, reveals to her daughter, Ellen, "People want everything. That's their problem" (343). Clare may have created problems along with its products, but consumers ask for those products... and keep asking. Clare and P&G keep doing what they do because what they do *works*. And, what the companies do allows them to become ever more ubiquitous. After the phosphates controversy and the TSS scare, P&G continued to appear near the top of the *Fortune* 500 and still does today. This mode of progress—the optimization of all human effort and the drive for innovations—has costs that are downplayed even as they are widely distributed. As mentioned previously, human progress, even while bringing improvements and successes for some, tends to be accompanied by serious problems and losses for others. Agriculture occurs on a scale that makes "even grass pay"; P&G's eagerness to enter the personal hygiene market may have caused illness and death from TSS; Clare's monumental size and competitive nature encourage the selling of products that haven't been thoroughly tested for adverse effects. Production and distribution are so sped up and widespread that potential dangers are ignored.

One of P&G's most serious controversies fully illustrates this point. In 1980, at the height of the TSS scare, P&G claimed that because no one could definitively prove the link between Rely Tampons and TSS, no one could force the company to remove the product from the market. The corporation's insistence that researchers provide incontrovertible evidence—which would have required prohibitively costly testing in order to gather satisfactory results, but is typical of American corporate attitudes about expert authorities—allowed the company to avoid responsibility: "Company lawyers warned that the ads should be worded so that 'we do not leave ourselves open for other manufacturers to make claims against us.' The solution: don't mention tampons in the ads" (Swasy 1993, 137). Yet, when P&G finally discontinued the Rely product line, it proudly proclaimed that it did so because the company always acted on "conscience" and valued the consumer's trust above all else (Decker 1998, 65). As former P&G CEO Ed Artzt once said at a banquet awarding P&G's corporate citizenship, "Conscience is a wonderful thing. It can change the world. It can do what no laws, no rules, no threat of punishment or penalty can ever do; because it is an enduring, self-regulating force" (qtd. in Swasy 1993, 308). This comment is probably more telling than Artzt would have liked—rather than extolling the virtues of conscience, it actually suggests the depths of P&G's extreme version of risk management: a laissez-faire philosophy that flaunts regulations and lets the buyer beware.

BACKGROUND RADIATION

Even if we leave aside the question of risk management, responding to risk is a difficult proposition, given the widespread presence of corporations (and the effects of their practices) in everyday life. The largest U.S. companies, like P&G, manifest themselves in unexpected corners of our existence, yet are difficult if not impossible to pin down at precise locations. Many contemporary discourses and technologies operate to extend corporate presence well beyond office walls. This is not necessarily a conscious matter of rendering business influences somehow "invisible" to trick people into working and spending money, but is instead a matter of spreading the workings of corporate power over a wide network, so that even the most local decisions and events might be governed by business ideals and needs, such as lax environmental regulations or corporate-friendly tax cuts.[15] Meanwhile, the availability of corporate products widens, the presence of advertising and marketing deepens, and the effects of manufacturing and distribution reach increasing numbers of people. As Hardt and Negri put it, "[Empire]... is crisscrossed with so many fault lines that it only appears as a continuous, uniform space. In this sense, the clearly defined crisis of modernity gives way to an omnicrisis in the imperial world. In this smooth space of Empire, there is no *place* of power—it is both everywhere and nowhere. Empire is... really a non-place" (2000, 190). The history of P&G and Powers's history of the fictional Clare illustrate the process of becoming ubiquitous: the widening and deepening of corporate presence as well as companies' ability to impose their logic on everyday life.[16]

P&G's massive expansion began in the 1920s, when the company acquired several smaller, struggling firms in the United States. By 1955, P&G was already well established overseas; total net earnings from subsidiaries abroad were approximately $8 million. In the 1980s, that earnings figure increased to $149 million "with over 200 brands in 24 nations and almost a third of P&G's 60,000 employees working overseas" (Schisgall 1981, 185). Overall, by 1980, there were more than 10 billion consumer transactions per year involving P&G products. That same year, it was estimated that 97 percent of American households contained at least one P&G product (ix). The company's PR indicates that P&G products "touch the lives of people around the world" two billion times a day and that there are approximately 300 P&G brands distributed in over 160 countries worldwide (P&G "P&G Pharmaceuticals" 2003). The corporation's presence, however, is not only spread through product purchases, but through a variety of channels that seem to grow in number each year: advertising, marketing, lobbying, performing community work, and even providing teaching aids for school classrooms.[17] P&G was one of the first companies to sponsor daytime serials on radio and television—and profits boomed, thanks in part to this revolutionary advertising tactic (Schisgall 1981, 124). While P&G is an outspoken critic of governmental regulation of business, it sees fit to regulate television programming by placing monetary pressure on networks: "The company has long demanded the right to preview shows on which its commercials might appear" (279).

As *Gain* points out, a corporation like P&G can also literally *enter people's bodies* through the foods they eat, the medicines they take, the air they breathe, and the water they drink. Laura Bodey learns that

> we are all surrounded. Cucumber and squash and baked potato. Fish, that great health food she's been stuffing down the kids for years. Garden sprays. Cooking oils. Cat litter. Dandruff shampoo. Art supplies. Varnish. Deodorant. Moisturizers. Concealers. Water. Air. The whole planet, a Superfund site. Life causes cancer. (Powers 1998, 284)

The sense of being "surrounded," with no chance for escape, is repeatedly invoked in *Gain*. Laura notes that she and her family "live in a house trapped in its own made things, hard on the coast of a man-made ocean" (50). Cute, nostalgic refrigerator magnets featuring old brand logos hold up a reminder of her post-op appointment at Mercy Hospital. Where else can she live, besides in the world of corporate products? As a resident of Lacewood, she is especially unlikely to live free of Clare (much as a resident of Cincinnati is unlikely to live free of P&G): "The firm built her entire town… She knows where her lunch comes from" (6). Clare is ubiquitous and inevitable, always in the background even for townspeople like Laura, who have no direct connection with it. The company sponsors her son's soccer team. The company enters her home through telemarketing calls and mail solicitations. Don, Laura's ex-husband, compares their children to French kids who live in a village under the shadow of a medieval castle and therefore believe that every town has a medieval castle of its own. Clare itself proudly points out its omnipresence in its PR statements, listing all of the wonderful, widespread benefits it has brought to Lacewood. Powers juxtaposes such Clare-produced human-interest stories with Lacewood newspaper articles about the rise in cancer cases—the two kinds of omnipresence go hand in hand.

Laura's response to Clare goes beyond the idea of escape or a quest for freedom:

> Every hour of her life depends on more corporations than she can count. And any spray she might use to bomb the bugs would have to be Clare's, too... Who told them to make all these things? But she knows the answer to that one. They've counted every receipt, more carefully than she ever has. And wasn't she born wanting what they were born wanting to give her?... She brought them in, by choice, toted them in a shopping bag. And she'd do it all over again, given the choice. Would have to. (304)

As these lines indicate, *Gain* is very much about how corporate values (not only consumer desires, as in this example) are disseminated, spread so that they are shared even by people who don't work for corporations. In previous chapters, I suggested that workers' lives are profoundly affected by the cultures of the companies where they work and, more generally, by prevailing trends in management and employee relations. But people don't have to be employed by P&G or Clare to be influenced by those companies' values. In short, many Americans seem socialized to want precisely what corporations want: a competitive and "free" market, minimal government regulations, constant improvements to products and processes, the right to pursue more and more profits, the right to expand, the drive for progress. Julia Clare, *Gain*'s passionate champion of capitalism and democracy, "led [her husband] Resolve to the gradual realization that what was good for soap was good for America. And better still: the other way around" (95). From that moment—the realization that business and national ideals can be one and the same—Powers's Clare narrative focuses on those shared values or, more specifically, on how the needs and desires of the business world become entwined with broader cultural values. The Clare-sponsored soccer team inculcates the enjoyment of competition in children, which meshes perfectly with their already-competitive experiences at suburban public school, which meshes perfectly with popular advertising slogans like "Fear is for the Other Guy," which meshes perfectly with the needs of corporate offices seeking brash go-getters, who will stop at nothing to succeed. Business values are widely disseminated and self-replicating.

Despite being everywhere, however, corporations are also nowhere. An attempt to find all of the P&G products in an average American house would be an arduous, time-consuming process. As Decker points out, many people don't even know what, exactly, P&G makes—they know the brand names but not the manufacturer behind them.[18]

And P&G reinforces this phenomenon by refusing to allow the brands to associate themselves directly with the manufacturer in television, radio, and print advertising: "P&G will allow each new brand to say, 'New, from Procter & Gamble,' but only for the first six months and only as a closing announcement in the advertising. After that, every P&G brand must stand on its own" (Decker 1998, 41). The corporation remains behind the scenes while spending over $3 billion per year on promoting its brands—brand recognition, after all, is what helps to move products from supermarket shelves and into consumers' homes, and downplaying the manufacturer allows P&G to dissociate itself from possible risks posed by its products. Similarly, according to Swasy, P&G exerts a subtle but strong influence on the American scientific community: "Through money, P&G can control research. Doctors have testified that the grant applications stipulate that research has to be submitted to P&G twenty-one days prior to submission for publication in a research journal" (Swasy 1993,142). Swasy stipulates that this "control" over researchers contributed to the downplaying of TSS risk from Rely Tampons—and that the connection between P&G and its Rely brand was further downplayed by the scientific investigation.

Due to a different sort of corporate invisibility, Laura's initial attempt to hold Clare accountable for her cancer—an attempt shared by the equally frustrated Don—proves insurmountably difficult. There's no one to talk to, no one to hear their concerns. She can find no contact information for Clare offices, other than a consumer hotline run entirely by computers. Don visits Clare headquarters, only to find that "real business doesn't care diddly for its regional agents. Doesn't give a squat for setback or inconvenience ... Just so long as people want what it does. Just so long as we have no real alternative. The truth of the matter is: there is no ground zero" (Powers 1998, 257). Corporate capitalism has no central point that people can attack—how much agency do people really have in a free market they supposedly control? As Laura and Don learn, agency is not even a relevant question. The only choice is response—people cannot remove Clare from their lives, but they *can* try to negotiate with Clare's inevitable presence. And the Bodey family does, finally, respond: Don convinces Laura to join a joint lawsuit against Clare. The money can't save Laura's life, but it eventually allows her son, Tim, to begin his *own* corporation, one devoted to researching a cure for cancer. Thus, the corporation—with its notion of progress—remains, but Tim's organization demonstrates how corporate values can be leveraged to ends other than financial profit. The conclusion of *Gain* (which is eerie given the events of 9/11, subsequent to the novel's publication) hints at other possibilities, new values and logics: "Existence lies past price, beyond scarcity. It breaks the law of supply and demand. All things that fail to work will vanish, and life remain. Lovely lichen will manufacture soil on the sunroofs of the World Trade" (344).

But will corporations "fail to work" as they are expected to work? One could point to high-profile business scandals and reply in the affirmative, but those failures are but a few among so many companies. And, despite fluctuations in profits and consumer confidence ratings, there is no compelling reason to believe that firmly entrenched notions of business progress are going to change anytime soon. If anything, the presence of these notions has deepened and widened with intensive capitalism's globalization. For now, commerce and its deadly by-products remain in the air everyone breathes, and corporate presence is naturalized so that it becomes paradoxically invisible. As Powers puts it, corporate effects are "mixed together in the air's cross-breeze, these smells sum to a shorthand for freshness. The day's background radiation" (49).

NOTHING CAN KEEP IT FROM COVERING THE EARTH?

To return to the issue with which I began this chapter, P&G's approach to product research and development is a particularly revealing instance of intensified, accelerated progress. Oscar Schisgall describes a time not so long ago, when P&G was well known—and even criticized—for its painstaking research process. Crest toothpaste's successful formula was developed through such a process: "The company's investment in long and patient research, with clear proof of a consumer benefit, was thus justified" (Schisgall 1981, 209). Howard Morgens, who became president of the company in 1957 and chairman of the board in 1971, insisted on protecting the integrity of P&G's separate research department, so that company scientists would have adequate time and resources to study particular products without pressure from the managers and marketers in the corporate offices. By the 1970s, however, P&G management and shareholders expressed concern that competitors were gaining market share by getting more products to store shelves at a faster pace than P&G. Manufacturers with smaller, less strictly regulated R&D departments seemed better able to respond to market circumstances and consumer research findings. This issue (epitomized by consumers' lackluster response to Pringles potato chips, a product that was once the pride of the R&D staff) led to changes in how P&G management interacted with company researchers (Swasy 1993, 75). The pressure was on, and, Swasy claims, the pressure led to speedy but careless product development, a tendency to rush goods to market without adequate assessment of their possible risks and effects.

Unlike Swasy, P&G fans like Schisgall and Decker are quick to point out the company's consistent emphases on integrity and service—providing the best possible products for consumers while maintaining the same values that the firm's founders insisted upon: honesty, fairness, and careful decision making. But P&G seems markedly less concerned about these age-old traditions now than it was even a decade ago—and this particular corporation is certainly not alone in this profound shift. The business world's celebration of "change" and "change agents"—which itself can be as much of a knee-jerk reaction to contemporary circumstances as blind adherence to tradition and status quo—underscores just how deeply rooted are the notions of progress I have analyzed throughout this chapter. As noted in previous chapters, the rhetoric of individualism as well as the corporate focus on flexibility and adaptability both link change—moving forward, doing things differently—with progress, improvement, success. P&G, in its PR materials, online information for job applicants, and executive speeches, makes the same sort of equation. Change is good and so is progress. As P&G CEO A. J. Lafley puts it, "Change is pervasive, inevitable, and accelerating in our world today. Avoiding or resisting change is a losing strategy. Adapting to change results in survival at best. But if we are proactive, if we lead change, then we will thrive, and win. I embrace change. I welcome it" (Lafley 2001).

Lafley's speech interests me for two reasons: he indicates that P&G will lead change and perhaps even further accelerate the progress process, but he also sounds resigned, even reluctant. Change is "inevitable" and "avoiding" or "resisting" will result in destruction. In *Gain,* too, business progress takes on a depressing, destructive inevitability that people—even, at times, corporate executives—seem powerless against. Indeed, the progress itself is described as a process increasingly out of human control:

> In turn, the energies released by this energy launched ocean steamships and set machine presses stamping out the tools needed to make their own replacements. Infant factories forced a self-cleaning steel plow, which beat a reaper, which called out for vulcanized rubber, which set in inexorable motion a sewing machine that left half of Boston out of work, turning upon itself, poor against poorer.   (Powers 1998, 67)

And this is just the beginning—these are nineteenth- and early twentieth-century stirrings of the way progress marches on while its negative effects are downplayed or ignored. Clare becomes too large an entity for its founders to handle. Incorporation comes to seem "necessary," despite the founders' less-than-enthusiastic feelings about the strategy: "Time and Clare required one more catalyst to render life's waste fat and solidify it, stainless and inexorable" (159). Combining the Fifth and Fourteenth Amendments to the U.S. Constitution, the U.S. government granted incorporated entities like Clare every legal right and protection afforded to human individuals. Powers suggests that this moment is when corporations become, perhaps, more powerful than the people who created them, manage them, and work for them: "What *human* dared oppose the inevitable logic of a good deal?" (211, italics mine). More importantly, the deepening power and presence of Clare—and the growing speed of progress—amplify the company's effects on everyday life; Don, angered by Clare's refusal to respond to charges that its factory causes cancer, remembers the words of Winston Churchill: "*We shape our buildings. Thereafter they shape us*" (qtd. in Powers 1998, 261, italics in original).

Shortly before she dies, Laura Bodey meditates on the possibility that Clare caused her cancer. Despite her intense physical pain and her misery about saying goodbye to her children, she will not blame any single person or entity for what has happened to her. This is not a matter of noble strength, martyrdom, or even resignation on Laura's part; rather, she has come to realize the complexity of the relationship between people and corporations, the possibly inextricable links between consumers and producers: "It makes no difference whether this business gave her cancer. They have given her everything else. Taken her life and molded it in every way imaginable, plus six degrees beyond imagining" (320). Powers's novel can be seen as a call to stop and try to imagine those six degrees, but the intensified speed of progress—and the emerging ubiquity of corporate presence that accompanies it—would make the imagining quite a challenge. Long-held, optimistic notions of progress as development or success likewise present barriers to the imagination, as do the multiple effects of corporate practices—the problems they cause linked together with the life-improving (or even life-saving) products they may provide. Business progress is an ever-quickening process that simultaneously widens and deepens corporate presence, to the point where the corporations themselves may seem invisible. But the concept of progress described in these pages existed long before corporations did. Will the process eventually slow down or stop? The more appropriate question is, if it does, what, if anything, might change?

CHAPTER 6

STUDENTS AND STAKEHOLDERS: BUSINESS WRITING COURSES AND CORPORATE CULTURAL LITERACY

TEACHING THE EMPLOYEES OF TOMORROW

My first semester teaching business writing was not a happy one. I remember worrying about lesson plans during sticky summer morning walks to the classroom. I fretted not only about the usual, minor teaching problems—dealing with obnoxious grade grubbers and plagiarists, losing my train of thought mid-lecture, or losing a heel from the same, now-ancient, cheap shoes I wore throughout my temp-work days in California—but also about bottom-line issues. What was I teaching my students, and why? Though my experiences working at high-profile companies had left me skeptical about (and, occasionally, hostile toward) corporate America, I found myself demonstrating the proper protocols of business letter and memo writing to the entry-level employees of tomorrow. I found myself teaching undergraduates how to write effective resumes and cover letters so that they could obtain the same kinds of jobs I once held. Many of my students—most of them, it seemed—*wanted* to know more about persuasive report writing strategies and were effusively grateful to me when their painstakingly edited application materials landed them positions at top advertising agencies and investment banking firms. Despite their enthusiasm, however, I still felt gloomy... and guilty. Sometimes, I felt like a business-suited Charon ferrying souls into corporate hell.

Even after several semesters of experience, my business writing classes remained less than pleasant for me. I struggled through explaining and grading the six required writing projects, including the aforementioned job application unit, a packet of business letters, and a series of three linked assignments: a research proposal, a progress report, and a formal business report analyzing the feasibility of solutions to a problem of the student's choosing. The required textbook readings touched upon key topics in contemporary business communication, such as dealing with angry customers, breaking bad news to downsized employees, and appealing to treasured clients by utilizing the "you attitude"—the second-person address that allegedly forges a bond between reader and writer and lets the reader know that his/her opinions are valued. All of these aspects of the course materials may seem relatively harmless and even benevolent. But, given my own job experiences and my ongoing research about corporate discourses and cultures, I couldn't help wondering if teaching business writing was implicating me in some sort of sinister process. Was I "indoctrinating" students into corporate culture? Or, was I just giving students what they wanted out of a college education? What choice, if any, did I have? Was there any possible middle ground between the two positions?

I have found that many scholars of business writing and communication share the concerns described above, but I have also noticed that many other researchers *celebrate* the status of business writing courses as stepping stones for students entering corporate America and as paradigms of pragmatic training for the so-called real world. Given the issues described and analyzed in the pages of this book, it is important for me to consider the role of my own teaching work in the spread and maintenance of corporate practices and, more importantly, of the values that define and drive those practices. I am also interested in the tension within academia surrounding roles like mine—specifically, the pedagogical and philosophical conflicts between scholars from various fields (such as English, communication, and business) who teach writing skills. For example, some researchers with work published in one of communication's most respected journals, *Business Communication Quarterly* (henceforth *BCQ*), argue that English departments unfairly marginalize business writing and foster an individualistic writing style ill suited for corporate jobs. They also contend that universities should make a stronger effort to satisfy companies' desires for well-trained entry-level employees. Meanwhile, some communication and rhetoric/composition scholars, including Deborah Cameron and James Paul Gee, are ambivalent about the encroachment of business values and interests in universities and suggest that writing courses too focused on such values risk undermining students' critical thinking abilities. I have come to feel that all of the researchers just mentioned could frame their questions somewhat differently, judging from my research and from my own experiences teaching business writing (undergraduate courses at Drake University, Penn State, and Penn State's online World Campus, plus a semester spent instructing a weekly seminar for shift workers at an aluminum plant in Lancaster, Pennsylvania). Rather than focusing so tightly on the pros and cons of corporate influence on universities, I will examine business writing's power to naturalize values, to affect what counts as "truth," to advise which ideas should be believed or disregarded, and to foster particular types of workplace environments.

First, I will describe some ways in which business writing conventions, whether learned in the university classroom or onsite in the workplace, can help to construct and disseminate corporate values, thus working to enculturate students and new employees into the business world. It is important to note that such enculturation is not lockstep brainwashing; students (and instructors) can negotiate with the conventions they're taught. Second, I will establish additional context for this issue by describing in more detail the debate between scholars about the pros and cons of business writing education—a debate centered on the efficacy of providing students with practice dealing with "authentic" workplace situations. Third, I will discuss possibilities for improving business writing instruction, including a way to negotiate with the demand for "realness" espoused by many communication researchers. My analysis in these pages is not comprehensive, nor is it meant to be so. My goal here is to wrap up this investigation of corporate culture by closely examining one of its many possible entry points and modes of distribution.

BUILDING THE "WE" OF BUSINESS

When brainstorming for this assignment, envision yourself as an employer evaluating resumes and cover letters for an open position at your firm. Write a letter informing a hopeful applicant that s/he has not been selected for the job. In this letter, you must clearly and authoritatively explain the reason for the rejection (do not apologize!), and you must ensure that the applicant retains a sense of goodwill toward your company. You must find a way to convey the bad news as honestly and concisely as possible, but you must also avoid alienating your reader. Good luck.

Some variant of the assignment described above—often called the "bad news letter"—appears in all of the business writing syllabi I have ever used or read. The general consensus appears to be that bad news crops up on a fairly regular basis in the business world. Someone will get rejected or fired or demoted; someone's request for a raise or for maternity leave will be denied; someone's ideas will be dismissed. One could say the same of any professional field—there's bad news in academia, in government, in the military, and at the circus—but the protocols for presenting a potentially upsetting decision in business seem unusually standardized (judging by what business writing textbooks and similar course materials have to say on the matter). Students are told to use specialized distraction tactics, including a scheme memorably described by one of my Penn State colleagues as "pat, rap, pat" ("pat the reader gently on the head with an upbeat opening statement, rap him with the bad news, and close by patting him again with a kind compliment or hopeful remark about his future"). The business communication textbook I use in my courses advises student writers to defuse emotional situations and avoid blame by keeping bad news letters short and neutrally worded: "Try using third-person, impersonal, passive language... This approach downplays the doer of the action because the doer is not specified" (Bovée, Thill, and Schatzman 2003, 229). The textbook does not call attention to some of the other possible effects of its recommended strategy: the distribution of fault away from the writer and, more generally, the ongoing distribution of corporate authority away from any centralized locus of power.[1] The "we" of business writing—as in, "We were impressed with your background and skills, but..."—is a savvy strategy meant to convey a neutral, inoffensive, united front, and calculated to discourage the reader-outsider from taking any action other than what the united front desires. The strategy may not always work, but, as I tell my business students every semester, the strategy is doing its job if it works even half the time.

Such writing conventions do not merely reflect currently accepted business practices, but help to create and replicate those practices and values. When students learn the accepted strategies for organizing and tailoring bad news letters, they simultaneously learn how contemporary corporations—often so quick to celebrate the "always right" customer—typically mete out rejections and disappointments to outsiders. The *Business Communication Today* textbook I often use in my courses also instructs students about the finer points of delivering bad news to "insiders," such as employees and coworkers. Students can easily see how companies try to prevent feelings from getting in the way of commerce, and they may well take this knowledge with them when they join the workforce, thus reinforcing and replicating the values and practices set forth in business communication classes. In the case of the "bad news" letter assignment, students may "learn" that difficult emotions are always to be squelched in the workplace, even when those emotions—anger, for instance—are justified by problematic workplace situations. Also, textbooks and course materials for business writing classes suggest that success at writing and communication—attained by utilizing the strategies advocated by instructors and textbook writers, for example—leads to success at managing and, therefore, to professional advancement: "[This textbook] gives specific examples of the communication techniques that have led to sound decision making and effective teamwork. In addition, its insights into the way organizations operate help clarify student career interests by identifying the skills needed for a lifetime of career success" (Bovée and Thill 1999, xvii) As Deborah Cameron puts it, business communication training focuses on "teaching [students] to discipline themselves so they can operate more easily within [workplace] constraints: become more flexible, more team-oriented, better at resolving the conflicts and controlling the emotions that threaten to disrupt business as usual" (2000, 179). In other words, while writing classes do not brainwash students, such classes do impart a strong sense of workplace parameters and expectations—and of the communication styles most likely to be rewarded or punished. Business writing classes are among the many technologies that can groom workers for optimal performance and encourage a good attitude toward workplace regulations and activities. As the study guide for one of my business writing courses notes, effective business communication strategies "prevent disagreements by establishing the bases on which people can reach common ground and work together" (Lyday 2002, 2). Similarly, one edition of my course's business writing textbook trumpets its emphasis on teamwork and collaboration— an emphasis entirely unsurprising given trends in management theory and business self-help (see the analysis, in Chapter 2, of the tension between the corporate celebration of individualism and the "return to ethics").

Indeed, "working together" is a much-discussed concept in both business writing courses and literature about business writing and communication. In *The New Work Order: Behind the Language of the New Capitalism* (1996), James Paul Gee, Glynda Hull, and Colin Lankshear contend that communication training works cumulatively to foster particular corporate environments: "A business adopts a set of tools and procedures, often emanating from consultants or business schools, designed to change social relations in the workplace (a form of sociocultural engineering) and thereby create a new workplace culture or new workplace 'core values'" (xiv).[2] While this description neglects to mention the important roles of the mainstream business press and business self-help books in this process, the basic premise rings true: "The new capitalism is now quite open about the need to socialize people into 'communities of practice' that position people to be certain kinds of people" (21). In the classroom and in the office, students and new employees learn how to fit into such corporate communities—how to present instructions for a task in a logical, concise manner; how to show deference to managers when requesting funding; or how to convince a disgruntled department to stay focused on a project. As Cameron notes, "Education is not only supposed to equip future workers with the skills and competencies their jobs will require, but also to socialize them in particular ways—to inculcate certain social habits, dispositions and values" (19–20). Once students enter the workforce, their communication training will no doubt continue; even when writing and verbal communication techniques are not explicitly regulated (and they often are—consider the scripted greetings and gestures used by Walt Disney World or Wal-Mart employees), rewards and criticisms function to regulate what workers do and don't do in their documents and perhaps even in their everyday conversations with coworkers.[3] While reinforcing corporate values and strengthening corporate cultures are not necessarily overtly stated goals of business writing and communication courses (or onsite training), these aspects of such courses undeniably exist, providing employers not only with grammatically correct writers, but also with employees trained to fit in and cooperate: "A person who learns to control the use of language in the writing of effective business documents is often the same person who learns to use language creatively and flexibly in order to lead others to work productively and harmoniously" (Mandel and Vassallo 1999, 347).

Business writing students are urged to "control" their language through close attention to audience. As in other rhetoric and composition classes, in business writing courses audience dictates students' tone, style, and organization strategy: what do the readers need to know, and how can the writer convey the necessary information in a persuasive and appealing manner? Tailoring one's writing to suit one's audience is a fine strategy for success, but it's frustrating to see that some researchers and instructors characterize writing that does not precisely fit the business model (a model that entails blatantly audience-oriented, action-driven, and concise prose) as insulting to readers. According to Penn State World Campus's official grading standards for the courses I used to teach there, people whose writing diverges from the audience-based model are supposed to be penalized—and the threat of negative consequences is another opportunity to groom students for the corporate sector. Indeed, the attitude of consultants Barrett J. Mandel and Philip Vassallo toward writing outside the business field moves beyond mere punishment of student writing "flaws" and into a kind of contempt; so-called academic writers are portrayed as navel gazing, inefficient, and selfish, while business writers bask in the glory of crystal-clear, "we-oriented" prose: "We consider it a necessary task to help new business writers transition from the me of the university to the us of business... gratification that comes from effective business writing is embedded in the tradition of excellence that emerges from working with others to craft a product" (Mandel and Vassallo 1999, 345). But, this focus on "us" necessarily excludes a "them": those who don't know how to communicate according to typical corporate standards or would prefer not to do so. One communication researcher even hints that writing instructors who do not actively encourage their students to follow current business writing conventions and who attempt to teach their students values other than business values are living in dreamland, hopelessly naïve; Malcolm Richardson contends that there is a "persistent myth" within the humanities of "the university of pure knowledge, the great and good place where, just beyond the grasp of living memory, students come for the love of learning and not lucre" (2003, 106).

Also ominous is the use of business writing and communication conventions to win and enforce worker loyalty. As Mandel and Vassallo suggest, good writing is good management. It is therefore unsurprising when, in an article for *BCQ*, university professor William Wardrope finds through surveys that the academic chairs of management departments in business schools—more so than chairs of any other business school departments—deem business communication classes highly important (Wardrope 2002, 66). Of course management professors rate business writing and communication highly; these skills help to establish the importance of corporate values, and communication is what disseminates those values in the first place. The use of motivational language—so pervasive that it is often parodied in popular comic strips and television shows—is one prime example of a business writing skill (or "competency," as current corporate lingo might have it) that may encourage readers to make the best of any given work situation and remain devoted to organizational goals despite problems, conflicts, or questions. For instance, one of the very first exercises that appears in Penn State's standard business writing syllabus involves comparing two sample memos—one of them angrily berates workers for submitting incorrect time cards, and the other methodically explains the new time card system and the advantages of using it. Identifying the "better" memo is easy for students to do, especially because the angry version also includes unfounded accusations and misogynistic slurs. But few students criticize the "better" memo at all, even though the system it so cheerfully describes sounds like one of constant worker surveillance, painted in the document as "helpful to those of us who are making a New Year's resolution to be more punctual" (Bovée, Thill, and Schatzman 2003, 20). Instead of inviting questions or comments from workers, the "better" memo curtly ends with holiday greetings. There is no doubt that upbeat writing is more pleasant to readers than a document chock-full of vicious insults, but the sample memo held up as a model for students is an underhanded attempt to motivate workers to accept surveillance, and the underhanded quality is ignored in the course materials.

Motivational language is not confined to "bad news" scenarios or documents explaining new workplace regulations. As Kitty Locker notes in an article for *BCQ*, "Business communication focuses on persuasion. The communicator's problem is not primarily exposition—though some business issues can be highly arcane—but motivation: how do you make people adopt common goals? How do you make their commitment to work not merely a matter of mechanically meeting minimum expectations, but rather one of intelligence, creativity, and energy?" (2003, 129). Locker's article celebrates the role of business communication in forging commitment, but as a business writing instructor and researcher of corporate culture, I feel that this role should not go unremarked and unquestioned. I mentioned a similar point in Chapter 2 of this book, but it seems worth mentioning again here, because current trends in business writing education show that the process of job training (in this case, shaping corporate-friendly attitudes and loyalty) can begin well before people ever enter the workplace. Corporations, communication researchers, and instructors seem aware of this possibility, which may explain the phenomena discussed in the next section of this chapter: the insistence on optimally "authentic" training in business writing courses and the related conflict between communication and English departments.

Keeping It Real

For this timed, in-class assignment, pretend that you are a busy lower-level marketing executive at XYZ, Inc. You have been away at a conference for the past two business days, and you return to your office to find the following items in your desk inbox: a solicited report from the company's research and development manager regarding product tests for XYZ's new potato chip brand, a request for maternity leave from your assistant, a letter from a consumer claiming dissatisfaction with a six-pack of XYZ's soda, and a request for holiday sales statistics from your department's supervisor. All of these documents require a written response from you today. For the assignment, submit your written responses to each inbox document, plus a brief memo explaining your writing strategy. In the memo, be sure to explain the order in which you would respond to the requests described above. You have three hours to complete your work.

The elaborate business writing exercise outlined above is derived from the work of professors James M. Stearns, Kate Ronald, Timothy B. Greenlee, and Charles T. Crespy, who advocated such case-based in-basket exercises (CIBEs) in an issue of the *Journal of Education for Business*. As Stearns and his coauthors point out, "Requiring that students contextualize their analytical skills by writing solutions, suggestions, and directives to 'real' audiences... helps students see writing as a real-world skill with consequences that affect their success as managers" (2003, 215). Similarly, Jerome Curry, in an article for *BCQ*, argues for the integration of highly contextualized rhetorical situations in business writing assignments: "Almost certainly all business writing instructors realize the importance of introducing real-life challenges into the classroom... confronting students with situations replicating those that they will actually encounter in the world of work" (1996, 77). The insistence of these scholars that business students get a reasonably "authentic simulation" of so-called real-life writing experience in the classroom haunts much of the communication field's commentary on effective teaching and program design. In this section of the chapter, I will explore the significant tension surrounding the issue of realness in writing and communication studies—and that tension's various implications for students, instructors, and administrators. The next section will suggest some ways in which the realness question could productively point toward improvements in current business writing/communication curricula—improvements that could address many of the corporate cultural issues raised throughout this book. If, as argued previously, business writing instruction can function as a conduit for corporate values, perhaps instructors can adapt this emphasis on realness so that students are not constantly and exclusively taught that what's best for the company is all that matters or that the company is always an entity to be judged as "good" or "bad."

First, it's necessary to examine why real-life experience has been deemed such a crucial component of business communication courses. One oft-cited reason is the benefit of students, who—in part by preparing to tackle the contents of an inbox or to send a rejection letter to a job candidate—may position themselves to win coveted jobs in a competitive market: "Research validates the importance of communication skills for job applicants and for career success" (Krapels and Davis 2003, 90). While many communication scholars, such as Patrick Dias, Mark Mabrito, Aviva Freedman, and Christine Adam, lament the impossibility of exactly replicating workplace scenarios within the confines of the university classroom, all agree that instructors should strive for optimal authenticity and immersion into corporate conventions and expectations.[4] Some researchers even suggest that neglecting to foster such immersion in the classroom places students at a significant disadvantage once they enter the workforce. For instance, Freedman and Adam contend that standard grading processes—which offer feedback but usually do not demand rewrites and revisions—ill-prepare students for "document cycling," the multi-draft process by which corporate documents are usually developed. Instead of cheerfully accepting critiques and rewriting as instructed by managers or coworkers, unprepared students might become defensive and even refuse to edit their writing. Similarly, Adam argues that a lack of group assignments causes students to be uncomfortable with teamwork at the office, and Mandel and Vassallo describe an entry-level employee frustrated by what she perceives as constraints on her individual writing style:

> She did not know whom to blame—her professors for misleading her about her ability in college, her present boss for not recognizing that everyone has an individual style, or her new writing coaches who wanted her to give up her own style... [other] participants [were] either sharing similar woes or expressing cynicism about what they have had to surrender to write "the way they want me to write here." (Mandel and Vassallo 1999, 339)

More realistic and pragmatic undergraduate business writing course design, say Mandel and Vassallo, would help to avoid or ameliorate such frustrations.

The second reason why scholars advocate writing courses that incorporate real-world scenarios is the benefit for businesses: "Evidence suggests that employers in all occupational fields place greater value on employees' communication skills than they do on their technical skills" (Wardrope 2002, 61–62). Many researchers in the communication field (much fewer in the fields of English and composition) seem eager not only to give students the pragmatic training they supposedly need for the workforce, but also to please employers, business schools, and affiliated organizations, such as the Association to Advance Collegiate Schools of Business International (AACSBI). Stearns and his coauthors survey corporate desires and suggest that instructors should immediately go about fulfilling them: "Corporate recruiters consistently place written communication at the top of their criteria in selecting job candidates... Recruiters strongly advise business faculty to 'prepare [students] more to work and communicate with others rather than strictly with books.' And 'bring in as much "real life" business experience to the class as possible'" (2003, 213). The language here—particularly the phrase "strongly advise"—is noteworthy for its forcefulness and authoritarian tone. Indeed, several of the authors published in Patrick Dias and Anthony Paré's *Transitions: Writing in Academic and Workplace Settings* (2000) collection claim that corporations are growing impatient with students who "can't write well" and adamant about the idea that instructors need to do their jobs better (e.g., by adding real-world experiences to their syllabi). Meanwhile, Deborah Cameron hints at some disagreement on the subject of capitulating to corporate demands without questioning them:

> There is a particularly strong link between the sphere of work and that of education. This is not surprising: from the point of view of employers, and of many politicians, parents and students, schools and colleges are there in large part to provide an appropriately skilled workforce. Educators themselves may take a somewhat different view, but few would deny entirely that it is part of their mission to prepare students for future employment. In any case, they are subject to both political and financial pressure to take notice of what employers want. (2000, 17)

This issue—are instructors obligated to provide the training that corporations want for their job candidates and entry-level employees?—brings me to the third reason why classroom realism is considered important by communication scholars: integrating such authentic, pragmatic training into course design can benefit administrators and professors themselves. As Wardrope writes, "A strong impetus provided by the academic and corporate sectors, as well as by accrediting bodies, continues to justify the presence of business communication as a core business component... the need for good communication skills by business practitioners is not going away" (Wardrope 2001, 243). While, as I will discuss in a moment, business communication researchers often characterize their field as marginalized within the academy, Wardrope and others suggest that business writing programs and communication departments have a strong (but, perhaps, not silent) partner, corporate employers.[5] Because these employers want students to get real-world preparation, it behooves instructors in these supposedly marginalized programs to comply. Such arguments have an ominous undertone, though: what happens to these university programs when business trends shift (as they so often do) and communication and teamwork are no longer so highly valued in the workplace?

As may be apparent from many of the comments quoted in the last few paragraphs, communication researchers' insistence on realistic, pragmatic job training—and the worry that failing to provide such training will displease corporations—has found a scapegoat, English departments. Articles like Wardrope's, Mandel and Vassallo's, and Adam's set up a stark contrast between the ideal business writing course (realistic, pragmatic) and the supposedly problematic ones currently offered, which focus on students finding an individual voice or style; allegedly, these problematic writing courses are often housed within English departments. The difference in pedagogical philosophy between English and other fields, some writers claim, has led to major, long-standing institutional conflicts. As long ago as 1943, an article in *College English* argued that "while [business writing] is gradually making a place for itself in the college curriculum, it is still being mistreated in many places... the English department maintains that it is a 'practical' course and belongs in the business department" (Horning 381). Kitty Locker, writing for *BCQ* in 2003, contends that the tension between English departments and business writing programs began well before Horning's World War II era claim of "mistreatment," with the Morrell Acts of 1862 and 1867. These acts, Locker claims, indicated a profound shift in American higher education, from liberal arts colleges meant to prepare students for the ministry (or to educate the sons of wealthy families about history and culture), to land grant universities offering training in business, farming, and engineering. This shift may be an emblematic moment in the development of the tendency to characterize "liberal arts" and "pragmatic training" as fundamentally and irreconcilably different categories of education.

This tendency, and the suspicion that English departments are undermining business writing programs and therefore alienating students and employers, is central to several angry articles denouncing the allegedly lowly status of business communication in the academy. Locker tells her own story of abuse at the hands of an English department: "The term ['professional communication'] is acceptable to English departments who associate 'business' with filthy lucre. In 1977 in the English department at Texas A&M University, I was told that we couldn't use any textbook with the word 'business' in the title" (123). Similarly, Malcolm Richardson scoffs at the snobbery and esoteric interests of his English department colleagues, for example, the "hirsute John Clare specialist in the next office" (2003, 108). The accusations and defensiveness evinced in these quotations are especially counterproductive because they are based on shopworn stereotypes and outdated portrayals of how writing courses generally work. Before admitting that many courses have moved away from such a philosophy, Mandel and Vassallo make the imprecise claim that "an ancient notion of the author as a solitary figure struggling to develop not only an argument, but a personal style as well, still prevails in the universities" (Mandel and Vassallo 1999, 341). This claim seems misguided, given the heavy emphasis in rhetoric and composition programs on peer review and following genre conventions. Even the gentler critiques of the alleged "English department approach" to writing instruction seem unfair; Adam complains,

> Even when the professor reads case studies that are prepared and presented in what seems to be carefully simulated workplace conditions, his response is still shaped by the exigence present in the university, namely that he determine if the students have learned what has been taught, compare their texts to others in the class, and give the assignments appropriate grades. (2000, 173)

The same could be said of any kind of academic training, though, including business school classes. Adam's article repeatedly implies that students and instructors are incapable of making the mental leap from classroom experience to workplace knowledge. However, instructors can easily envision themselves in the employer's role when reading student job application assignments, and students can envision themselves as job candidates when they research and tailor their "applications." In this way, the insistence on the importance of optimal authenticity found in many business communication scholars' work gives students and teachers very little credit.

As frustrating and misguided as such academic conflicts may seem, the pedagogical philosophy driving the conflicts has very real effects on instructors, students, and administrators. The push for "authenticity" in business writing classrooms has further inserted corporate values into higher education and, more importantly, has helped to naturalize those values. There is increased pressure on educators to tailor their courses in certain ways—to emphasize the training so strongly advocated by employers (and, perhaps, administrators) hoping to curry favor and funding. Deborah Cameron, James Gee, and others have described the high-pressure academic atmosphere that discourages writing instructors from diverging from corporate interests. Cameron argues that this trend has been on the rise for a long time, but that it has recently intensified:

> What is striking... is the *scale* of the changes now being advocated. Just as business organizations are told by management consultants and "gurus" that to survive in new conditions they must break radically with the past, so schools and colleges are now hearing the same message from employers and politicians. The ability of the education system to respond to economic change is seen as crucial for the future competitiveness, not just of individual companies but of whole nations. (2000, 128)[6]

The emphasis on (and debate over) authentic training furthers the intensification of corporate influence on higher education. For some researchers, the paramount importance of corporate desires is simply a given; colleges should just give employers what they want, without question. Wardrope writes, "Employers still tell us, 'teach your graduates to write well,' and that is exactly what we should unabashedly do" (2001, 244). Stearns and his coauthors note that "educators no longer can ignore the need to integrate meaningful writing into business curricula. This need is well documented by the experiences of a variety of stakeholders" (2003, 217). While it is true that college professors and administrators cannot simply choose to jettison corporate influence and demands, they can find different ways to negotiate with those forces. Some examples of different possible responses appear in the next section of this chapter. But the possibility of different responses and negotiation with corporate forces is made ever more daunting by the continuing naturalization of business values and the fierce disciplinary debate that contributes to that naturalization process.

CORPORATE CULTURAL STUDIES, REVISITED

Select two advertisements for open positions at different companies that interest you. Apply for both jobs by tailoring a resume and cover letter for each of them. Before you begin writing your drafts, research each company to learn about its mission, values, culture, and strengths. Let the information you find direct your writing strategies (e.g., the skills and experiences you choose to emphasize in your cover letter, the organization of your resume, and the tone and layout of your documents). Also, write a memo, addressed to me, providing information about the companies, the jobs, and your writing strategies. Think of your resumes and cover letters as "sales pitches" for yourself: always accentuate the positive, and do your best to present yourself as a memorable, interesting candidate.

"But that's a lie! Technically it's a lie, right?"

Jill raised her hand and blurted out this question when I called on her. The class was discussing job application documents at the time. I was describing various methods for downplaying less-than-impressive details in resumes: a dismissal from a job, a low grade point average, or even a criminal record. Jill wasn't sure that such strategies were ethical. Specifically, she thought that camouflaging her low grades might be unfair to the nonprofit organization to which she planned to apply for work. "They have a right to know so they can really make a fair decision who to hire," she said.

Later during that same class, Jill's friend Sean had questions as well:

> It's cool that there're all these ways to make yourself stand out in your cover letter, but if everyone uses the same ways, all the letters will just look the same again, won't they? I mean, what's the point of nonconforming if everyone's nonconforming the same way?

Sean's question could apply to situations far beyond the business writing classroom, to be sure, and the class murmured in agreement. "What *is* the point?" I wondered aloud. My students seemed about half satisfied with my improvised answer, which had something to do with the clear differences between individuals' employment histories and academic training. I recount this story here not to interrogate the nature of nonconformity, but to illustrate the much-overlooked ability of students to ask pointed questions about business practices and conventions. This ability is a central component of my thinking on possible changes to business writing instruction. Given claims presented in previous chapters of this book, my ideas for improving business writing curricula will probably come as no surprise. Ultimately, I feel that students, instructors, and even corporations could benefit from the introduction of "cultural studies of business" into business writing and communication programs. As noted in the introduction of this book, cultural studies of business entail examining the origins, mechanisms, and effects of business knowledge, discourse, and practice. Implementing cultural studies of business in the business writing or communication classroom, however, does not mean assuming that students—many of them soon to enter the corporate workforce—are woefully naïve about corporate cultures. Instead, I hope that instructors who teach business writing will do so not by simply following and replicating its conventions, and not through simply critiquing corporations and arrogantly assuming that students who "don't know better" must be led to some properly radical stance, but by committing themselves to sustained, skeptical engagement with the ever-changing discourses of business—and sustained, skeptical engagement with their own classroom and research practices.

How can such engagement(s) be incorporated into the business writing classroom? One possibility is mentioned in passing by Zaidee Green in her 1942 essay in *College English:* "The college course in business writing should, I think, be a course in which the student is motivated to collect and study business materials, to observe business policies and practices, to reflect upon improvements in the business communications which he studies" (742). What interests me most here is Green's use of the word "observe." Rather than simply telling students how workers at today's businesses are asked to write and communicate with each other, instructors could provide concrete examples, culled from their own workplace experiences or direct observations of workplaces, from the latest management books and journals, from case studies (as done in law schools), or from corporate websites, to provide a few options. Many business writing classes already collect and analyze business documents, from interoffice memos to resumes to sales reports; this practice provides opportunities to observe the workings of corporate discourses as well, as long as the contexts where such documents are composed and circulated are continually discussed. Also, students themselves could be tasked with observations of their own—"fieldwork" at their jobs or internships (or at the jobs or internships of friends and family). While ethnographic approaches to teaching and learning are not without drawbacks, an emphasis on observation (participant or otherwise) in business writing and communication courses could have multiple productive effects. This tactic—an improvement over authenticity-obsessed attempts to replicate business situations in the classroom—could teach students and instructors alike how particular documents function within particular contexts, from management structures to interpersonal dynamics between coworkers to market concerns. Seeing how the same document has different effects in different contexts demonstrates that conventions are never set in stone, that corporate values don't dictate worker (or manager) decisions in the same way every time.

By contrast, "teaching" business writing students to *critique* corporations would almost certainly be counterproductive. Some instructors might dream of teaching students exactly how to stick it to The Man, but consider how such dreams would pan out when these rebel students eventually enter the workforce. As noted in Chapter 2, corporate cultures that welcome dissent have a funny way of defusing its capacity for change, and corporate cultures that discourage dissent may well fire, demote, or simply ignore the dissenter. Gee, Hull, and Lankshear take a similarly dim view of the efficacy of dissent: "Genuine contestation is ultimately problematic in a business setting where, in the end, profit is the goal and the competition is at one's heels" (1996, xvi). Despite this pessimism, which sounds a bit wistful ("in a different world, dissent would work!"), Gee and his coauthors remain clearly committed to the idea that education can play some kind of role in preparing students for the workplace—a commitment that I share. The question is what kind of role is possible and worthwhile, and their answer has to do with fostering literacy—giving students practice in reading "social, institutional, and cultural relationships" (1). Realistically presenting hypothetical workplace situations and asking students to respond to them is one method of giving students such practice, but these artfully directed exercises may simply replicate conventions without showing how they work. A less problematic method is letting students see for themselves how social relationships and practices play out in offices or factories (or even in web-based, "virtual" workplaces). Some instructors already do this through service learning projects, which give students hands-on, participatory workplace experience. What students see will inevitably include a complex array of practices, some they might consider "good" and others they may consider "bad." The role of the instructor is to encourage students to look beyond these value judgments and "take apart" workplace practices (many of which are so naturalized as to seem inevitable) to see how they function in different contexts. The instructor must also remember to move beyond acts of judgment and critique.

As a business writing instructor, I hope to encourage the "corporate cultural literacy" that many of my students already possess, but I must do so with the knowledge that students will wield that literacy in a variety of ways; some will embrace their entry-level jobs wholeheartedly, while others will constantly request department meetings to discuss policy changes, while others will post confidential company documents on the web, just for revenge against despised employers. Some will use the business writing conventions they've observed to impress their supervisors, while others will use those conventions to persuade the CEO to rethink his decision to outsource the entire customer service division. In cultural studies of business based on observation and analysis, when a student responds with enthusiasm or disgust to corporate discourses, that response will be informed by some understanding of the reasons behind business writing conventions and the multiple contexts that affect those conventions, as discussed in the university classroom and observed firsthand.

Recently published textbooks suggest another potentially fruitful approach to incorporating sustained, skeptical engagement with business discourses into the undergraduate classroom—one that could easily fit with the cultural studies of business approach described above: a focus on ethics. Although it is unfortunate that many business communication programs needed the prod of Enron to induce them to include ethics within their curricula in the early 2000s, the growing presence of ethics in such programs (and of ethics classes in business schools) seems like a productive trend, providing another opportunity for students to practice "reading" workplace situations and practices. Kitty Locker argues that business writing instruction is more beneficial for students, instructors, and employers than technical writing instruction, precisely because of this emerging emphasis on ethics in business communication: "Chapters on ethics in technical communication texts rarely deal with the ways in which organizations create and enforce norms for language and actions" (2003, 124). Having used several business writing texts in the past, however, I am not convinced that the material on ethics is as nuanced as Locker claims—do business communication books really acknowledge how norms are "created" and "enforced"? From what I have observed, such books offer advice for behaving ethically and ask students to record their reactions to hypothetical workplace situations, but they do not acknowledge how corporate structures and power relations might affect ethical decisions, nor do they carefully examine how those relations and structures work. Locker writes that "many people who would not undertake dubious or illegal actions on their own will do so at the behest of... a culture that rewards or seems to demand such behavior. Organizations affect the way people act and interact, and business communication studies just these interactions" (130–131). I agree that business communication should study such things if it really wants to help students, but I don't think the field accomplishes this goal… yet. Business writing courses, while focusing—as many administrators and students wish—on pragmatic skills, should more fully incorporate another sort of pragmatic skill: close observation and analysis of everyday workplace practices and values (which are, after all, the forces driving the use of business writing conventions in the first place). In this book, I have endeavored to perform these kinds of observations and analyses of American corporate cultures, of individuality and conformity in the workplace, of flexibility as a popular business value, of corporate health discourses and policies, and of current notions of what business "progress" entails.

Gee, Hull, and Lankshear contend that "language is both an instrument *of* change and a target *for* change" (14). In the case of business writing, such an important factor in how corporate cultures are built, maintained, and circulated, this claim seems particularly true. If we concede that higher education is a kind of "training" to equip students for postgraduation life, that training ought to include practice examining the reasons why certain conventions and practices are in place and the various ways these conventions and practices work within different contexts. It is my hope that this book might serve as an example for future directions in research and teaching. To improve my classes (and to ease my own feelings of ambivalence about business writing instruction in general) I will incorporate such business studies into my courses. Will the task of implementing cultural studies of business in the classroom be easy? No. But, to borrow a phrase that business management gurus are fond of saying, a challenge is not a problem, but an opportunity.

CHAPTER 7

CORPORATE CULTURE
OUT OF CONTROL?

NOTES FROM AN ABANDONED WEBSITE

The company's website was clearly expensive to design, featuring artsy black-and-white photos and the latest in slick animations. Its colors—cashmere gray, mineral green, tangerine—immediately signal class, taste, and money to spare. But these eye-catching elements are little more than an elegant frame for an intriguing text, a seductive tale of workplace wonders. The company describes itself as a "thought leader," encouraging job applicants to "engage [their] passion" and welcoming employee creativity. Extensive training programs are spotlighted, programs for workers at any stage of their career, workers eager to excel: "We are committed to educating and developing our people." Some of the people in question appear in the "Profiles" section of the site, where pictures reveal well-coiffed 20- or 30-somethings in designer eyewear, confident employees who say things like "There is a tremendous sense of relentlessness and optimism for helping our clients win," and "the firm's senior bankers are exceptionally talented and experienced and provide you with a steep learning curve." The words of the profiled analysts, associates, and vice presidents bolster the company's overall message and mission: "We are One Firm, defined by our unwavering commitment to our clients, our shareholders, and each other. Our mission is to build unrivaled partnerships with and value for our clients, through the knowledge, creativity, and dedication of our people, leading to superior returns for our shareholders." When the corporation posted these words, it must have envisioned a sparkling future.[1]

Lehman Brothers, the financial services firm responsible for the corporate cultural rhetoric quoted and described above, filed for Chapter 11 bankruptcy on September 15, 2008. Lehman's bankruptcy was the largest in U.S. history up to that date, with a record debt of $613 billion against assets of $639 billion and more than 100,000 creditors. That same day, the value of Lehman shares dropped more than 90 percent. Thanks in part to Lehman's collapse, the Dow Jones Industrial Average suffered its steepest-ever drop, which in turn intensified an already-brewing global financial crisis.

Lehman, founded in 1850 and long known as a leader in investment banking and management, is gone now. Barclays PLC purchased its North American divisions, and Nomura Holdings, Inc., bought its Asian, European, and Middle Eastern divisions. The Lehman website still remains, a ghostly remnant of the company's glamorous, go-go days. Hints of the firm's fate—including a slapped-together homepage with news of the bankruptcy and information about their former subsidiaries—occasionally intrude on the haunting optimism of this Titanic of a site, seemingly fathoms-deep, littered with shattered crystal chandeliers and the slowly dulling gleam of pricey silverware. Exploring the wreckage, I cannot help but suspect that the corporate culture that Lehman celebrated not so long ago contributed to the company's bankruptcy and liquidation. As I conclude this study of corporate culture, I will address this issue, as well as a few related, broader questions. How did certain aspects or strands of corporate culture impact other struggling companies, thus playing a part in the financial crisis? Can corporate culture be used strategically to prevent future bankruptcies and bailouts? If so, how?

Much of Lehman's discourse about itself is forward looking, emphasizing the contribution of employees and managers to an ongoing culture of trust and success. Such an emphasis makes sense, given the ways in which publicizing corporate culture is a strategy used to attract job applicants, retain the workforce, and bolster firm morale. But this sense of optimism, accompanied by a focus on the future rather than the present, can have multiple effects, including a propensity among workers to downplay, or even ignore, problems in need of solving. For example, the practices eventually leading to Lehman's 2008 downfall had by then been in play for at least 13 years, according to the *Wall Street Journal*. In 1995, the firm sent one of its vice presidents, Eric Hibbert, to California, where he was charged with the task of investigating an intriguing business strategy being used by First Alliance Mortgage Company, subprime lending. Despite Hibbert's strongly worded report that First Alliance was a "sweatshop" encouraging unethical practices and taking advantage of "people in a weak state," Lehman senior management opted to lend the California company "roughly $500 million and helped sell more than $700 million in bonds backed by First Alliance customers' loans" (Hudson 2007). In this way, Lehman pioneered a type of securitization, "taking over individual mortgage loans and packaging them as high-interest paying investment vehicles for Wall Street" (Ross 2008). After the Federal Trade Commission deemed its lending practices illegal in 2002, First Alliance went out of business, but Lehman Brothers continued to ride high on the profits of securitization until vast numbers of loans began to go into default; this subprime mortgage crisis is one of the major factors contributing to the global economic insecurity of 2008.

Yet, though Lehman had been involved in subprime lending for over a decade, it seems that Lehman's collapse took its staff by surprise. Also, voices of dissent, like Eric Hibbert's, seem exceedingly rare in the discourses surrounding Lehman's failure. Interviews with former Lehman employees confirm these observations. When interviewed for the *Daily Princetonian* just after the bankruptcy was announced, Anita Gupta commented that the mood around the Lehman offices had been upbeat until the very end: "Over the summer, people were really confident... People here have always been committed regardless of the economy, but it was very different. It was great" (qtd. in Wolff 2008). One senior vice president specifically noted the dramatic differences between senior managers' continued, confident focus on corporate strength and the alarming signals sent by the stock market (Wolff 2008).

The firm's strong corporate culture is one possible reason for these anomalies. The insistence on trust and confidence, repeated many times within Lehman Brothers' descriptions of itself, helped to prevent employees from acknowledging the firm's less ethical practices and noticing the signs of impending disaster. More frightening still is the fact that the firm's culture may have actively discouraged whistleblowers from airing their concerns; prior to the bankruptcy, the *Wall Street Journal* found some ex-Lehman employees who claimed that Lehman Brothers "retaliated against workers who complained about fraud" (Hudson 2007). In response to this allegation, Lehman argued that "most of [these employees] never raised concerns during their tenures at Lehman lending units, even though that was a requirement of their jobs," and the *Wall Street Journal* also found Lehman employees who claimed to have no knowledge of the developing problems (Hudson 2007). If Lehman's official statement on the matter is accurate, why didn't the employees speak up, and why were other employees seemingly unaware of the firm's lapses—lapses that seem obvious now? Perhaps because the culture discouraged questions that imply distrust and lack of confidence.

Though Lehman's culture may not have explicitly advocated risk taking, the comforting reminders of trustworthiness may well have served to make even upper-level managers complacent about problematic business practices. For example, the senior vice president interviewed in the *Princetonian* article said that "he did not blame the senior management for the decisions that led to Lehman's bankruptcy because those decisions did not seem imprudent to him at the time they were made" (Wolff 2008). Indeed, some Lehman spokespeople, as late as 2007, were still proudly trumpeting the firm's role in popularizing the practice of securitization, because (in their view) the practice nobly helped people who otherwise would not have been able to afford a home (Hudson 2007). As noted in this book's introduction, corporations typically are what they say they are, and I am not suggesting here that the concept of "corporate culture" is used as a ruse to hoodwink unsuspecting employees into following orders and buying into business policies without question. Instead, because corporate culture is a set of values and practices that shape the environment in which people work, a culture emphasizing trust and confidence in one's "team" also encourages faith that the team (including its leaders) is doing the right thing. In other words, the Lehman culture was genuinely a culture of trust, with employees trusting each other to act in ways that would ultimately benefit the company, its clients, and its shareholders. Sadly, by emphasizing future profit (and progress, as described in Chapter 5) rather than studying and reflecting on policies and practices, the culture also helped to doom Lehman Brothers.

Some of the firms most shaken by the 2008 financial crisis, such as Merrill Lynch and Citigroup, have (or had) corporate cultures similar to that of Lehman Brothers. Merrill Lynch, acquired by Bank of America in September 2008, claims to have an "open, collaborative" culture, while Citigroup publicizes its commitment to communicating with employees about management strategies and decisions, thus making them feel empowered. (Cassano 2008; Citigroup 2007). Some corporate cultures, however, were (and are) more overt in their endorsement of risk-taking behavior. Consider the case of one of the world's largest insurance companies, American International Group (AIG). As loan defaults on subprime mortgages piled up, AIG announced significant financial losses, which in turn led credit rating agencies to lower AIG's rating. This downgrading meant that the company was considered high risk for defaulting on loans—a development that deflated AIG's stock prices. After trying in vain to secure a loan, AIG went to the U.S. government for assistance. AIG's heavy involvement in subprime lending, which led to its collapse, is obviously not unique, but the practice dovetails quite smoothly with the company's rhetoric about itself. As a leader in the risk management industry, AIG inevitably mentions risk in its publicity, but does so in such a way that the company seems to embrace, or even celebrate, the necessity of confronting risk. A particularly telling statement on AIG's "Vision and Values" website applauds employees who take initiative: "Entrepreneurship is about continuous improvement, and success-fully managing change. Entrepreneurs champion new initiatives with energy and urgency. They act decisively without complete informa-tion" (AIG 2008). Another description of AIG's entrepreneurship echoes the "individuality" theme discussed in Chapter 2; the firm wants to "encourage innovation and creative problem solving" and "leverage the power of each employee acting like an owner of the firm every day" (AIG 2008). A corporate culture that consistently advo-cates speedy decision making and constant striving for future success may not encourage taking time to reflect, implementing or heeding institutional checkpoints, or avoiding choices motivated solely by the desire for immediate profits. While statements like those found on AIG's website cannot fully explain the problematic business decisions eventually leading to AIG's bankruptcy, they do strongly suggest that corporate culture is far more than an empty buzz-phrase.

With many once-proud firms and industries struggling—and some even begging the U.S. government for help, despite the busi-ness world's usual tendency to champion free market, laissez-faire ideology—the "survival" theme explored in Chapter 3 is taking on new importance. One afternoon, in September 2008, I happened to glance at the front page of the *New York Times* Sunday Styles section, and suddenly I felt like I was reliving a moment from my past. The lead article's headline, "Dim Lights, Big City: Cast in 'Survivor,' the Wall Street Edition," echoed the Sunday Styles piece that had helped to instigate my Chapter 3 investigation of Darwinian discourse in the workplace. While John Schwartz's 2001 article focused on the bursting of the dot-com bubble, Alex Williams's article focuses on the aftershocks of "seismic disruptions" in the world of high finance. Williams posits a shift in the circumstances of bank workers—more layoffs and regulation, lower salaries and bonuses—but also describes a change in corporate cultures: in light of the financial crisis, we will see "a more subdued Wall Street, one where professionals make a comfortable living but where the enormous payouts and outrageous bravado have faded" (Williams 1977, 8). Given the serious consequences of Wall Street bravado, such a change sounds welcome, especially as the article turns to dark depictions of pre-crisis, kill-or-be-killed firms where "young traders and bankers were willing to endure punishing workweeks for huge pay down the road" (8). As the promised bonuses and salaries dwindle, freshly minted MBAs and seasoned employees alike are looking elsewhere for work, and Williams links this development to the possibility of a kinder, gentler financial sector. But the intense quest for success is also being reconfigured as a struggle for "survival" as rounds of layoffs shrink staffs: more applicants for fewer jobs in all sectors, increasing competition to keep existing jobs, and so forth. Even those who remain employed are adrift and nervous as the world of investment banking vanishes; as the *Wall Street Journal's* Dennis Berman reports, "Yes, there are tens of thousands of people still with jobs. They just don't have much work. Debt and stock markets are virtually shut, merger volume is down by 28%, and whole lines of structured finance are closed for good" (2008).

This "survival" discourse extends beyond high finance, just as the impact of investment banks collapsing extends beyond Wall Street. Advice columns instructing readers to stay constantly alert, flexible, and competitive in a high-stress corporate environment (much like the books described in Chapter 3) are especially common since September 2008. An October 2008 *Business Week* column, part of the magazine's "Recession Survival Guide," notes that "the workplace will become increasingly Darwinian" and cautions readers that "team leaders will be watching everyone a lot more closely than before" (Conlin 2008). The column also warns that employees should not succumb to the temptation to duck for cover; instead, they should prove their value by looking for ways to help workplaces struggling through troubled times. The process of proving one's value while companies look to reduce staff is a daunting challenge, however; *Business Week* advocates remaining unflappably upbeat (even in the face of upsetting circumstances) and being "tireless" in the pursuit of sales, new clients, and the like (Conlin 2008). Meanwhile, the *Wall Street Journal's* "careers" section, normally optimistic in tone, has been featuring dour headlines about looking for work in a tough economy. One article recommends that job applicants demonstrate that they are "flexible and not fussy" in order to impress interviewers (Needleman 2008). In an interview with *U.S. News and World Report,* executive search firm president Stephen Viscusi, who wrote *Bulletproof Your Job: 4 Simple Strategies to Ride Out the Tough Times and Come Out on Top at Work,* claims that employees wishing to stay employed should avoid being "high-maintenance" and notes that people who stay later than the boss without complaining are likeliest to survive rounds of layoffs: "Bosses seem to love people who love the company. They want you to 'drink the Kool-Aid.'" (qtd. in Wolgemuth 2008). Taken together, these pieces of career advice strongly suggest that now is a particularly good time for workers to swallow any doubts they might have about their employers, stay ever vigilant, and commit themselves to being adaptable to any and all circumstances.

The "survival" discourse also goes beyond the question of employment. President Obama once hopefully described the financial crisis as an opportunity for corporate America to become "leaner and meaner," but—if his prediction comes true—I wonder how this leanness and meanness might impact the work-life, diversity, and health programming examined in chapters 2 and 4, all of these ways in which corporate cultural values are put into practice (Bellantoni 2008). Can such programs survive? As of this writing, companies do still seem committed to such programs, despite cutbacks. The companies discussed as examples in chapters 2 and 4 continue to advertise policies aimed at improving employees' work-life balance and wellness as well as programs meant to foster a diverse, inclusive workplace environment. As of this writing, Ford is requesting financial assistance from the U.S. government, but it has nonetheless retained its many employee resource groups and benefits for working parents (Ford 2002). An example mentioned in Chapter 4, Johnson & Johnson, still has extensive health and wellness programs for employees and their families, including counseling, "on-site fitness centers, personal training, and exercise classes" (Johnson & Johnson 2008). The websites of corporations directly involved in the 2008 financial meltdown, such as Ford, General Motors, Chrysler, and AIG, all describe these firms' ongoing diversity initiatives.[2] Corporate culture may well escape a recession relatively unscathed. Firms will continue to look for ways to cultivate a sense of community belonging amongst workers and managers. Doing so will continue to benefit the bottom line by attracting top applicants, retaining staff (avoiding hiring and training costs), and, most importantly, inspiring employees to contribute as much time and effort as possible to the company.

As I have argued throughout this book, the cultures of individual corporations are powerful influences on employees and managers alike, but the power of culture extends beyond a single organization's offices. In Chapter 1, I alluded to Doug Henwood's ideas about the "macro-effects" of the economy: while the market can dictate the policies and decisions of specific companies and managers, it can also influence the business environment in general—mass layoffs at one high-profile firm may cause employees at other firms to work longer and harder because they, too, fear layoffs. Similarly, when one corporation profits via risk-taking strategies like extending mortgages to people without the resources to pay their bills, other corporations are likely to follow suit, because they are also driven by a desire for profit and/or because they need to stay competitive. This phenomenon may explain one mystifying fact of the financial crisis: a *lot* of banks engaged in sub-prime lending—a practice which, in hindsight, seems an obvious invitation to trouble.

Some corporate cultures, including those of Nomura Holdings and Barclays Capital (which each bought divisions of the now-defunct Lehman Brothers), suggest a somewhat more sustainable model that might help to protect firms from ethical blunders and poor decisions like sub-prime lending. Nomura, based in Japan, describes its workplace structure as open, with transparent strategies and policies: "We take a positive approach, communicating messages from management and important decisions to the entire staff through our intranet and in-house magazine" (Nomura 2008). Barclays, based in the United Kingdom, claims that it "applies an intellectual rigour to its strategy and day-to-day management, questioning each decision on the basis of its value to clients and shareholders" (Barclays 2008). The "Our Culture" section of the Barclays website also states, "We acknowledge mistakes and encourage constructive disagreement. In everything we do, we focus on the processes and controls to protect the Barclays brand and our shareholders" (Barclays 2008). There are several unusual words and phrases worth noting here. First, while "communication" is often mentioned in corporate culture descriptions—a buzzword, often signifying opportunities for even entry-level employees to express ideas to management—Nomura's emphasis on top-down communication is less common. Second, while many corporations are eager to trumpet their creativity and innovation (as seen in Chapter 2), Barclays' references to the careful use of intellect are relatively rare. Finally, direct references to mistakes and checkpoints in the decision-making process are quite rare indeed, especially given the fact that descriptions of corporate culture are often used as advertising to job applicants.

There are some mitigating factors and concerns to keep in mind when examining these slight anomalies, though. Neither Nomura nor Barclays is a U.S.-based firm, and while many of the corporations discussed in this book are transnational, the "national headquarters" may well impact corporate cultural discourse; as Andrew Ross has argued, the phenomenon of "corporate culture" is often seen as peculiarly American (2003, 120). More importantly, just as corporate culture can be used as a strategy to improve a corporation's bottom line through attracting and retaining enthusiastic employees, it can also be used, abused, or ignored in the service of the profit motive or in the drive for so-called progress as defined in Chapter 5. For example, Nomura stays true to its promise of clear, top-down communication by announcing an embarrassing disclosure on the front page of its website. But this disclosure—the fact that the company risked 27.5 billion yen in its dealings with former chairman of the Nasdaq stock market Bernard Madoff, arrested in December 2008 for running a $50 billion Ponzi scheme—stands as suggestive evidence that companies will continue to be involved in problematic practices, even when they promise trustworthiness and transparency. Similarly, Lehman Brothers, even when engaged in sub-prime lending, described itself as a paragon of ethical, careful strategizing. One of the more disturbing aspects of this phenomenon is that—as noted in Chapter 2 and elsewhere—companies' descriptions of their cultures are, often, remarkably similar to each other. Plenty of corporations claim to be cultures of trust, oriented toward future progress, celebrating independent decision making at every turn. Which of these corporations might be next to crumble?

Despite the problems I have enumerated in these pages, the phenomenon of corporate culture may still represent an opportunity for significant changes in the business world and beyond. After all, culture is more than a buzzword; it has a significant impact on company policy and worker conduct. Since corporate culture has from the start been primarily a series of managerial directives rather than organically grown values and practices, management, if it cares enough to do so, can use it strategically to help protect companies from hurried, unreflective decisions; ethical lapses; and other problems potentially leading to lawsuits, financial losses, bankruptcies, and wider economic instability. Joel Bakan, in *The Corporation: The Pathological Pursuit of Profit and Power* (2004), argues that all privately held, publicly traded companies—even those most devoted to being worker friendly or "green" or creative or flexible—ultimately exist for one reason alone: to benefit shareholders—in other words, to make money. In Bakan's view, corporate culture can never be as important a priority as the profit motive. While this argument is persuasive, I wonder if increasing numbers of managers might find ways in which ethical cultures and profit-making strategies are ultimately aligned. In the short term, sub-prime lending (and the competitive culture fostering the practice) did improve the bottom line, but in the longer term, the strategy and the culture colluded to bankrupt a 158-year-old firm. In light of these kinds of findings, and at the risk of sounding like a business advice book, I contend that culture really can make a difference. What kind of difference—an improvement or a deepening crisis—remains to be seen. As such, I hope that the future will bring not only more ethical cultures, but also greater numbers of scholars to remain vigilant about the manifestations and effects of corporate culture.

NOTES

CHAPTER 1

1. Even if its popular usage is not limited to American companies and management gurus, I suspect that the concept of corporate culture is strongly associated with the U.S. context. For example, according to Andrew Ross, workers he interviewed at the London office of Razorfish were prone to "exercise some native skepticism about the company culture, which they tended to view as a product of American business schtick" (Ross, *No-Collar: The Humane Workplace and Its Hidden Costs* [New York: Basic Books, 2003], 120). Also, corporate culture-based approaches have occasionally been applied to nonprofit organizations—see management guru Peter Drucker's *Managing the Non-Profit Organization: Principles and Practices* (New York: HarperBusiness, 1992).
2. Alexandra Moses, "Workplace Wellness: From Yoga to Walking, Employers Finding Ways to Encourage Good Health," *Centre Daily Times*, April 28, 2002.
3. Bill Readings, *The University in Ruins* (Cambridge: Harvard University Press, 1996).
4. The plethora of similar-yet-not-quite-alike definitions of corporate culture reminds me of Doug Henwood's opinion of the overused word "globalization," which he calls "a pretty spongy concept... it's rarely defined explicitly; everyone is expected to know what it means" (Henwood, *After the New Economy* [London and New York: The New Press, 2003], 145).
5. This emphasis on ethics seems more than slightly disingenuous, given *Business Week's* unabashed celebration of Enron and other now-disgraced companies during the bubble years of the 1990s. Indeed, as the editorial staff of the *Baffler* remind us, "Thanks to advertising pressure and conglomerate ownership, business journalism—the institution that bore primary responsibility for warning of the impending disaster—became so deeply committed to business ideology that it often read more like stock-selling than stock-taking" (Thomas Frank, Greg Lane, David Mulcahey, and Emily Vogt, "This Car Climbed Mount Nasdaq," in *Boob Jubilee: The Cultural Politics of the New Economy,* eds. Thomas Frank and David Mulcahey [New York and London: W. W. Norton, 2003], 6).

These same *Baffler* writers attribute the magnitude of the so-called New Economy's various disasters to the blunting of criticism by corporate ownership and political conservatism: "Financial abuses… are not some random misfortune resolved by a few mea culpas; they are systemic. They are what happens when we let our guard down" (7).

6. Frederick Taylor's work will be discussed in more detail in Chapter 2.

7. Here is Taylor on "systematic soldiering":

> This man deliberately plans to do as little as he safely can—to turn out far less work than he is well able to do—in many instances to do not more than one-third to one-half of a proper day's work. And in fact if he were to do his best to turn out his largest possible day's work, he would be abused by his fellow-workers for so doing, even more than if he had proved himself a "quitter" in sport. Underworking, that is, deliberately working slowly so as to avoid doing a full day's work, "soldiering," as it is called in [the United States], "hanging it out," as it is called in England, "ca canae," as it is called in Scotland, is almost universal in industrial establishments, and prevails also to a large extent in the building trades; and the writer asserts without fear of contradiction that this constitutes the greatest evil with which the working-people of both England and America are now afflicted. (Taylor, *The Principles of Scientific Management* [New York: Norton, 1967], 23)

8. Jay M. Shafritz and J. Steven Ott contend that another school emerged during the 1930s—a "Neoclassical Organization Theory" school including such authors as Herbert A. Simon, Talcott Parsons, and James G. March. This school distinguished itself from the Classical School in two ways: an increased emphasis on empirical data and a sociology-based perspective on management that acknowledged the crucial role of environment on organizations.

9. Despite multiple and serious objections to it, scientific management isn't dead yet. As Andrew Ross notes, the 1972 strike at the General Motors Lordstown plant was initially prompted by "resentment of GM time-study inspectors" and speedup on the assembly line (Ross, *No-Collar,* 6). Eric Schlosser's best-selling indictment of McDonald's and other restaurants chains, *Fast Food Nation: The Dark Side of the All-American Meal* (Boston and New York: Houghton Mifflin, 2001), amply demonstrates the ongoing use of scientific management techniques at American meat-packing plants.

10. Some mid-twentieth century organization theorists, notably Douglas McGregor, lamented the naïveté of some management strategies based on Human Relations theory, but also acknowledged the profound effects of Mayo's original findings on manager-worker

relations. McGregor was particularly concerned about management becoming too lenient and coddling workers too much:

> We have now discovered that there is no answer in the simple removal of control—that abdication is not a workable alternative to authoritarianism. We have learned that there is no direct correlation between employee satisfaction and productivity. We recognize today that "industrial democracy" cannot consist in permitting everyone to decide everything, that industrial health does not flow automatically from the elimination of dissatisfaction, disagreement, or even open conflict. (McGregor, *The Human Side of Enterprise* [New York: McGraw-Hill Book Company, 1960], 46)

11. The Nietzsche quotation used by Peters and Waterman originally appeared in the "Maxims and Arrows" chapter of *Twilight of the Idols* and has also been translated as follows: "If we possess our why of life we can put up with almost any how" (Friedrich Nietzsche, *Twilight of the Idols and The Anti-Christ: Or How to Philosophize with a Hammer* [New York: Penguin Classics, 1990], 33.

12. Systems theory—specifically, its famous precursor, Norbert Wiener's *Cybernetics* (1948)—is examined in Chapter 3. Currently available as Wiener, *Cybernetics, Second Edition: Or Control and Communication in the Animal and in the Machine* (Cambridge: The MIT Press, 1965).

13. Stanley Davis, author of *Managing Corporate Culture* (Cambridge, MA: Ballinger, 1984), claims to have coined the term "corporate culture" circa 1970 (Avery Gordon, "The Work of Corporate Culture: Diversity Management." *Social Text* 44, no. 13.3 [Fall/Winter 1995]: 6).

14. Arlie Hochschild, *The Commercialization of Intimate Life: Notes from Home and Work* (Berkeley and London: University of California Press, 2003), describes the formation of corporate culture using terms that underscore management's control of the process: "In certain sectors of the economy cultural engineers are busy adding ritual to work" (204).

15. As Henwood notes in his work on the so-called New Economy, the idea of measuring productivity (and making business decisions based on that measurement) is problematic in and of itself. He argues that commonly used statistical indicators of productivity can be misleading and inaccurate and that the link between productivity and greater profits is not definitive. Andrew Ross specifically addresses Deal and Kennedy's multiple references to productivity: "[They] provided a widely cited estimate (on the basis, apparently, of zero research or evidence) that a firm with a strong culture can 'gain as much as one or two hours of productive work per employee per day'" (Ross, *No-Collar*, 102). Regardless of the veracity of Deal and Kennedy's claim

or the accuracy of productivity statistics, lots of people bought *Corporate Cultures*, and it's likely that lots of people based their business decisions on it.

16. Multiple versions of this idea appear in Foucault's work. Here are two specific examples:

> When you have thus formed the chain of ideas in the heads of your citizens, you will then be able to pride yourselves on guiding them and being their masters. A stupid despot may constrain his slaves with iron chains, but a true politician binds them even more strongly by the chain of their own ideas... this link is all the stronger in that we do not know of what it is made and we believe it to be our own work. (Michel Foucault, *Discipline and Punish: The Birth of the Prison*, trans. Alan Sheridan [New York: Vintage Books, 1991], 102–103)
>
> One had to speak of sex... one had to speak of it as a thing to be not simply condemned or tolerated but managed, inserted into systems of utility, regulated for the greater good of all, made to function according to an optimum. Sex was not something one simply judged; it was a thing one administered. (Michel Foucault, *The History of Sexuality: An Introduction, Volume I*, trans. Robert Hurley [New York: Vintage Books, 1990], 24)

17. This idea will be discussed in more detail in Chapter 5.

18. I can only hope that this reference to trains running on time, so strongly associated with unnerving images of Nazism, was used innocently or in error.

19. Ross, *No-Collar*, 102.

20. Tony Bennett, in *Culture: A Reformer's Science* (London: Sage, 1998), describes the debate as being between academics who want to intervene in matters of policy (political, corporate, medical, etc.) and those who prefer to remain within the realms of theory and criticism. He has suggested that this binary is far too polarized, but is nonetheless often invoked within cultural studies.

21. The International Labor Organization reports that Americans put in longer work hours than any other industrialized nation. Americans work two weeks more per year than the Japanese, who are frequently stereotyped for their intense devotion to work (Hochschild, *Commercialization of Intimate Life*, 145).

22. Additional justification for including a novel among the sources used in this book appears in Chapter 5.

23. The application of cultural studies of business to classroom practices will be taken up again in Chapter 6.

24. Indeed, it would be difficult to argue that these allegations are not true; yet, people from politicians to pundits to paper pushers do so every day.

CHAPTER 2

1. Theodor Adorno and Max Horkheimer, "The Culture Industry: Enlightenment as Mass Deception." *Dialectic of Enlightenment*, trans. John Cumming (New York: Continuum, 1994), 123.
2. This aggressively ungrammatical phrase was a popular advertising slogan introduced by Apple Computers in 1997. The print ads featured arty black-and-white photographs of various well-known "free thinkers" (an eclectic group including Mahatma Gandhi, Miles Davis, Amelia Earhart, Cesar Chavez, and Bob Dylan) emblazoned with the message, "think different." The television commercial that jump-started the campaign featured the following voice-over, performed by Richard Dreyfuss: "Here's to the crazy ones. The misfits. The rebels. The troublemakers. The round pegs in the square holes. The ones who see things differently. They're not fond of rules. And they have no respect for the status quo. You can praise them, disagree with them, quote them, disbelieve them, glorify or vilify them. About the only thing you can't do is ignore them. Because they change things. They invent. They imagine. They heal. They explore. They create. They inspire. They push the human race forward. Maybe they have to be crazy. How else can you stare at an empty canvas and see a work of art? Or sit in silence and hear a song that's never been written? Or gaze at a red planet and see a laboratory on wheels? We make tools for these kinds of people. While some see them as the crazy ones, we see genius. Because the people who are crazy enough to think they can change the world, are the ones who do" (http://web.archive.org/web/20010228171255/http://www.apple.com/thinkdifferent/). Possibly, Apple's grammatical error was meant to be seen as an act of rebellion against the oppressive standards of English syntax.
3. The direct quotations in this paragraph are from, in order, the official corporate websites of Accenture (www.accenture.com), Exxon Mobil (www.exxonmobil.com), Fannie Mae (www.fanniemae.com), and the Altria Group (www.altria.com). Please look for these company names in the references for more specific web addresses.
4. This is not to say that brutally and violently repressive tactics never exist in any context—some nations, religious groups, and sweatshops thrive on them.
5. In a later section of this chapter, I will briefly return to the central roles of nonconformity and individualism in consumerism and advertising.
6. The volatility of business in the past decade is also a concern of John Grahl, who, in "Globalized Finance," *New Left Review*, no. 8 (March–April 2001), offers a very different interpretation of individuality in the workplace: despite lip service to the importance of employees' individual self-expression, another business model has supplanted "voice-based" management. Basing his article on economist Albert

Hirschman's *Exit, Voice, and Loyalty: Responses to Decline in Firms, Organizations, and States* (Cambridge and London: Harvard University Press, 1970), Grahl argues that the "voice" model—which entails long-term relationships between business partners; community embeddedness; loyalty; and "close, individual knowledge" of all participants in transactions—is becoming obsolete (3). Global finance today, Grahl notes, can be better characterized as operating according to an "exit-based" approach, which "controls economic relations by the threat of departure" (3). One example of "exit" could be selling shares in a corporation or selling off one's ownership of a company (a strategy often utilized just before the profits of a particular company or industry bottom out). These two models configure corporate individuality in very different ways. The voice model retains a sense that individual input is indeed significant—to the workings of a company or economy, but in the exit model—which, as Grahl points out, is dominant today—individualism still matters, but only insofar as self-interested decisions affect the big picture. In Grahl's view, believing in the power of one's individual voice becomes a kind of nostalgic romanticism: voice gets you nowhere in today's market, but exit—letting go of your loyalties, ties, and embeddedness—is what makes profits.

7. For an account of the psychological effects of downsizing on out-of-work executives and their families, see Jonathan Mahler's excellent report, "Commute to Nowhere," *New York Times Magazine*, April 13, 2003.

8. Evan Watkins, "Introduction." *Social Text* 44, no. 13:3 (1995): 2–3.

9. In *The One Best Way: Frederick Winslow Taylor and the Enigma of Efficiency* (New York: Viking, 1997), Robert Kanigel provides an extremely detailed account of the development of scientific management.

10. An interesting aside: the term "scientific management" was coined by former Supreme Court justice Louis T. Brandeis. He was an associate of Taylor's and appeared before the Interstate Commerce Commission to testify against American railroad companies that were threatening to raise their rates. Brandeis said that the railroads could save "a million dollars a day" by applying Taylor's ideas to their everyday operations (Jay M. Shafritz and J. Steven Ott, eds., *Classics of Organization Theory*, 2nd ed. [Chicago: The Dorsey Press, 1987], 11).

11. Kanigel, *One Best Way*, 444–449.

12. Critiques of Taylor's work and of management strategies based on it still appear, notably in Tom Peters's writings.

13. Elton Mayo (1880–1949) is best known for his involvement in the Hawthorne Studies on worker motivation and loyalty; as I will suggest, his Human Relations theory strongly influenced later management theory.

14. Mayo acknowledges that his ideal of friendly management is based in part on direct surveillance of workers (and workers' subsequent inter-

nalization of the all-seeing supervisor's eye)—a tactic that does not seem very "humanistic" on the face of things (Mayo, *The Human Problems of an Industrial Civilization* [New York: Macmillan, 1933], 77).

15. Whyte suggests that the supplanting of the Protestant Ethic by the Social Ethic actually began in the late nineteenth century. Despite the emphasis on individual success through competitiveness and diligence in the popular culture of that era (exemplified by the stories of Horatio Alger), corporate structures even then did not necessarily reward the hardest-working employees or managers. Instead, the system often prized bureaucrats with smooth social skills or people with prominent social connections. In Chapter 3, I will briefly return to this twist on the "survival of the fittest" model in the business world. Also, Whyte notes that late nineteenth- and early twentieth-century marketers, eager to spur American consumerism, worked relentlessly to downplay the element of thrift central to the traditional Protestant Ethic, thus contributing to an overall weakening of that Ethic's influence (William H. Whyte, *The Organization Man* [New York: Simon and Schuster, 1956]).

16. In a tentative gesture toward this idea, Whyte notes that the "talking cure" aspect of Human Relations was borrowed from the tenets of psychotherapy and argues that the problems workers described to management were frequently attributed to personal, inner conflicts, rather than to actual issues in the workplace (Ibid.).

17. In *Dilemmas of the American Self* (Philadelphia: Temple University Press, 1989), sociologist John P. Hewitt offers a detailed account of this misreading of Riesman. Hewitt also argues that a similar misreading took place when Christopher Lasch's *The Culture of Narcissism: American Life in an Age of Diminishing Expectations* (New York: W. W. Norton, 1979) became surprisingly popular in the 1970s.

18. *The Man in the Gray Flannel Suit* (New York: Simon and Schuster, 1955) reached number five on the *Publisher's Weekly* Best Seller List for 1955 (Cader Books 2002).

19. Thomas Frank argues that because *The Lonely Crowd, The Organization Man, and The Man in the Gray Flannel Suit* were so influential, there really were not many "conformists" during the 1950s—they had all been forewarned. John P. Hewitt makes a similar point, which also acknowledges the widespread misreading of Riesman's ideas: "The paradox lies in the fact that Americans of the 1950s, who were supposedly becoming other-directed, were alarmed by the prospect and took up the cry against the dangers of conformity by purchasing and talking about a book that could easily have been read as a sympathetic description of the other-directed character" (Hewitt, *Dilemmas of the American Self* [Philadelphia: Temple University Press, 1989], 38).

20. As Hewitt points out, the humanistic, client-centered psychology of the 1970s, exemplified by the work of Carl Rogers and Abraham

Maslow, also contributed to a sense that one's everyday activities were part of a self-actualization process (Ibid., 40).

21. Henry Ford and Samuel Crowther, *My Life and Work* (Garden City, NY: Garden City Publishing Company, 1922).

22. Many companies, such as Accenture and Deloitte, carefully phrase their policies so that they do not seem specifically and solely tailored for parents. Deloitte's human resources website refers to employees who take time off from work to write novels, do volunteer work, or compete in sporting events.

23. Diane Lewis, "More Bang, No Bucks: GOP Battles Labor on Overtime." *Intelligencer Journal Business Monday* (March 31, 2002): 2+.

24. The word "solution" has another meaning in business lingo as well. "Solutions" is a popular marketing term implying a bundling of products and services. In the case of Bright Horizons Family Solutions, those products and services are the education and care that children need on a daily basis and the assistance that parents need so that they can work. Whether education should be considered a "product" and care should be considered a "service" is an issue for another study.

25. Business journalists report that many corporations have returned to formal dress, including on Fridays. They attribute the change to a variety of developments, including the shaky economy, the increased competition for available jobs, the bankruptcy of many dot-com companies (known for their lack of office formality), and the somber national mood that followed September 11, 2001.

26. As might be expected, despite lip service to the importance of ethical business conduct, serious repercussions remain for the whistle-blower: lawsuits or countersuits from employers and former employers, discrimination, and difficulty getting jobs. The title of a newspaper article on this topic says it all: "Blowing the Whistle at Work: Heroic or Dumb?"

27. Michael Hardt and Antonio Negri argue that "diversity management" played a role in American business practices long before the term was coined. In the nineteenth century, when the immigrant work force expanded, "Bosses... did not shy away from bringing together this potentially explosive mix of workers... The linguistic, cultural, and ethnic differences within each work force were stabilizing because they could be used as a weapon to combat worker organization" (Hardt and Negri, *Empire* [Cambridge, MA, and London: Harvard University Press, 2000], 200). They go on to point out that "difference" was a key strategic factor in this practice—maintaining the separation between different ethnic groups within the work force was precisely the way to discourage unionization.

28. I did not find any books about what Andrew Ross describes as the "silicon ceiling"—"the older, higher-priced information workers were being filtered out in favor of young blood or overseas labor. Recruiting

for 'diversity' had become a code word for hiring much cheaper Asian employees on the H1-B visa track" (Ross, *No-Collar: The Humane Workplace and Its Hidden Costs* [New York: Basic Books, 2003], 203).

29. Many companies use this exact phrase: "leveraging diversity." It can be found, for example, in the websites of AT&T, Ford, and Microsoft.

30. John A Byrne, Louis Lavelle, Nanette Byrnes, Marcia Vickers, and Amy Borrus, "How to Fix Corporate Governance." *Business Week,* May 6, 2002, 69–78.

31. Patrick McGeehan, "Executive Pay: A Special Report—Again, Money Follows the Pinstripes." *New York Times,* April 6, 2003.

CHAPTER 3

1. These Walt Disney and Ray Kroc comments were unearthed by Eric Schlosser in *Fast Food Nation : The Dark Side of the All-American Meal* (Boston and New York: Houghton Mifflin, 2001), 37.

2. Cader Books, *"Publisher's Weekly* Bestseller Lists 1900–1995." *Caderbooks.com.* 2002, http://www.caderbooks.com/best80.html (accessed on Nov. 26, 2008).

3. The links between Foucault's work and self-help discourses—both within and outside the business realm—have been usefully traced by Heidi Marie Rimke, "Governing Citizens through Self-Help Literature." *Cultural Studies* 14:1 (2000): 61–78, and Nikolas Rose, *Inventing Our Selves: Psychology, Power and Personhood* (New York: Cambridge University Press, 1996), and *Powers of Freedom: Reframing Political Thought* (New York: Cambridge University Press, 1999). Also, Alan McKinlay and Ken Starkey's edited essay collection, *Foucault, Management and Organization Theory: From Panopticon to Technologies of Self* (London: Sage Publications, 1998), provides important perspectives on these links from business, economics, and management scholars.

4. It is important to underscore here Deleuze's insistence on the coexistence of discipline and control models of power. For example, the American corporate offices of a transnational company like Nike may exhibit many of the tendencies described by Deleuze in his essay, but the people who provide Nike's outsourced sweatshop labor may (and often do) live under a discipline-oriented management regime. Physical, factory-based, and just-plain-unglamorous labor is too often ignored by business writers and management gurus. As Doug Henwood notes in his discussion of George Gilder's work, Gilder celebrates New Economy knowledge workers and their lifestyles, but overlooks "the teenage women going blind from soldering circuits in the Philippines, the low-wage workers packed six to a room in the Silicon Valley, the reporters and data-entry clerks paralyzed by

repetitive strain injury" (Henwood, *After the New Economy* [London and New York: New Press, 2003], 11).

5. Heidi Marie Rimke argues that self-help texts about relationships—notably the well-known phenomenon of codependency—demonstrate that "the self-help genre presents individual 'development' and 'personal growth' as a free moral and ethical decision... Individuals are rendered entirely responsible for their failures as well as their successes, their despair as well as their happiness" (Rimke, "Governing Citizens," 63).

6. Whether or not business writers use Darwinian imagery in an "accurate" manner is not my primary concern here, except in one important respect: the way corporate culture tends to focus on individually willed survival rather than species survival. This chapter is not a science studies approach to evolution and business practices, and I am not a Darwin scholar. I am more interested in how Darwinian ideas and images get taken up in various ways by American corporate cultures.

7. In *Darwinian Myths: The Legends and Misuses of a Theory* (Knoxville: University of Tennessee Press, 1997) Edward Caudill notes, "That social Darwinism could be derived from *On the Origin of Species* is obvious, but it is debatable whether Darwin supported the idea. Although he never endorsed the idea, Darwin did not protest the application of his biological theory to society, and passages from his writings even suggest that Darwin himself made such applications" (64).

8. Ibid., 71.

9. For detailed accounts of the history of social Darwinism, I recommend the works of Caudill (*Darwinian Myths*); Mike Hawkins (*Social Darwinism in European and American Thought, 1860–1945: Nature as Model and Nature as Threat* [Cambridge: Cambridge University Press, 1997]); Michael Rose (*Darwin's Spectre: Evolutionary Biology in the Modern World* [Princeton: Princeton University Press, 1998]); and Alexander Rosenberg (*Darwinism in Philosophy, Social Science and Policy* [Cambridge: Cambridge University Press, 2000]).

10. Bill Boisvert argues that organization theory was once dominated by vocabulary and imagery culled from physics (as seen in the work of Frederick Taylor and his followers), but later, by mid-twentieth century, emphasized concepts derived from biology, including evolution and symbiosis. He also discusses the valorization of "predators" in business literature—for example, the admiration expressed in several business advice books for Attila the Hun. The Mongols, it seems, were best suited to adapt to harsh environments and to run roughshod over naïve believers in order and stability as success strategies (Boisvert, "Apostles of the New Entrepreneur: Business Books and the Management Crisis," in *Commodify Your Dissent: The Business of Culture in the Gilded Age: Salvos from the Baffler*, eds. Thomas Frank and Matt Weiland [New York and London: W. W. Norton, 1997], 92–93).

11. See Chapter 5 for further discussion of human "progress" as a potentially endless process.

12. Eric Schlosser, *Fast Food Nation: The Dark Side of the All-American Meal* (Boston and New York: Houghton Mifflin, 2001), 36.

13. Ibid., 24.

14. Greil Marcus, *Lipstick Traces: A Secret History of the Twentieth Century* (Cambridge: Harvard University Press, 1989), 46. Marcus also provides a lengthy list of 1970s rock and disco song or album titles that contain some variant of the verb "survive."

15. The downfall of the New Economy probably began earlier than September 11, as many writers, including John Schwartz of the *New York Times,* have noted.

16. To cite just a few of many available examples, the *Los Angeles Times* called Peters "the father of the postmodern corporation," and Southwest Airlines CEO Herbert D. Kelleher described Peters as "a mental catapult crashing ideas into the walls of conventional thinking." These quotations and many others just like them are available in reviews of Peters's books at www.amazon.com.

17. There are many Peters's apologists. For example, in an article justifying *Forbes* magazine's naming of *In Search of Excellence* as the number one most influential business book of the last several decades, Dan Ackman writes that the book contains "just a few arguably embarrassing picks" among its list of excellent companies (Ackman, "Excellence Sought—And Found." *Forbes,* October 4, 2002). Ackman does not mention the data-faking controversy. Still, more recent Peters's books, such as *Re-Imagine!: Business Excellence in a Disruptive Age,* have yet to appear on the *New York Times* best seller list—an omission unusual for an author whose past publications have seemed to be surefire successes.

18. Viewing *Wall Street* today, it is striking how Gekko's business practices seem about as quaint as the technology featured in the film (gigantic mobile phones, dot matrix printers, and computers with the telltale black and green screens of MS-DOS operating systems). The "survival of the fittest" model he advocates in the "Greed is Good" speech has been surpassed tenfold since 1987.

19. Despite his policy of sending job candidates to an industrial psychologist for training, Mackay only seems interested in how employees think when it affects what they do on the job.

20. Mackay is equally insistent on knowing and documenting information about his customers. For example, he advocates what he calls the "Mackay 66," which is essentially a customer profile comprising 66 questions. All of Mackay's employees, not just official sales representatives, must be able to answer these questions—some fairly straightforward, others oddly private (about medical history, drinking habits, marital status)—about each regular customer and potential client. This information, he argues, is key to establishing any lucrative business relationship.

21. Age-related anxiety permeates *Swim with the Sharks without Being Eaten Alive: Outsell, Outmanage, Outmotivate, and Outnegotiate Your Competition* (New York: Fawcett Columbine, 1988). For instance, Mackay advises parents to "tell... kids to take chances... The wheel is tilted in their favor, the system is biased on their side, because it is based on change. On destroying the old" (258).

22. In terms of the evolution argument, it is interesting to note that the mice in Johnson's book are depicted as being much better suited for survival than the humans are. Johnson repeatedly reminds readers that the mice survive because they don't stop to think about things and don't spend any time moping about what they lose.

23. This passage is a strange maneuver on Johnson's part, considering that many self-help books are explicitly marketed to people who believe themselves to be victims and seek reassurance and support from such books.

24. Unfortunately, Kelly's lively and freeing version of New Economy lifestyles and technologies may be based on a rather selective worldview. As Doug Henwood writes of an interview he conducted with Kelly, "I interrupted his effusions to ask him what relevance they had in a world where the statistics showed that the gap between rich and poor—nationally and globally—has never been so wide, a world where half the population has never even made a phone call. Kelly responded by saying that there's never been so good a time to be poor, though he didn't offer any evidence" (Henwood, *After the New Economy*, 24).

25. John Schwartz, "Dot-Com is Dot-Gone, and the Dream with It." *New York Times*, November 25, 2001, 4.

CHAPTER 4

1. Because diet and exercise have long been significant factors in medical discourse, my discussion of medicalization will focus on sleep, a relatively new, emerging subject of medical inquiry.

2. Another of Foucault's concepts—"governmentality," or "the encounter between the technologies of domination of others and those of the self"—further complicates this issue by adding the component of authority; people learn to regulate their own behavior when met with criteria and instructions from authority figures (Foucault, "Technologies of the Self" in *Ethics: Subjectivity and Truth*, ed. Paul Rabinow [New York: New Press, 1997], 225).

3. Foucault's use of Christian traditions as examples in his argument does not imply that only persons of Christian faith are affected by the social phenomena he describes.

4. Jeremy Howell and Alan Ingram describe the self-help phenomenon as a "class struggle" that has been "couched in politically innocuous

language—lifestyle management—and self improvement policies that leave most of us saying 'What fool would argue with that?'" (Howell and Ingram, "From Social Problem to Personal Issue: The Language of Lifestyle." *Cultural Studies* 5.2 [2001]: 346).

5. Other kinds of workplace health promotion include blood pressure screening, smoking cessation programs, cancer screening and informational sessions, Alcoholics or Narcotics Anonymous meetings, prenatal testing, and support groups.

6. On its website, the Henry J. Kaiser Family Foundation carefully emphasizes its lack of affiliation with Kaiser Permanente (the insurance company) and Kaiser Aluminum. It's quite possible that the organization is "protesting too much" and does in some sense remain associated with these Kaiser family companies, but this statistic about insurance costs does not appear to favor corporate interests.

7. For a detailed discussion of the early twentieth-century fascination with new scientific theories and technologies, see Tim Armstrong, *Modernism, Technology, and the Body: A Cultural Study* (Cambridge: Cambridge University Press, 1998).

8. Doug Henwood also notes that "productivity" does not translate into better wages or working conditions. In a 1999 survey by *Business Week*, "Almost two-thirds of those polled—63%—said that the celebrated productivity boom hadn't raised the level of their income, and 62% said it hadn't raised their job security" (Henwood, *After the New Economy* [London and New York: New Press, 2003], 32).

9. Similarly, it's interesting that while the nature of work can be blamed for people's high stress levels (another health no-no) many workplaces offer "stress management" programs rather than making significant changes that would actually reduce stress. The Workplace Resource Center of the Substance Abuse and Mental Health Services Administration notes, "It has been shown that 60–90% of all visits to health professionals are for some sort of stress-related disorder. Employers invest in stress reduction programs in order to minimize these costs. Programs that have been shown to give the highest rate of return for the employer include: stress reduction, smoking cessation, and nutrition" (Substance Abuse and Mental Health Services Administration, "Workplace Health/ Promotion Wellness Fact Sheet," 1998, http://workplace.samhsa. gov/ResourceCenter/r305.pdf [accessed on Dec. 15, 2008]).

10. Society for Human Resource Management, "2001 Benefits Survey," 2001, http://www.shrm.org/hrresources/surveys_published/ archive/12001%20Benefits%20Survey.asp (accessed on Dec. 13, 2008). Also, 44 percent of businesses that are open 24 hours a day, seven days a week officially permit workplace napping, according to Circadian Technologies' "Shiftwork Practices" survey (Ami Randall, "Napping on the Job: Policies and Benefits in Extended Hours Operations." *Circadian Technologies, Inc.*, 2003, http://www.

circadian.com/download/11_napping_on_the_job_policies_benefits. pdf_[accessed on Dec. 13, 2008]). As for the plentitude of sleep-related self-help materials currently available, a keyword search of books in print from Amazon.com yields 1,787 books on the subject of sleep; 51 of the first 500 search results are self-help books written for a general audience, most of them published during and after 1998. In my tally of the results, I eliminated books specifically tailored for parents with newborn children (there are many of these) or for adolescent or elderly populations. I also eliminated religious and New Age "dream books," audio books, and books about specific sleep disorders and syndromes (such as sleep apnea, restless legs syndrome). A keyword search for "sleep self-help" yields 85,100 results from Yahoo. com's directory of websites.

11. For up-to-date statistics on work hours, consult the website of the U.S. Department of Labor, listed in the references section.

12. Herbert Marcuse wrote that in capitalist systems, the idea of a productive work ethic "came to smack of repression or its philistine glorification: it connotes the resentful defamation of rest, indulgence, receptivity—the triumph over the 'lower depths' of the mind and body, the taming of the instincts by exploitative reason" (Marcuse, *Eros and Civilization: A Philosophical Inquiry into Freud*, 2nd ed. [Boston: Beacon Press, 1966], 156). A significant number of self-help books and consulting firms related to the "taming" of sleep—one of the most basic or "lowest" human bodily needs—have emerged over the past decade.

13. According to William Dement, there is some disagreement amongst medical researchers as to how much sleep humans need. Some researchers have even claimed that people can stay awake for several days straight without severe physical or mental impairment (William C. Dement and Christopher Vaughn, *The Promise of Sleep: A Pioneer in Sleep Medicine Explores the Vital Connection between Health, Happiness, and a Good Night's Sleep* [New York: Dell, 1999], 88).

14. Certainly, the introduction of sleep into official corporate policy has met with some resistance; a *Washington Post* article claimed that despite consultants' recommendations, the vast majority of American companies were choosing to eschew workplace naps. Sleep consultant Tom DeLuca claims that when he was scheduled to appear on NBC's popular news program, *Dateline*, in fall 2000, he could not find a single client who would admit to using his services on the air. "There's still a stigma attached to it," he hypothesized (qtd. in Liz Stevens, "Close Your Eyes: Midday Dozes Are Stripping Away Stigma of Siestas." *Centre Daily Times,* March 26, 2001, 2C).

15. Maas's work is more specifically tailored for a corporate audience, as immediately suggested by the review blurbs from well-known business management guru Tom Peters and former Ogilvy & Mather CEO William E. Phillips printed on the first pages of the book.

16. I used PubMed, a database of professional and research journal articles pertaining to the medical field, to perform a keyword and title search for the words sleep and performance. I further limited the search by looking only at clinical trials, randomized controlled trials, meta-analyses, and reviews published in English.

17. In a 1995 review article discussing writing styles in the social and medical sciences, Robert Madigan, Susan Johnson, and Patricia Linton note that hedged conclusions are quite common in research reports. While the inconclusive nature of medical findings about sleep may be attributed in part to this convention of scientific writing, the tendency of popular, corporate, and self-help sources to suggest that these findings are conclusive, despite the hedging of reports, is significant.

18. Again, these articles were found through the PubMed database's search engine, using criteria and limits described in note 19. Here, I also read through article abstracts, selecting only titles relevant to the issue of sleep's link with performance.

19. In April, 2003, The Federal Motor Carrier Safety Administration (FMSCA) issued Hours-of-Service regulations limiting the amount of time a truck driver can drive without rest. This rare example of curtailed work hours is more in line with the "NASA Nap" and other sleep policies based on worker and customer/client safety than it is with office sleep promotion (and the barely regulated hours of office workers).

20. The Provigil prescribing information for health professionals lists the side effects most frequently reported by users during clinical trials (such as headache, nausea, anxiety, and dizziness) but also alludes to more serious issues, such as a post-marketing fatality and a serious, life-threatening rash (Cephalon, "Provigil Prescribing Information." *Provigil.com*, 2008, http://www.provigil.com/Media/PDFs/prescribing_info.pdf [accessed on Nov. 26, 2008]). Also, the Food and Drug Administration's official label for the drug notes that the "precise mechanism(s) through which Modafinil [Provigil] promotes wakefulness is unknown" and that the relationship of findings from animal testing to human applications is not established (Food and Drug Administration, "FDA Approved Labeling Text for NDA 20-717/S-005 &S-008: Provigil (modafinil) Tablets [C-IV]," 2004, http://www.fda.gov/cder/foi/label/2004/20717se1-008_provigil_lbl.pdf [accessed on Dec. 15, 2008]).

21. It's perfectly legal, however, to charge smokers more for health and life insurance, because smoking is considered to be a preventable condition/behavior.

22. Certain more rudimentary kinds of on-the-job health testing are already very common in the United States—cholesterol screening, cancer screening, and drug testing, to name a few. These kinds of tests could also be used to screen unwanted workers.

23. Some examples of discourses about Attention Deficit Disorder in workplace environments include Kathleen G. Nadeau's *ADD in the Workplace: Choices, Changes, and Challenges* (New York and London: Routledge, 1997); Lynn Weiss's *ADD on the Job: Making Your ADD Work for You* (New York: Cooper Square Press, 1996); and Anne Field's September 22, 2002, *New York Times* article, "Attention Deficit Is in the Office, Too."

CHAPTER 5

1. Richard Powers, *Gain* (New York: Farrar, Straus and Giroux, 1998), 295.

2. In an interview with Laura Miller of *Salon*, Powers says that he based his fictional corporation, Clare International, on the histories of Procter & Gamble (P&G), Colgate, and Lever, among others. He mentions P&G first, which is probably not accidental; the particulars of Clare's long history as well as its "contemporary" status very closely resemble those of P&G.

3. For a firsthand account of the Pat Kehm case, see Kehm family attorney Tom Riley's 1986 book, *The Price of a Life: One Woman's Death from Toxic Shock* (Chevy Chase, MD: Adler & Adler, 1986).

4. Gilles Deleuze's concept of "control society," as defined in "Control and Becoming" (1990) and "Postscript on Control Societies," 1990, *Negotiations: 1972–1990,* trans. Martin Joughin (New York: Columbia University Press, 1995), also figures prominently in Michael Hardt and Antonio Negri's *Empire* (Cambridge, MA, and London: Harvard University Press, 2000). Because this concept has been discussed at length elsewhere in this book, I am leaving it aside here.

5. See the "careers" section of www.pg.com for more details about P&G's work-life programs.

6. I am reminded here of contemporary debates about higher education: what, exactly, is the purpose of going to college? Many argue that college should consist of purely "pragmatic" coursework—departments (or majors) like English or Classics must recast themselves as useful for corporate jobs postgraduation.

7. This mentality is discussed in more detail in Chapter 3.

8. Swasy also argues that this internal competition may have serious health consequences for P&G employees: "A report on the top medical claims by P&Gers shows that three of the four top claims were stress-related, such as heart attacks" (Alecia Swasy, *Soap Opera: The Inside Story of Procter & Gamble* [New York: Times Books, 1993], 11).

9. See Chapter 2 for a longer discussion of consumers-as-individuals. Also, it is worth noting here that Powers's *Gain* includes a fictionalized version of this statement from Butler. Franklin Kennibar, a Clare CEO of the 1990s, says in a speech, "The very notion of

'consumer advocacy' is a well-meaning mistake, for there are as
many consumer interests as there are consumers. Only by leaving consumer interests to the market have we managed the whole
mind-boggling transformation of life since the days when Americans
boiled dead animal scraps... to make a little liquid soap" (Powers,
Gain, 338).

10. Interestingly, the "immaculate molecules" referred to here are phos-
    phates—the very same molecules that led P&G into crisis in the
    1970s.

11. Slightly earlier in the novel, Laura tries to help her son, Tim, with
    his homework: an analysis of Walt Whitman's poem "Crossing
    Brooklyn Ferry." She finds herself feeling unnerved by several lines of
    Whitman's tribute to human invention and progress: "We use you,
    you objects, and do not cast you aside—we plant you permanently
    within us... We fathom you not—we love you... You furnish your
    parts toward eternity" (qtd in Powers, *Gain*, 89). The "plant you
    permanently within us" line is a disturbing reminder of her cancer,
    probably caused by everyday household products.

12. For a longer discussion of *Gain* and risk theory, see Ursula Heise,
    "Toxins, Drugs, and Global Systems: Risk and Narrative in the Con-
    temporary Novel." *American Literature* 74.4 (2002): 747–778.

13. P&G also began struggling with risk management in the nineteenth
    century, as executives debated how best to handle labor disputes
    and other individual versus corporation issues. By the mid-twentieth
    century, though, the risks brought about by P&G had spread well
    beyond the walls of the company's Cincinnati headquarters. The
    phosphates, TSS, and Fenholloway River stories—to cite just a few
    of Swasy's examples—illustrate the deepening presence of business-
    related dangers.

14. Powers himself has remarked on the complexity of corporate risk and
    responsibility:

    To say that markets, that commerce gives with one hand
    and takes away with the other is not to satisfy anyone, or to
    potentially alienate everybody. But it seems to me true, finally.
    I don't think that's defeatist and, in fact, in some ways it's a
    necessary first step toward intelligent activism. Externalization,
    vilification, saying "We're decent human beings and this CEO
    of Dow Chemicals is out to get us," isn't really historically
    informed. It's not really coming to terms with the size and
    scale and scope of the problem. And in some ways... it's that
    attitude that channels alienation and makes people continue to
    lead the lives that they've been leading... it makes it seem as
    if everything would be fine if the guy at the top wasn't being
    greedy or trying to poison us. We don't consider the roles that
    we're taking in making the world the way it is. These things

are the realizations of our desire to conquer matter and time and to live on our own terms, and it behooves us to look at the degree to which we can't have life on our own terms and the attempt to do so is deeply poisoning and alienating. (qtd. in Laura Miller, "The Salon Interview: Richard Powers." *Salon,* July 23, 1998)

15. In *The Ecology of Commerce* (New York: HarperCollins, 1993), Paul Hawken, cofounder of the successful mail-order company Smith & Hawken, argues that lax environmental regulations are not truly necessary for lucrative business ventures. Hawken's book suggests ways in which companies might easily align their goals and needs with what's best for the natural environment.

16. As Fredric Jameson writes about capitalist globalization, "The system is better seen as a kind of virus... and its development as something like an epidemic (better still, a rash of epidemics, an epidemic of epidemics). The system has its own logic, which powerfully undermines and destroys the logic of more traditional or pre-capitalist societies and economies... But epidemics sometimes play themselves out, like a fire for want of oxygen, and they also leap to new and more propitious settings, in which the preconditions are favorable to renewed development" (Jameson, *The Cultural Turn: Selected Writings on the Postmodern, 1983–1998* [London and New York: Verso, 1998], 139–140).

17. Oscar Schisgall provides a dubious description of the latter: "After extensive consultation with educators in many states, [P&G's] educational services group—as part of its consumerism program—offered teaching aids free to teachers. Soon some 50,000 educators were using P&G teaching guides and films. One reason for the broad acceptance of the program was its noncommercial, objective tone. Emphasis lay on how new products are tested, on the importance of consumer reaction, and on the role of advertising behind a brand" (Schisgall, *Eyes on Tomorrow: The Evolution of Procter & Gamble* [Chicago: J. G. Ferguson Publishing, 1981], 275).

18. Powers describes a similar scenario in *Gain*:

> Brought to you by Snowdrop, Gristo, Tar Baby, Flapperjack Pancake Mix, Mentine Gargle and Breath Repairer: as if these things themselves were doing the bringing. Through radio, these names grew as easy to flesh out as any phantom... Each brand was a wooden puppet longing to be a little boy. The best of them grew lives of their own, until not even their most devoted listeners could say who made them anymore. America knew what Gristo brought you, but not who brought you Gristo. (311)

Chapter 6

1. James Gee, Glynda Hull, and Colin Lankshear argue that students are being specifically trained to handle such dispersed, noncentralized corporate structures:

> We see a movement away from schooling as reproducing the identities and practices of disciplinary experts, away even from schooling as producing individually "smart people." We see, rather, a movement toward [educating] people [so that they] can work collaboratively (in teams) to produce results and add value through distributed knowledge and understanding. Such students are much better suited... to be modules in a distributed non-authoritarian system, than are traditional students (Gee et al., *The New Work Order: Behind the Language of the New Capitalism* [Boulder, CO: Westview Press, 1996], 59).

2. Some scholars persuasively argue that developments in writing-related technologies, such as typewriters, shorthand, and word processors, have also significantly shaped workplace culture. In her review of Bernadette Longo's *Spurious Coin: A History of Science, Management, and Technical Writing* (Albany, NY: State University of New York Press, 2000), Martha Wetterhall Thomas writes,

> As the technological capacity for producing communications grew, so did the volume of communications produced. Business documents became less personal, more standardized in form and content, and thus more easily generated by workers a step removed from the composing process... The ability to efficiently generate internal documents further encouraged the division of labor within a system of continual performance review, leading to a divide-and-conquer effect on workers at all levels of the business hierarchy. (Thomas, "Book Review: *Spurious Coin: A History of Science, Management, and Technical Writing.*" *Journal of Business Communication* 40.4 [2003]: 307)

> Friedrich Kittler's *Gramophone, Film, Typewriter,* trans. Geoffrey Winthrop-Young and Michael Wutz (Stanford, CA: Stanford University Press, 1999) also provides a detailed discussion of the effects of writing technologies on writing conventions.

3. Deborah Cameron provides a detailed analysis of the "scripted greeting" phenomenon:

> Without disputing that anything that goes on in talk has in the final analysis to be accomplished by the participants, I think there are cases where institutions (or to be more exact, people with certain kinds of authority in institutions) do define the kinds of talk produced within them... I am especially interested in professional

identities and ways of talking that are not so much negotiated by participants "on the ground" as imposed on them from above by training, scripting, and surveillance. It is my contention that many kinds of "talk at work" are increasingly subject to this explicit codification. Today it is not always left to workers to construct a suitable professional identity and "somehow" make it relevant in talk; instead, approved forms of interactive discourse are prescribed in advance, and often in detail.   (Cameron, *Good To Talk?: Living and Working in a Communication Culture* [London: Sage, 2000], 55–56)

4. Aviva Freedman and Christine Adam are particularly pessimistic about the ability of instructors to provide adequately authentic training. They state that "a potential conclusion . . . is that it is simply not possible at all to prepare students for the rhetorical demands of a workplace while operating within the institutional constraints of a university classroom" (Freedman and Adam, "Bridging the Gap: University-Based Writing That Is More Than Simulation," in *Transitions: Writing in Academic and Workplace Settings,* eds. Patrick Dias and Anthony Paré [Cresskill, NJ: Hampton Press, 2000], 130). Such as statement evinces little faith in students' ability to use their imagination—even if an assignment cannot precisely duplicate a specific workplace scenario, can't students still see the basic connection and write/learn accordingly?

5. William J. Wardrope writes of business communication's marginalization: "Like many of my readers, I have witnessed the elimination of the graduate business education programs which produced so many of our current faculty, the re-structuring of academic units in which business communication is housed, the consistently lower salaries paid to business communication teachers, and our heavy teaching loads" (Wardrope, "'Challenge Is a Positive Word: Embracing the Interdisciplinary Nature of Business Communication." *Journal of Business Communication* 38.3 [2001]: 242–243).

6. An article written in 1944 by Robert Aurner demonstrates that the idea that college instructors must bow to corporate demands has been in circulation a long time. Aurner writes,

Instructors in the field of English of business, particularly at the collegiate level, carry an obligation to prepare their students in such a way that those students will be of at least initial value to their employers upon graduation. A reasonable familiarity with the major types of communication with which our graduates will have to deal after they have taken their diplomas will make our product valuable to society in the short view as well as in the long view.   (Aurner, "The English of Business and its Significance: An Approach to the Collegiate Course." *College English* 5.8 [1944]: 449)

CHAPTER 7

1. The quotations in this paragraph come from the following pages of the Lehman Brothers website, in order: http://www.lehman. com/who/intellectual_capital/, http://www.lehman.com/careers/ workatlehman/index.htm, http://www.lehman.com/careers/ lifeatlehman/career_development.htm, http://www.lehman.com/ careers/profiles/gaddy_ib_vp_us.htm, http://www.lehman.com/ careers/profiles/tomoyuki_ib_vp_asia.htm, and http://www.lehman. com/who/mission/.

2. Please see references for citations of specific web addresses where information about these firms' diversity programs can be found.

REFERENCES

Accenture. "Diversity and Inclusion." *Accenture.com*. 2008. Nov. 23, 2008. http://careers3.accenture.com/Careers/Global/WorkingHere/Diversity.
———. "Meet Our People." *Accenture.com*. 2001. Nov. 25, 2008. http://careers3.accenture.com/Careers/UK/BHSPprofiles.
———. "Teamwork and Collaboration." *Accenture.com*. 2002. Nov. 25, 2008. http://careers3.accenture.com/Careers/Global/WorkingHere/OurCulture/Teamwork_Key.htm.
Ackman, Dan. "Excellence Sought—And Found." *Forbes*. Oct. 4, 2002. Dec. 11, 2008. http://www.forbes.com/2002/10/04/1004excellent.html.
Adam, Christine. 2000. "What Do We Learn from the Readers?: Factors in Determining Successful Transitions between Academic and Workplace Writing." In *Transitions: Writing in Academic and Workplace Settings*, eds. Patrick Dias and Anthony Paré, 167–182. Cresskill, NJ: Hampton Press.
Adorno, Theodor, and Max Horkheimer. 1944. "The Culture Industry: Enlightenment as Mass Deception." *Dialectic of Enlightenment*. Trans. John Cumming. New York: Continuum, 1994, 120–167.
Åkerstedt, Torbjörn, P. Fredlund, M. Gillberg, and B. Jansson. 2002. "A Prospective Study of Fatal Occupational Accidents: Relationship to Sleeping Difficulties and Occupational Factors." *Journal of Sleep Research* 11.1: 69–71.
Alertness Solutions. "About Us." *Alertness Solutions.com*. 2000. Nov. 26, 2008. http://www.alertness-solutions.com/About_AS/about_AS.html.
Allmon, Stephanie. 2002. "I'll Get Back to You After My Nap: 'Power Napping' during Workday Can Be a Great Thing." *Intelligencer Journal*: A2.
Althusser, Louis. 1969. "Ideology and Ideological State Apparatuses (Notes toward an Investigation)." *Lenin and Philosophy and Other Essays*. Trans. Ben Brewster. New York: Monthly Review Press, 1971, 127–186.
Altria Group. "Our Values." *Altria.com*. 2008. Nov. 23, 2008. http://www.altria.com/about_altria/1_1_2_values.asp.
American International Group. "Careers: People." *AIG.com*. 2008. Dec. 11, 2008. http://www.aig.com/people_547_104706.html.
———. "Vision and Values." *AIG.com*. 2008. Nov. 30, 2008. http://www.aig.com/culture_547_104154.html.
American Management Association. *AMA.net*. 2004. Mar. 30, 2004. www.amanet.org.
American Medical Association. "Genetic Discrimination." *Ama-assn.org*. 2004. Nov. 26, 2008. <http://www.ama-assn.org/ama/pub/category/print/2312.html>.

Andrews, Kenneth R. 1968. Introduction to *The Functions of the Executive,* by Chester I. Barnard, vii–xxi. Cambridge, MA: Harvard University Press.

Anthony, William A., and Camille Anthony. *Napping.com.* 1998. Nov. 26, 2008. http://www.napping.com.

Apple Computers. "Here's to the Crazy Ones." *Apple.com.* 1997. Nov. 26, 2008. http://web.archive.org/web/20010228171255/http://www.apple.com/thinkdifferent/.

Armstrong, Tim. 1998. *Modernism, Technology, and the Body: A Cultural Study.* Cambridge, UK: Cambridge University Press.

Arnott, Dave. 2000. *Corporate Cults: The Insidious Lure of the All-Consuming Organization.* New York: AMACOM American Management Association.

AT&T. "Diversity at AT&T." *Att.org.* 2004. Nov. 25, 2008. http://www.league-att.org/diversity/brgs.html.

———. "Why AT&T." *Att.org.* 2008. Nov. 24, 2008. http://www.att.jobs/culture.aspx.

Aurner, Robert. 1944. "The English of Business and its Significance: An Approach to the Collegiate Course." *College English* 5.8: 448–449.

Bakan, Joel. 2004. *The Corporation: The Pathological Pursuit of Profit and Power.* New York: Free Press.

Bank of America. "My Work." *Bankofamerica.com.* 2008. Nov. 25, 2008. http://careers.bankofamerica.com/learnmore/mywork.asp.

Barboza, David. 2001. "Victims and Champions of a Darwinian Enron." *New York Times,* Dec. 12, sec. C: 5.

Barclays Capital. "Our Culture." *Barclays.com.* 2008. Dec. 16, 2008. http://www.barcap.com/sites/v/index.jsp?vgnextoid=d6fb15cd3f4f8010VgnVCM1000002581c50aRCRD.

Barnard, Chester I. 1938. *The Functions of the Executive.* Introduction by Kenneth R. Andrews. Cambridge, MA: Harvard University Press, 1968.

Barrett, Jennifer. "Wealth and Waistlines." *Newsweek Online.* Dec. 28, 2007. Dec. 15, 2008. http://www.newsweek.com/ID/82258.

Barringer, Felicity. 2003. "Readers, Like Investors, Are Tiring of C.E.O.'s." *New York Times,* Jan. 19, sec. D: 4.

Bauman, Zygmunt. 1992. *Mortality, Immortality and Other Life Strategies.* Cambridge, UK: Polity Press.

Beebe, Dean W., and David Gozal. 2002. "Obstructive Sleep Apnea and the Prefrontal Cortex: Toward a Comprehensive Model Linking Nocturnal Upper Airway Obstruction to Daytime Cognitive and Behavioral Deficits." *Journal of Sleep Research* 11.1: 1–16.

Beck, Ulrich. 2000. *The Brave New World of Work.* Trans. Patrick Camiller. Cambridge, UK: Polity Press, 2000.

———. 1986. *Risk Society: Toward a New Modernity.* Trans. Mark Ritter. London and Newbury Park, CA: Sage Publications, 1992.

Belkin, Lisa. 2000. "Your Kids Are Their Problem." *New York Times Magazine,* Jul. 23, 30+.

Bellantoni, Christina. "Obama Puts Deficit on Back Burner." *Washington Times.* Dec. 8, 2008. Dec. 11, 2008. http://washingtontimes.com/news/2008/dec/08/obama-puts-deficit-on-back-burner/.

Bennett, Tony. 1998. *Culture: A Reformer's Science.* London: Sage Publications.

———. 1990. *Outside Literature.* New York and London: Routledge.

Berman, Dennis. "On the Street, Disbelief and Resignation." *Wall Street Journal Online.* Dec. 9, 2008. Dec. 9, 2008. http://online.wsj.com/article/SB122878309173989913.html.

Boeing. "Employment—Culture: Diversity." *Boeing.com.* 2002. Nov. 25, 2008. http://boeing.com/employment/culture/diversity.html.

Boisvert, Bill. 1997. "Apostles of the New Entrepreneur: Business Books and the Management Crisis." In *Commodify Your Dissent: The Business of Culture in the Gilded Age: Salvos from the Baffler,* eds. Thomas Frank and Matt Weiland, 81–98. New York and London: W.W. Norton and Company.

Bovée, Courtland L., and John V. Thill. 1999. *Excellence in Business Communication.* 4th ed. Upper Saddle River, NJ: Prentice Hall.

Bovée, Courtland L., John V. Thill, and Barbara E. Schatzman. 2003. *Business Communication Today.* 7th ed. Upper Saddle River, NJ: Prentice Hall.

———. 2003. *Instructor's Manual: Business Communication Today.* 7th ed. Upper Saddle River, NJ: Prentice Hall.

Brown, Wendy. 1995. *States of Injury.* Princeton, NJ: Princeton University Press.

Byrne, John A. "The Real Confessions of Tom Peters." *Business Week Online.* Dec. 3, 2001. Dec. 11, 2008. http://www.businessweek.com/magazine/content/01_49/b3760040.htm.

Byrne, John A., Louis Lavelle, Nanette Byrnes, Marcia Vickers, and Amy Borrus. 2002. "How to Fix Corporate Governance." *Business Week,* May 6, 69–78.

Cader Books. "*Publisher's Weekly* Bestseller Lists 1900–1995." *Caderbooks.com.* 2002. Nov. 26, 2008. http://www.caderbooks.com/best80.html.

Cameron, Deborah. 2000. *Good To Talk?: Living and Working in a Communication Culture.* London: Sage Publications.

Carlone, David. 2001. "Enablement, Constraint, and *The 7 Habits of Highly Effective People.*" *Management Communication Quarterly* 14.3: 491–497.

Carnegie, Andrew. 1920. *Autobiography of Andrew Carnegie.* Boston and New York: Houghton Mifflin Company.

Cassano, Eric. "Bullish on Culture." *Smart Business.* 2008. Dec. 9, 2008. http://www.sbnonline.com/National/Article/15733/0/Bullish_on_culture.aspx?Category=102.

Caudill, Edward. 1997. *Darwinian Myths: The Legends and Misuses of a Theory.* Knoxville: University of Tennessee Press.

Center for Narcolepsy, Sleep and Health Research. "Excessive Daytime Sleepiness." *University of Illinois at Chicago College of Medicine.* 2002. Nov. 25, 2008. http://www.uic.edu/nursing/CNSHR/NewFiles/EDSfill.html.

Cephalon. "Provigil Prescribing Information" *Provigil.com.* 2008. Nov. 26, 2008. http://www.provigil.com/Media/PDFs/prescribing_info.pdf.

ChevronTexaco.com. 2002. ChevronTexaco. Jul. 2, 2002. http://www.chevrontexaco.com.

Chrysler, LLC. "Diversity." *Chryslerllc.com*. 2008. Dec. 11, 2008. http://www.chryslerllc.com/en/community/diversity/.

Citigroup. "Citi Graduate Recruitment: Our People." *Citi.com*. 2008. Nov. 18, 2008. http://www.oncampus.citi.com/our_people.aspx.

———. "Working at Citi." *Citi.com*. 2007. Dec. 9, 2008. http://www.citigroup.com/citi/citizen/data/cr07_ch14.pdf.

Conlin, Michelle. "Career Advancement in Tough Times." *Business Week Online*. Oct. 23, 2008. Dec. 9, 2008. http://www.businessweek.com/magazine/content/08_44/b4106052111185.htm?chan=careers_managing+your+career+page_top+stories.

Curry, Jerome. 1996. "Introducing Realism into Business Writing: Extended Conflict with a Hostile Audience." *Business Communication Quarterly* 59.3: 77–87.

Davis, Stanley. 1984. *Managing Corporate Culture*. Cambridge, MA: Ballinger Publishing Company.

Deal, Terrence E., and Allan A. Kennedy. 1982. *Corporate Cultures: The Rites and Rituals of Corporate Life*. Reading, MA: Addison-Wesley Publishing Company.

De Certeau, Michel. 1984. *The Practice of Everyday Life*. Trans. Steven Rendall. Berkeley, LA, and London: University of California Press, 1984.

Decker, Charlie L. 1998. *Winning with the P&G 99 : 99 Principles and Practices of Procter & Gamble's Success*. New York: Pocket Books.

Deetz. Stanley. 1998. "Discursive Formations, Strategized Subordination and Self-Surveillance." In *Foucault, Management and Organization Theory*, eds. Alan McKinlay and Ken Starkey, 151–172. London: Sage Publications.

Deleuze, Gilles. 1990. "Postscript on Control Societies." *Negotiations: 1972–1990*. Trans. Martin Joughin. New York: Columbia University Press, 1995, 177–182.

Deleuze, Gilles, and Félix Guattari. 1980. *A Thousand Plateaus: Capitalism and Schizophrenia*. Trans. Brian Massumi. Minneapolis and London: University of Minnesota Press, 1987.

TomDeLuca.com. 2000. DeLuca Enterprises. Aug. 12, 2002. http://www.tomdeluca.com.

Dement, William C., and Vaughan, Christopher. 1999. *The Promise of Sleep: A Pioneer in Sleep Medicine Explores the Vital Connection between Health, Happiness, and a Good Night's Sleep*. New York: Dell.

Derer, Mike. "Corporate Benefits Take Aim Against Obesity." *USA Today Online*. Sept. 1, 2003. Dec. 11, 2008. http://www.usatoday.com/money/workplace/2003-09-01-obesity-benefits_x.htm.

Drummond, Sean P. A., J. Christian Gillin, and Gregory G. Brown. 2001. "Increased Cerebral Response during a Divided Attention Task Following Sleep Deprivation." *Journal of Sleep Research* 10.2: 85–92.

Ehrenreich, Barbara. 2001. *Nickel and Dimed: On (Not) Getting By in America*. New York: Henry Holt and Company.

Exxon Mobil. "Careers." *Exxonmobil.com*. 2003. Nov. 23, 2008. http://www.exxonmobil.com/Corporate/careers.aspx.
———. "Flexible Workplace Program." *Exxonmobil.com*. 2003. Nov. 25, 2008. http://www.exxonmobil.com/Corporate/careers_dev_flex.aspx.
Fabius, Raymond, Sharon Glave Frazee, Thomas Sabia, Rochelle Broome, and Pam Dulaney. "Creating a Competitive Advantage by Investing in Health and Productivity." *Health and Productivity Management*. Spring 2008. Dec. 15, 2008. http://www.takecareemployersolutions.com/tpl/articles/CHDM_IHPM_Spring_2008.pdf.
Fannie Mae. "Careers." *Fanniemae.com*. 2002. Nov. 23, 2008. http://www.fanniemae.com/careers/.
Fayol, Henri. 1916. "General Principles of Management." In *Classics of Organization Theory*, eds. Jay M. Shafritz and J. Steven Ott, 51–66. 2nd ed. Chicago: The Dorsey Press, 1987.
Featherstone, Mike. 1991. "The Body in Consumer Culture." In *The Body: Social Process and Cultural Theory*, eds. Mike Featherstone, Mike Hepworth, and Bryan S. Turner, 170–196. London: Sage Publications.
Food and Drug Administration. "FDA Approved Labeling Text for NDA 20-717/S-005 &S-008: Provigil (modafinil) Tablets [C-IV]." 2004. Dec. 15, 2008. http://www.fda.gov/cder/foi/label/2004/20717se1-008_provigil_lbl.pdf.
Ford, Henry, and Samuel Crowther. 1922. *My Life and Work*. Garden City, NY: Garden City Publishing Company.
Ford Motor Company. "On the Team." 2002. Nov. 25, 2008. http://www.mycareer.ford.com/ONTHETEAM.ASP?CID=15.
Foucault, Michel. 1975. *Discipline and Punish: The Birth of the Prison*. Trans. Alan Sheridan. New York: Vintage Books, 1991.
———. 1978. *The History of Sexuality: An Introduction, Volume I*. Trans. Robert Hurley. New York: Vintage Books, 1990.
———. 1982. "Technologies of the Self." In *Ethics: Subjectivity and Truth*, ed. Paul Rabinow, 223–250. New York: New Press, 1997.
Frank, Thomas. 1997. *The Conquest of Cool: Business Culture, Counterculture, and the Rise of Hip Consumerism*. Chicago and London: The University of Chicago Press.
———. 2000. *One Market under God: Extreme Capitalism, Market Populism, and the End of Economic Democracy*. New York: Doubleday.
Frank, Thomas, Greg Lane, David Mulcahey, and Emily Vogt. 2003. "This Car Climbed Mount Nasdaq." In *Boob Jubilee: The Cultural Politics of the New Economy*, eds. Thomas Frank and David Mulcahey, 3–8. New York and London: W.W. Norton & Company.
Freedman, Aviva, and Christine Adam. 2000. "Bridging the Gap: University-Based Writing That Is More Than Simulation." In *Transitions: Writing in Academic and Workplace Settings*, eds. Patrick Dias and Anthony Paré, 129–144. Cresskill, NJ: Hampton Press.
Gee, James Paul, Glynda Hull, and Colin Lankshear. 1996. *The New Work Order: Behind the Language of the New Capitalism*. Boulder, CO: Westview Press.

Geller, Adam. 2002. "Blowing the Whistle at Work: Heroic or Dumb?" *Intelligencer Journal*: D1+.

General Electric. "Annual Report 1999: Initiatives." *GE.com*. 1999. Nov. 25, 2008. http://www.ge.com/annual99/initiatives/index.html.

General Motors. "I Am GM: Diversity." *GM.com*. 2008. Dec. 11, 2008. http://www.gm.com/corporate/responsibility/diversity/.

Godin, Seth. 2002. *Survival Is Not Enough: Zooming, Evolution, and the Future of Your Company*. New York and London: The Free Press.

Goldman Sachs. "Goldman Sachs Annual Report 2000." *Goldmansachs.com*. 2000. Nov. 25, 2008. goldmansachs.com/our_firm/.../annual_reports/2000/pdfs/GSAR_pp1-24.pdf.

———. "Your Career." *Goldmansachs.com*. 2008. Nov. 23, 2008. http://www2.goldmansachs.com/careers/your-career/index.html.

Gordon, Avery. 1995. "The Work of Corporate Culture: Diversity Management." *Social Text* 44, no. 13.3: 3–28.

Grahl, John. "Globalized Finance." *New Left Review*, no. 8 (March–April 2001). Jun. 14, 2002. http://www.newleftreview.net.

Green, Zaidee E. 1942. "Increasing the Profit of the Course in Business Writing." *College English* 3.8: 742–750.

Greenhouse, Steven. 2004. "Workers Assail Night Lock-Ins by Wal-Mart." *New York Times*, Jan. 18, 1+.

Groopman, Jerome. 2001. "Eyes Wide Open: Can Science Make Regular Sleep Unnecessary?" *New Yorker*, Dec. 3, 52–57.

Hardt, Michael, and Antonio Negri. 2000. *Empire*. Cambridge, MA, and London: Harvard University Press.

Harper, Philipp. "Shape Up Your Company with a Wellness Program." *Microsoft Small Business Center*. 2004. Dec. 11, 2008. http://www.microsoft.com/smallbusiness/resources/management/recruiting-staffing/shape-up-your-company-with-a-wellness-program.aspx#Shapeupyourcompanywithawellnessprogram.

Harvey Mackay. 2000. Oct. 15, 2002. http://www.mackay.com.

Hawkins, Mike. 1997. *Social Darwinism in European and American Thought, 1860–1945: Nature as Model and Nature as Threat*. Cambridge, UK: Cambridge University Press.

Heise, Ursula K. 2002. "Toxins, Drugs, and Global Systems: Risk and Narrative in the Contemporary Novel." *American Literature* 74.4: 747–778.

Hellmich, Nanci. 2001. "When Sleep Is but a Dream." *USA Today*, Mar. 27, 1–2D.

Henry J. Kaiser Family Foundation. "Employer Health Benefits: 2003 Summary of Findings." 2003. Dec. 11, 2008. http://www.kff.org/insurance/ehbs2003-abstract.cfm.

Henwood, Doug. 2003. *After the New Economy*. London and New York: The New Press.

Hewitt, John P. 1989. *Dilemmas of the American Self*. Philadelphia: Temple University Press.

Hochschild, Arlie Russell. 2003. *The Commercialization of Intimate Life: Notes from Home and Work.* Berkeley and London: University of California Press.

Holliday, Chad, and John E. Pepper. "Sustainability through the Market." 2001. Dec. 15, 2008. http://www.wbcsd.org/DocRoot/ihlC8nJnH2pOLpa23tNc/stm.pdf.

Horibe, Frances. 2001. *Creating the Innovation Culture: Leveraging Visionaries, Dissenters, and Other Useful Troublemakers in Your Organization.* Toronto and New York: J. Wiley & Sons.

Horning, Kenneth Baker. 1943. "Approaching the Course in Business English." *College English* 4.6: 381–383.

Howell, Jeremy, and Alan Ingram. 2001. "From Social Problem to Personal Issue: The Language of Lifestyle." *Cultural Studies* 5.2: 326–351.

Hudson, Michael. "How Wall Street Stoked the Mortgage Meltdown." *Wall Street Journal Online: Real Estate Archives.* Jun. 28, 2007. Nov. 23, 2008. http://www.realestatejournal.com/buysell/mortgages/20070628-hudson.html.

Hultman, Ken. 2002. *Balancing Individual and Corporate Values: Walking the Tightrope to Success.* San Francisco: Jossey-Bass/Pfeiffer.

IBM. "Valuing Diversity." *IBMcom.* 2002. November 5, 2002. http://www-03.ibm.com/employment/us/diverse/executive_corner_vp.shtml.

Jameson, Fredric. 1998. *The Cultural Turn: Selected Writings on the Postmodern, 1983–1998.* London and New York: Verso.

Johnson & Johnson. "Careers: Health and Wellness." *JNJ.com.* 2007. Dec. 11, 2008. http://careers.jnj.com/careers/global/rewards/health/index.htm.

Johnson, Spencer. 1998. *Who Moved My Cheese?: An A-Mazing Way to Deal with Change in Your Work and in Your Life.* New York: G. P. Putnam's Sons.

Juffer, Jane. 2005. *The Single Mother.* New York: New York University Press.

Kanigel, Robert. 1997. *The One Best Way: Frederick Winslow Taylor and the Enigma of Efficiency.* New York: Viking.

Kaiser, Emily. "Wal-Mart on PR Offensive to Repair Image." *China Daily.* Feb. 2, 2004. Dec. 11, 2008. http://www.chinadaily.com.cn/en/doc/2004-02/02/content_302266.htm.

Kelly, Kevin. 1999. *New Rules for the New Economy: 10 Radical Strategies for a Connected World.* New York: Penguin.

Kingshott, Ruth N., Richard J. Cosway, Ian J. Deary, and Neil J. Douglas. 2000. "The Effect of Sleep Fragmentation on Cognitive Processing Using Computerized Topographic Brain Mapping." *Journal of Sleep Research* 9.4: 353–357.

Kitchen, Patricia. 2002. "Leadership Styles Changing as Distrust Rises." *Intelligencer Journal:* D1+.

Kittler, Friedrich. 1999. *Gramophone, Film, Typewriter.* Trans. Geoffrey Winthrop-Young and Michael Wutz. Stanford, CA: Stanford University Press, 1999.

Krapels, Roberta H., and Barbara D. Davis. 2003. "Designation of 'Communication Skills' in Position Listings." *Business Communication Quarterly* 66.2: 90–96.

Lafley, A. G. "Chairman's Address: 2002 Annual Meeting of P&G Shareholders." *Pg.com.* Oct. 8, 2002. http://www.pg.com.

———. "Making a Meaningful Difference in Consumers' Lives." *Pg.com.* May 7, 2001. http://www.pg.com.

Lehman Brothers. "Career Development." *Lehman.com.* 2008. Nov. 30, 2008. http://www.lehman.com/careers/lifeatlehman/career_development.htm.

———. "Gaddy: Investment Banking Vice President, U.S.—Profiles—Careers." *Lehman.com.* 2008. Nov. 30, 2008. http://www.lehman.com/careers/profiles/gaddy_ib_vp_us.htm.

———. "Intellectual Capital." *Lehman.com.* 2008. Nov. 30, 2008. http://www.lehman.com/who/intellectual_capital/.

———. "Mission Statement." *Lehman.com.* 2008. Nov. 30, 2008. http://www.lehman.com/who/mission/.

———. "Tomoyuki: Investment Banking Vice President, Asia—Profiles—Careers." *Lehman.com.* 2008. Nov. 30, 2008. http://www.lehman.com/careers/profiles/tomoyuki_ib_vp_asia.htm.

———. "Work at Lehman: Careers." *Lehman.com.* 2008. Nov. 30, 2008. http://www.lehman.com/careers/workatlehman/index.htm.

Lewis, Diane. 2002. "More Bang, No Bucks: GOP Battles Labor on Overtime." *Intelligencer Journal Business Monday.* 2+.

Livingston, James. 1995. "Corporations and Cultural Studies." *Social Text* 44, no. 13.3: 61–69.

Locker, Kitty O. 2003. "Will Professional Communication Be the Death of Business Communication?" *Business Communication Quarterly* 66.3: 118–131.

Lyday, Margaret. 2002. *English 202D Study Guide: Effective Writing: Business Writing.* University Park: Pennsylvania State University.

Maas, James B., Megan L. Wherry, David J. Axelrod, Barbara R. Hogan, and Jennifer Bloomin. 1998. *Power Sleep: The Revolutionary Program That Prepares Your Mind for Peak Performance.* New York: Villard.

Mackay, Harvey. 1988. *Swim with the Sharks without Being Eaten Alive: Outsell, Outmanage, Outmotivate, and Outnegotiate Your Competition.* New York: Fawcett Columbine.

Madigan, Robert, Susan Johnson, and Patricia Linton. 1995. "The Language of Psychology: APA Style as Epistemology." *American Psychologist* 50.6: 428–436.

Mahler, Jonathan. 2003. "Commute to Nowhere." *New York Times Magazine,* Apr. 13, 44+.

Mahowald, Mark W. 2002. "What is Causing Excessive Daytime Sleepiness?: Evaluation to Distinguish Sleep Deprivation from Sleep Disorders." *Postgraduate Medicine* 107.3: 108–110, 115–118, 123.

Mandel, Barrett J., and Philip Vassallo. 1999. "From 'Me' to 'Us': Crossing the Bridge from Academic to Business Writing." *Etc.: A Review of General Semantics* 56.3: 338–347.

Manly, Tom, Geraint H. Lewis, Ian H. Robertson, Peter C. Watson, and Avijit K. Dattaa. 2002. "Coffee in the Cornflakes: Time-of-Day as a Modulator of Executive Response Control." *Neuropsychologia* 40.1: 1–6.

Maquet, Pierre, Phillipe Peigneux, Stephen Laureys, and Carlyle Smith. 2002. "Be Caught Napping: You're Doing More Than Resting Your Eyes." *Nature Neuroscience* 5.7: 618–619.

March, James G., and Herbert A. Simon. 1958. *Organizations.* New York and London: John Wiley & Sons.

Marcus, Greil. 1989. *Lipstick Traces: A Secret History of the Twentieth Century.* Cambridge, MA: Harvard University Press.

Marcuse, Herbert. 1966. *Eros and Civilization: A Philosophical Inquiry into Freud.* 2nd ed. Boston: Beacon Press.

Martin, Emily. 1994. *Flexible Bodies: Tracking Immunity in American Culture —From the Days of Polio to the Age of AIDS.* Boston: Beacon Press.

"Mary Parker Follett." *Organisations@Onepine.* 2005. Dec. 11, 2008. http://www.onepine.info/pfollett.htm.

Mayo, Elton. 1933. *The Human Problems of an Industrial Civilization.* New York: Macmillan.

McGeehan, Patrick. 2003. "Executive Pay: A Special Report—Again, Money Follows the Pinstripes." *New York Times,* Apr. 6, sec. 3: 1+.

McGregor, Douglas. 1960. *The Human Side of Enterprise.* New York: McGraw-Hill Book Company.

McKinlay, Alan, and Ken Starkey, eds. 1998. *Foucault, Management and Organization Theory: From Panopticon to Technologies of Self.* London: Sage Publications.

McLean, Bethany, and Peter Elkind. 2003. *The Smartest Guys in the Room: The Amazing Rise and Scandalous Fall of Enron.* New York: Portfolio.

Mednick, Sara C., Ken Nakayama, Jose L. Cantero, Mercedes Atienza, Alicia A. Levin, Neha Pathak, and Robert Stickgold. 2002. "The Restorative Effect of Naps on Perceptual Deterioration." *Nature Neuroscience* 5.7: 677–681.

Miller, Laura. "The Salon Interview: Richard Powers." *Salon.* July 23, 1998. http://www.salon.com.

Monster.com. "Deloitte." *Monster.com.* 2008. Nov. 23, 2008. http://company.monster.com/delllp/.

Moses, Alexandra R. 2002. "Workplace Wellness: From Yoga to Walking, Employers Finding Ways to Encourage Good Health." *Centre Daily Times,* April 28, E1+.

National Sleep Foundation. 2002. National Sleep Foundation. Nov. 14, 2002. http://www.nsaw.org.

Needleman, Sarah E. "Explaining your Layoff to a Job Recruiter." *Wall Street Journal Online.* Dec. 9, 2008. Dec. 11, 2008. http://online.wsj.com/article/SB122876529597488855.html.

Nelson, Cary, Paula A. Treichler, and Lawrence Grossberg. 1992. Introduction to *Cultural Studies,* eds. Lawrence Grossberg, Cary Nelson, and Paula A. Treichler, 1–16. New York and London: Routledge.

Newfield, Christopher. 1995. "Corporate Pleasures for a Corporate Planet." *Social Text* 44, no. 13.3: 31–44.

Nietzsche, Friedrich. 1874. "On the Uses and Disadvantages of History for Life." In *Untimely Meditations,* ed. Daniel Breazeale. Trans. R.J. Hollingdale. Cambridge, UK: Cambridge University Press, 1997.

———. 1889/1895. *Twilight of the Idols and The Anti-Christ: Or How to Philosophize with a Hammer.* New York: Penguin Classics, 1990.

Nomura. "Relationship with Employees: Supporting Unity among Diverse Personnel and Various Working Styles." *Nomuraholdings.com.* 2008. Dec. 16, 2008. http://www.nomuraholdings.com/csr/stakeholder/employee/support.html.

Patel, Dave. "SHRM Workplace Forecast: A Strategic Outlook, 2002–2003." *Society for Human Resources Management.* 2003. Dec. 11, 2008. http://www.shrm.org/trends/Forecast.pdf.

Peters, Tom. 1992. *Liberation Management: Necessary Disorganization for the Nanosecond Nineties.* New York: Knopf.

———. 2001. "Tom Peters's True Confessions." *Fast Company.* 78.

Peters, Thomas J., and Robert H. Waterman. 1982. *In Search of Excellence: Lessons from America's Best-Run Companies.* New York: Harper & Row.

Polman, Paul. "Linking Opportunity with Responsibility: Euro-Environment Conference, Aalborg." *Pg.com.* 2002. Dec. 13, 2008. http://pgdoc.nl/documenten/sustainability_report_2002.pdf.

Powers, Richard. 1998. *Gain.* New York: Farrar, Straus and Giroux.

Procter and Gamble. "Consumer Market Knowledge." 2003. Nov. 26, 2008. http://www.pgeverydaysolutions.com/en_CA/careers/looking_for/cmk.jhtml.

———. "P&G Pharmaceuticals." *Pg.com.* 2003. Nov. 26, 2008. http://www.pgpharma.com/licensing_whypg.shtml.

———. "U.S. Jobs: U.S. Career Advice—Functions: Customer Business Development." *Pg.com.* 2003. Nov. 25, 2008. http://www.pg.com/jobs/jobs_us/cac/f_cbd_opportunities.shtml.

Principal Financial Group. "Our Culture." *Principal.com.* 2008. Nov. 24, 2008. http://www.principal.com/careers/workinghere/ourculture.htm.

Rabinbach, Anson. 1990. *The Human Motor: Energy, Fatigue, and the Origins of Modernity.* New York: Basic Books.

Rabuzzi, Daniel A. "Business Needs the Humanities." *Liberal Education* 87.1 (2001). Nov. 22, 2008. http://web5.epnet.com/citation.asp.

Randall, Ami L. "Napping on the Job: Policies and Benefits in Extended Hours Operations." *Circadian Technologies, Inc.* 2003. Dec. 13, 2008. http://www.circadian.com/download/11_napping_on_the_job_policies_benefits.pdf.

RCPL Forex. "Careers." *Rcplforex.com.* 2006. November 25, 2008. http://www.rcplforex.com/careers.php.

Readings, Bill. 1996. *The University in Ruins.* Cambridge, MA: Harvard University Press.

Richardson, Malcolm. 2003. "Professional Communication Studies, the MLA, and Civic Discourse." *Business Communication Quarterly* 66.3: 105–112.

Riesman, David, Reuel Denney, and Nathan Glazer. 1950. *The Lonely Crowd: A Study of the Changing American Character.* New Haven and London: Yale University Press.

Rimke, Heidi Marie. 2000. "Governing Citizens through Self-Help Literature." *Cultural Studies* 14.1: 61–78.

Rose, Michael R. 1998. *Darwin's Spectre: Evolutionary Biology in the Modern World.* Princeton: Princeton University Press.

Rose, Nikolas. 1989. *Governing the Soul: The Shaping of the Private Self.* London and New York: Routledge.

———. 1996. *Inventing Our Selves: Psychology, Power and Personhood.* New York: Cambridge University Press.

———. 1999. *Powers of Freedom: Reframing Political Thought.* New York: Cambridge University Press.

Rosenberg, Alexander. 2000. *Darwinism in Philosophy, Social Science and Policy.* Cambridge, UK: Cambridge University Press.

Ross, Andrew. 2003. *No-Collar: The Humane Workplace and Its Hidden Costs.* New York: Basic Books.

Ross, Brian. "Lehman Had Long Relationship with Suspect Mortgage Brokers." *ABCNews.com.* Sept. 15, 2008. Nov. 24, 2008. http://abcnews.go.com/Blotter/story?id=5807408&page=1.

Rouse, Joseph. 1993. "What Are Cultural Studies of Scientific Knowledge?" *Configurations* 1.1: 57–74.

Schein, Edgar H. 1985. "Defining Organizational Culture." In *Classics of Organization Theory,* eds. Jay M. Shafritz and J. Steven Ott, 381–395. 2nd ed. Chicago: The Dorsey Press, 1987.

Schisgall, Oscar. 1981. *Eyes on Tomorrow: The Evolution of Procter & Gamble.* Chicago: J. G. Ferguson Publishing.

Schlosser, Eric. 2001. *Fast Food Nation: The Dark Side of the All-American Meal.* Boston and New York: Houghton Mifflin.

Schwartz, John. 2001. "Dot-Com is Dot-Gone, and the Dream with It." *New York Times,* Nov. 25, sec. 9: 1, 4.

Shafritz, Jay M., and J. Steven Ott, eds. 1987. *Classics of Organization Theory.* 2nd ed. Chicago: The Dorsey Press.

———. 1987. Foreword to *Classics of Organization Theory,* eds. Jay M. Shafritz and J. Steven Ott. 2nd ed. Chicago: The Dorsey Press.

Siehl, Caren, and Joanne Martin. 1984. "The Role of Symbolic Management: How Can Managers Effectively Transmit Organizational Culture?" In *Classics of Organization* Theory, eds. Jay M. Shafritz and J. Steven Ott, 433–445. 2nd ed. Chicago: The Dorsey Press, 1987.

Singer, Paul. 2002. "After Scandals, Business Schools Wonder Where to Put Ethics." *Intelligencer Journal Business Monday* : 11.

Society for Human Resource Management. "2001 Benefits Survey." 2001. Dec. 13, 2008. http://www.shrm.org/hrresources/surveys_published/archive/12001%20Benefits%20Survey.asp.

Stearns, James M., Kate Ronald, Timothy B. Greenlee, and Charles T. Crespy. 2003. "Contexts for Communication: Teaching Expertise through

Case-Based In-Basket Exercises." *Journal of Education for Business* 78.4: 213–219.

Stevens, Liz. 2001. "Close Your Eyes: Midday Dozes Are Stripping Away Stigma of Siestas." *Centre Daily Times,* Mar. 26, 1–2C.

Substance Abuse and Mental Health Services Administration. "Workplace Health/Promotion Wellness Fact Sheet." 1998. Dec. 15, 2008. http://workplace.samhsa.gov/ResourceCenter/r305.pdf.

Swasy, Alecia. 1993. *Soap Opera: The Inside Story of Procter & Gamble.* New York: Times Books.

Taylor, Frederick. 1911. *The Principles of Scientific Management.* New York: Norton, 1967.

Terry, Paul. "Rethinking Rewards: Using Incentives to Improve Workplace Wellness Results." *Human Resources Management Online,* 2008. Dec. 13, 2008. http://www.hrmreport.com/pastissue/article.asp?art=27214 3&issue=230.

Thomas, Martha Wetterhall. 2003. "Book Review: *Spurious Coin: a History of Science, Management, and Technical Writing.*" *The Journal of Business Communication* 40.4: 303–310.

Tortorello, Michael. "Richard Powers: Industrial Evolution." *Rain Taxi Online* 3.2 (1998). Dec. 13, 2008. http://www.raintaxi.com/online/1998summer/powers.shtml.

United States Department of Labor and Bureau of Labor Statistics. 1998. United States Department of Labor and Bureau of Labor Statistics. Dec. 13, 2008. http://www.bls.gov.

Vandewater, Judith. "Employers Control Costs by Promoting Health." *Boston Globe.* Sept. 14, 2003. Dec. 13, 2008. http://bostonworks.boston.com/globe/articles/091403_gym.html.

Wall Street. Dir. Oliver Stone. Perf. Michael Douglas, Charlie Sheen, and Daryl Hannah. 20th Century Fox, 1987.

Wal-Mart. "About Us." *Walmart.com.* 2008. Nov. 25, 2008. http://walmartstores.com/AboutUs/320.aspx.

Wal-Mart. "Sam's Rules for a Successful Business." *Walmart.com.* 2006. Nov. 25, 2008. http://walmart.nwanews.com/wm_story.php?storyid=3 5588&section=shareholder.

Wardrope, William J. 2001. "'Challenge is a Positive Word: Embracing the Interdisciplinary Nature of Business Communication." *Journal of Business Communication* 38.3: 242–247.

———. 2002. "Department Chairs' Perceptions of the Importance of Business Communication Skills." *Business Communication Quarterly* 65.4: 60–72.

Watkins, Evan. 1995. "Introduction." *Social Text* 44, no. 13.3: 2–3.

Weinger, Matthew B., and Sonia Ancoli-Israel. 2002. "Sleep Deprivation and Clinical Performance." *JAMA* 287.8: 955–957.

Whyte, William H. 1956. *The Organization Man.* New York: Simon and Schuster, Inc.

Williams, Raymond. 1977. *Marxism and Literature*. Oxford and New York: Oxford University Press.

Wilson, Sloan. 1955. *The Man in the Gray Flannel Suit*. New York: Simon and Schuster.

Wolff, Josephine. "Alums Face Hazy Future after Lehman Brothers Collapse." *Daily Princetonian*. Sept. 16, 2008. Nov. 23, 2008. http://www.dailyprincetonian.com/2008/09/16/21381/.

Wolgemuth, Liz. "How to Befriend Your Boss and Keep Your Job." *U.S. News and World Report*. Sept. 4, 2008. Dec. 9, 2008. http://www.usnews.com/articles/business/careers/2008/09/04/how-to-befriend-your-boss-and-keep-your-job.html.

WorldCom.com. 2001. WorldCom. Dec. 8, 2001. http://www.worldcom.com.

Yahoo. "Yahoo Careers." *Yahoo.com*. 2008. Nov. 25, 2008. http://careers.yahoo.com/.

Yahoo. "Life@Yahoo Employee Profiles." *Yahoo.com*. 2008. Nov. 25, 2008. http://careers.yahoo.com/eprofiles.php?prev=1&id=74.

Zernike, Kate. "Fight against Fat Shifting to the Workplace." *New York Times*. Oct. 12, 2003. Dec. 13, 2008. http://query.nytimes.com/gst/fullpage.html?sec=health&res=9407E0DB133FF931A25753C1A9659C8B63.

INDEX

Hewitt, John P., 191n
Hirschman, Albert, 190n
Hochschild, Arlie, 18, 25, 29, 61,
    187n, 188n
Horibe, Frances, 56, 68
Horkheimer, Max, 39, 41, 189n
Howell, Jeremy, 79, 102, 105, 110,
    196–197n
Hull, Glynda, 47, 156, 159, 168,
    171, 173, 203n
Hultman, Ken, 56–57
Human Relations theory, 12–16,
    18, 49–51, 105, 186–187n,
    190–191n
human resources, 2, 8, 30, 34, 57,
    60, 63, 65, 92, 125, 137–138,
    140, 192n

Iacocca, Lee, 77
IBM, 69
individuality, 4, 35, 40–42,
    44–48, 50, 57, 60–62,
    67, 69, 73, 123, 173,
    179, 190n
industrial/organizational
    psychology, 3, 92,
    120, 195n
Ingram, Alan, 79, 102, 105, 110,
    196–197n
intensive capitalism, 130–132, 145,
    152

Jameson, Fredric, 202n
Jaques, Elliott, 19
Johnson, Spencer, 34, 44, 77, 84,
    93–96, 99, 196n
Johnson & Johnson, 181
Juffer, Jane, 59

Kanigel, Robert, 48, 190n
Kelly, Kevin, 44, 77, 82, 84, 90,
    95–99
Kennedy, Allan, 10, 21–24,
    26–27, 72, 187n
Kroc, Ray, 75, 82–83, 85

labor unions, 14, 24, 47, 51, 57,
    61, 64, 82, 192n
Lankshear, Colin, 47, 156, 159,
    168, 171, 173, 203n
Lasch, Christopher, 191n
Lehman Brothers, 37, 176–178,
    182–183, 205n
Livingston, James, 32
Locker, Kitty, 162, 166–167, 172

Maas, James B., 114–115, 198n
Mabrito, Mark, 164
Mackay, Harvey, 77, 90–93, 96,
    99, 195n, 196n
Mahler, Jonathan, 190n
Man in the Gray Flannel Suit, The
    (Sloan Wilson), 52–53, 191n
Mandel, Barrett J., 160–161, 164,
    166–167
March, James G., 15, 32, 186n
Marcus, Greil, 84, 195n
Marcuse, Herbert, 198n
Martin, Emily, 29, 32, 84–85, 96
Martin, Joanne, 26
Martin, Randy, 29
Marx, Karl, 29
Mayo, Elton, 12–13, 15–16, 49–51,
    57, 73, 186n, 190–191n
McDonald's, 82–83, 186n
McGregor, Douglas, 16–19, 24,
    186–187n
McKinlay, Alan, 193n
Merrill Lynch, 178n
Microsoft, 7, 9, 66
motivation, 13, 15–17, 20, 78, 105,
    109–110, 120, 161–162, 190n
Mulcahey, David, 185n

Napping Company, The, 114
National Sleep Foundation
    (NSF), 110, 113
Negri, Antonio, 129–131, 135,
    148, 192n, 200n
Nelson, Cary, 30, 32

LaVergne, TN USA
23 June 2010
187060LV00003B/17/P

9 780230 618725